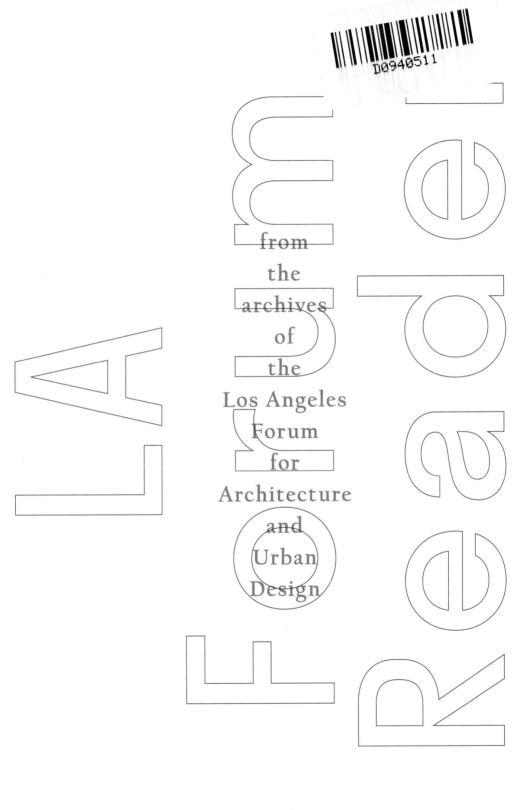

LA Forum Reader

from
the
archives
of
the
Los Angeles
Forum
for
Architecture
and
Urban
Design

LA Forum Reader
Edited by Rob Berry, Victor Jones, Michael Sweeney,
Mimi Zeiger, and Chava Danielson, Joe Day, Thurman Grant,
Duane McLemore

Design: Still Room, Jessica Fleischmann with Jenny Haru Kim

Copy Editor: Brigette Brown
Project Manager: Steven Chodoriwsky

This publication was made with the support and funding
of the Graham Foundation for Advanced Studies in
the Fine Arts and the National Endowment for the Arts

LA Forum
PO Box 291774
Los Angeles, CA 90029 USA
www.laforum.org
info@laforum.org

ISBN: 978-1-945150-99-9

Published by: Actar Publishers, New York, Barcelona

Los Angeles Forum for Architecture and Urban Design,
Los Angeles

Distribution
Actar D, Inc.

New York
440 Park Avenue South, 17th Floor
New York, NY 10016, USA
T +1 212.966.2207
E salesnewyork@actar-d.com

Barcelona
Roca i Batlle 2-4
08023 Barcelona, SP
T +34 933 282 183
E eurosales@actar-d.com

LA Forum Reader

Rob Berry
Victor Jones
Michael Sweeney
Mimi Zeiger

and
Chava Danielson
Joe Day,
Thurman Grant
Duane McLemore

Table of Contents

Acknowledgments

The contents of this book were produced with the support of multiple generations of LA Forum board members, volunteers, and friends, including John Dutton, Frank Escher, Todd Gannon, Christian Hubert, John Kaliski, Alan Loomis, John Southern, and Kazys Varnelis. Thank you to Siobhán Burke, Sara Daleiden, and Andrea Dietz for their fundraising prowess. We would be nothing without the dedicated assistance of Patricia Bacalao, Brigette Brown, Brian Daleiden, Khristeen Decastro, Anna Eremenko, Knarik Harutyunyan, Chris McMillan, Mark Montiel, and Oxana Yashenko. And we are indebted to Aaron Betsky, John Chase, Margaret Crawford, Tim Durfee, Merry Norris, Mohamed Sharif, and Roberto Sheinberg for their advice and critical belief in our institution.

Existing works included in this anthology are indebted to countless individuals over 30 years who wrote, designed, edited, or contributed to publications.

Many groups supported and published our work including Actar, RAM Publishers, Metropolis Books, Monticello Books, California Arts Council, City of Los Angeles Department of Cultural Affairs, Graham Foundation for Advanced Studies in the Fine Arts, Los Angeles County Arts Commission, National Endowment for the Arts, and Woodbury University School of Architecture.

Introduction
Victor Jones and Mimi Zeiger

The unverified garage myth is that the LA Forum began as a reading group. While it's difficult to envision Los Angeles designers so demurely domesticated, some of the early members were young transplants in search of a rigorous and intense discussion about architecture in a city they were eager to explore. What seems truer is that shortly after its founding in 1987, the Forum morphed into a new school of direct contact. It's pedagogical subject nothing less than the city in form, practice, and culture.

And what would be the freshly forged self-image? Gumshoe. Instigator. Nomad. All Angeleno identities held in contrapposto to the theoretical traditions privileged by East Coast entities such as Institute for Architecture and Urban Studies.

As the early 1990s saw the publication of two seminal texts, Ed Soja's *Postmodern Geographies* and Mike Davis' *City of Quartz*, fieldwork replaced literary analysis as Forum members combed the city for insights and lessons steeped in the morass of Los Angeles' uncharted architecture and urbanity. Events like *Suggestive Spaces* (1987), which featured panel discussions and lecturers in four not obvious locations (the top of City Hall, a freeway overpass, a filtration plant, and an oil refinery), were as much about being in the city as about the city itself.

This appetite for the *urbain* (over the cocoon-like atmosphere of a cozy salon interior) might explain why the Forum maintains a semi-permanent home on Hollywood Boulevard, shuffles a fragmentary archive of printed matter between random closets, file cabinets, and an occasional car trunk. Even its digital collection is not tethered to a single database, but floats freely in the proverbial cloud. As such, the archive always feels incomplete, even as the Forum board members and participants work diligently to retrieve and catalog misplaced documents. The extents to which mobility, temporality, and fluidity have shaped this roving institution are undeniable. And while these modes of operation define an attitude, their curatorial purpose is limited when it comes to the selection and organization of material for a book.

For three decades, the Forum's provisional nature has remained a core asset, held in tension by a commitment to produce public events, exhibitions, and publishing projects. Those efforts have spawned a myriad of artifacts: newsletters, pamphlets, posters, catalogs, and books—many with Los Angeles' key architects, artists, designers, and urban thinkers participating in their making. But parsing subject matter based on author, content type, or date would also be problematic, revealing flagrant irregularities in the Forum's output, not to mention ruthlessly dull. Certain moments are rich with production, others slim. Blank spots surround episodes where public programming such as exhibitions and special events dominated the calendar. It is reasonable to imagine that those lapses of quiet time were the consequence of intensive preparation periods surrounding significant events—not writer's block.

Perhaps the difficulty of our initial question about the Forum's identity has less to do with the organization itself and everything to do with our subject? Los Angeles, the protagonist (and, at times, antagonist) of all the stories told here, revels in the multiplication of plot lines. Tidy endings are avoided in favor of new diversions that rouse, advocate, and otherwise provoke. Each story opens up the possibility of a dozen others. Collected, organized, and newly presented as they are, the works included in the *Reader* naturally resist an underlying narrative or a convincing conclusion.

Arranged in four sections with three interludes punctuated between them, each section title reflects larger themes that have come to define the Forum's unique contribution to the discourse of architecture and urbanism in Los Angeles: Experiments, Detours, Hunches, and Santa Anas. Each section assembles reprinted texts from their original sources;

reproduced artifacts and documents ranging from dedications to experimental publications in which the design of the object is as important as the written words. Section summaries by individual editors frame and give context to the mixed bag of material, but do not necessarily aspire to smoothing the edges of the editorial selection. The interludes: Art and Architecture, The Newsletter, and Downtown, represent more narrow topics deserving of singular attention. They cover the role of public art in public space, the look and feel of the LA Forum's newsletter itself, and a continual revisiting of Downtown Los Angeles. In keeping with the Forum's ethos, this book avoids historicizing the institution and its material. Indeed, it begins with Aaron Betsky's *Fragments, Out There*, his early reflections on emergent practice, and ends with *Mock Up: The Persistence of Beige*, an excerpt from Tom Marble's suburban screenplay *After the City, This is How We (Live)*. It is no surprise that questions of practice versus questions of urbanism bookend the volume. These two positions—sometimes polar, sometimes not—track through our history, creating an active tension between writers.

More than an assemblage of the recent past's historical artifacts, the *Reader* offers character studies on the complexity of Los Angeles— its temperament, its quirks, its internal struggles. We could say that these texts are preludes for writing the city's perpetual next act, and indeed there's a latent hope that new readership will spur new (and renewed) discourses. The editors put forward this imperfect anthology as an unapologetic embrace of fragility as methodology. Recent dogmas tend to favor choate projects over anything eccentric—as if in preconceiving a whole it will bring outliers in line. But don't confuse this backward glance as a yearning for L.A. School redux or Decon nostalgia, the cultural context of that Los Angeles is as gone as Kate Mantilini's techno-expressionist restaurant in Beverly Hills. Today in our polarized era, which sees our disciplines, our practices split into binaries—between town and gown, between urbanism and form— we could benefit from more spaces of unpremeditated experimentation and exploration afforded by the LA Forum's publication history. And, perhaps, this looseness is the ultimate aspiration of the *LA Forum Reader*.

I.
Experiments

Embracing Experiments
Rob Berry

L.A.'s swagger comes from an unequivocal embrace of risk. Here, outsized ambitions of paradise confront headlong the existential realities of sudden tectonic shifts, bewildering winds, and debilitating drought. This intersection of the particular geography, climate, and geology of the place with a distinct set of social, cultural, and political conditions engenders an atmosphere of experimentation that extends from the city's creative and economic pursuits to its infrastructure and urban form. The result is a city that behaves differently than expected, that doesn't quite fit the existing models. It's the city's willingness to belie recognized patterns of behavior, organization, and form that exemplifies the risk of Los Angeles. But this doesn't make Los Angeles necessarily unique, particularly as other cities (and L.A. itself) take the same gambles and try to replicate the outcomes. As a result, there's a perceived ordinariness in the relentless repetition of familiar forms in Los Angeles that cloaks the profoundly experimental nature of the city.

Los Angeles and the L.A. School takes on the experiment of Los Angeles during a temporal and physical collision between the city's extreme risk and its utter ordinariness. Published by the LA Forum in 1993, the pamphlet appears just as the emerging narrative of Los Angeles as a paradigm for contemporary urban form was dramatically interrupted by civil unrest. The text outlines a series of challenges to the dominant readings of Los Angeles in development since the early 1980s by the loosely defined "L.A. School" of economists, sociologists, and urban scholars. Nuanced and varied in its subject and scope, the work of the L.A. School collectively identifies a restructuring of the city as an economic enterprise, a social apparatus, and an urban form. Fundamental to this restructuring is the recognition of a viable *other*—instances of cultural, temporal, and spatial specificity that offer distinct alternatives to the dominant trajectory of the city as defined by capital and development.

The risk of the restructuring identified by the L.A. School stems from the inevitable friction that results between the master narrative and the defiance of that narrative by the *other*. Under favorable circumstances, this friction offers a productive balance, a storyline underscored by the text. A situational or contextual shift, however, potentially leads to a moment of crisis and upheaval. The text outlines these conditions, but does not identify the risk explicitly. Instances of inequality and disparity are described, but the riots conspicuously are not mentioned anywhere. Instead, the text is interrupted graphically by images of *Skycam*, a 1992 series of paintings by Peter Alexander depicting the visual atmosphere of the riots.

The intertwining of Alexander's paintings within the text obviously simulates the disruption of the unrest, but more importantly allows the narrative of the L.A. School to remain relatively intact. This graphic pairing of the text and paintings with a marked degree of autonomy for each elicits a distinct paradox of the experimental. All experiments are wont to fail. The risk of failure is sometimes subtle, sometimes catastrophic, but always present. A failure, even a catastrophic one, however, doesn't dictate an obligatory end to the experiment. With each failure comes a recalibration of risk versus reward, a new wager is made, and the experiment continues. In this sense, the project of the L.A. School is not obliterated by the riots, but forced to attune to an extremely palpable risk of division and disintegration.

Potential recalibrations and wagers are evident in the positions put forth in editorials and essays from issues of the LA Forum's Newsletter published contemporaneously to *Los Angeles and the L.A. School*. Aaron Betsky, in a review of the LA Forum's "Out There Doing It" series, advances fragmentation and incompleteness as the defining contemporary condition of Los Angeles, one that finds expression in both architecture and urbanism. Sylvia Lavin and Frank Gehry, in a conversation ostensibly about Disney, implicate larger domains of cultural and urban production, with Gehry identifying the authenticity of art as the form of resistance to the ersatz culture propagated by capitalism.

While both Betsky and Gehry come down decidedly on the side of visual and formal complexity, John Chase counters with a stance that sees experimentation and ordinariness as equal participants in the ongoing evolution of Los Angeles. Chase argues not for reconciliation between the spectacular and the generic, but for recognition of the value and potential in the outward uniformity. In the repetitive sameness, difference and idiosyncrasy emerge from the diverse social and cultural influences found in the L.A. region. In this sense, Chase extends an inclusive position, more closely aligned with the L.A. School, which exudes an enthusiasm for Los Angeles as a captivating place for perpetual investigation and postulation.

Implicit in the debate engendered by these works is a fundamental risk posed to Los Angeles by a loss of the experimental in both theory and practice. Without continual questioning, Los Angeles risks abandoning the criticality exemplified by the L.A. School, along with architects of the same time period, in favor of safer, more established— and ultimately less rewarding—forms of architecture and urbanism. Two decades later, in the midst of another restructuring precipitated by an aging and antiquated infrastructure, looming climatic and ecological shifts, a crucial housing shortage, and uncertain political conditions, Los Angeles more than ever needs to gamble with conviction on its future. The components of the current restructuring— organizational systems, environment, and density—are not novel; the urban history of Los Angeles, in fact, can been seen as a series of reconciliations with the demands of these persistent issues. While the current mix may seem particularly volatile, the lessons of the L.A. School show that uncertainty breeds experimentation. Existing models or frameworks still don't matter, only the gumption to take a risk.

Fragments, Out There

Aaron Betsky

LA Forum Newsletter
October 1989

Out there, on the Plains of Id and in the Ranges of Romance, hidden in alleys and behind bougainvilleas, there are young men and women doing it. This was proven by the Forum series "Out There Doing It" this past Spring and Winter. What are they doing? They are densifying and complicating the metropolis. They are creating additions, alterations, and amendments that are symptomatic of a city struggling to evolve before it falls into the ocean, chokes on smog and social and economic disparities, or transforms itself into Alphaville-sur-Mer.

The simple economics of starting a practice means that the work presented took the form of fragmentary additions to the city: kitchen additions and remodels, a new bedroom here, a new entry there. But even freestanding buildings designed by the lucky few took on the character of the unfinished, with walls gesturing towards focal points that were never found, compositions finished in the void, and doorknobs or window frames that appeared to be parts of much larger, but invisible, orders. Such images signify several phenomena. First of all, they are simultaneously signs of the times in which it may be impossible, undesirable, or politically incorrect to make completed buildings. Second, they are the result of the desire of young practitioners to start building the grand plan even if they can only work on a few details. Finally, this fragmentary construction may be a necessary way of building in a city that delights in being continually in process.

Such collages of fragments make for a great deal of density and complication in all of the work, even in those designs that appeared at first to be spare and abstract. Again, such complexity can be attributed both to the energy of the new and untried and to the city's entropy. As a giant technological behemoth, Los Angeles is perfecting the systems that allow it to operate—real estate financing and codes, electrical, telephone, water and sewage lines, road grids— to such an extent that these orders are breeding ever more replicas of themselves at smaller scales, filling in all of the interstitial spaces of this once spread out city until it will become one completely solid urban mechanism perpetuating itself. For young architects, this means both that they are working for clients who are filling in their backyards, commissioning additions, and reclaiming the open warehouses that stretch along the previously endless boulevards, and that they feel an obligation to represent those technological systems whose formerly vast and open scale had made them invisible and taken for granted.

At the same time, the work presented was also enigmatic. It was strange stuff, often made up of blank walls, convoluted corners, and closed pavilions. Such is the nature of Los Angeles: a series of artificial oases hiding behind a gritty and indecipherable exterior. This is a city that hides from the sun, from the systems of transportation and communication that keep it going, and from the baggage it brought along across the ocean or over the mountains. Such is also the local architectural tradition, the strange hybrid mesas of Wright and the centrifugal, dense corners of Schindler, the blobs of the shopping centers, the snakes and fish of Frank Gehry. Only sometimes during this series did one suspect tactics of avoidance, of abstraction engendered by the inability to make up one's mind yet, of empty gestures for empty clients in the unfamiliar land of building in Los Angeles.

No doubt this work will coalesce into some form or order, but perhaps the stuff will continue to refuse closed forms and choose the orders of chaos— not only because such are the current lessons of the academies, but also because the unfinished is inherently more beautiful, more hopeful, more romantic, and more socially enabling than the closed monuments to a dead architecture in which the fathers, teachers, and employers of these young architects are buried.

Whose Beach Party Is This Anyway?

Architecture and its Audience

John Chase

LA Forum Newsletter
September 1992

In the Los Angeles of the 1990s, limited views of the architect's role, and a limited view of the region's architectural and urban context, have dangerously narrowed both the public and critical understanding of architecture's nature as a social art. Southern California is seen as lacking both in recognizable building types and clearly defined urban form. As a result, much importance is placed on the individual artifact, while far less attention is devoted to the relationship between the artifact and urban forms surrounding it. As Stefanos Polyzoides has pointed out, "Increasingly buildings here are a kind of selfish scream for attention. Everything has to be a thing in itself. The attitude about oneness has spawned such an interest in fashion." While it is true that Los Angeles is rightly perceived to be a place that is open to new ideas, personal expression, and experimentation, the current architectural avant-garde seems less interested in relating their work to this tradition of innovation in a meaningful way than in using this tradition as a license to make the kind of photogenic objects that get good press. This essay is a call for critical attention to the broad range of building types that, in Los Angeles, sprawl from the mall to the car wash and that are as valuable candidates for evaluation and understanding as are high-art artifacts of limited production. A work of architecture may begin as a private statement of taste, but all works of architecture inevitably become, to some degree, public artifacts that are part of everyone's daily life.

A perusal of the pages of *Experimental Architecture in Los Angeles* does not reveal that this city has a distinct context, history, and typology of vernacular architecture that is both all its own as well as part and parcel of American urbanism as a whole. Local avant-garde architects tend to behave as though these phenomena that unify urbanism in Southern California simply do not exist. As a result, reinforcing degrees of agreement between buildings or districts has generally been a low priority with recent architecture, just as the idea of taking cues from a neighborhood or regional repertoire of building types is seen here as a limitation on creativity. David Gebhard has pointed out that even the major architectural innovations of pioneer modernists, such as Frank Lloyd Wright, Irving Gill, and Rudolf Schindler, had little urbanistic impact, and Leon Whiteson notes that Los Angeles continues to be a place where small firms, however innovative they may be in the context of their small commissions, still have no real effect on the city as a whole. Given the mutual incompatibility of the agendas of high-art architecture as they inform many individual buildings and the agendas of popular taste as they inform the common landscape, it is difficult to understand how this could be otherwise.

Experimental Architecture does little to help overcome this incompatibility but does a lot to help one segment of architectural producers—"boutique" formalist offices—dominate the professional and public perception of architecture. This kind of domination is more acute in Los Angeles than perhaps anywhere else in the U.S. While Southern California may still be relatively isolated from East Coast publications, it has increasingly become mandatory for the established media to track activity here and to focus their evermore myopic eye on the most glamorous and the least socially relevant categories of building production. Each new wave of commodified architects is offered up as more daring, iconoclastic, and original than the last; "Los Angeles, where trends come from" proclaimed a 1989 issue of *Metropolitan Home* magazine devoted to architecture and design in the city.

As the speed of commodification increases, so does the speed of the star-making process. The *Metropolitan Home* issue, which typifies recent coverage of architecture in Los Angeles, featured a group of avant-garde architects with primarily sculptural or visual concerns. But the way these architects were presented seemed modeled after the media packaging of interior decorators, fashion designers, and most of all, movie stars. It would seem perfectly logical to view *Experimental Architecture* as part of this phenomenon that seeks to invent celebrities rather than provoke critical discussion.

Motivating the beachcombing to uncover the next media star lies the assumption that formal invention is the most important aspect of architecture. In other words, the more a building differs from the public's understanding of what building is, the more "information," and therefore the biggest possible media event, it generates. The more an avant-garde firm, such as Coop Himmelb(l)au, treats their work as pure formal abstraction, the more prestige

LA Forum Reader

they have—not with the public, but with their peers. The more the media treats "avant-garde" architects as they do artists, the more avant-garde architects are encouraged to treat their buildings as though they are walk-in sculpture. In the artificial land of the press, "movie star" architects often ignore the experiential character of their work, let alone the social and real world forces that are part of architecture. Without the burden of having to communicate with the public, these architects can exploit their fictitious freedom to gratify individual whim and pursue a course of self-aggrandizement.

Younger architects today seem to be disconnected from even the most recent architectural history of Los Angeles. In decades not very long past there was a local tradition of modernist architecture that often carried with it a moral imperative based on ambitious definitions of how much social change could actually be implemented by architects. Irving Gill was concerned with providing decent worker housing and in simplifying the amount of work that housewives had to do. Charles Eames explored the idea of using ready-made elements like a kit of parts, and even Wallace Neff experimented with simple concrete houses. This modernist imperative was exemplified by the Case Study Houses program, which was operated by the now legendary *Arts and Architecture* magazine between 1946 and 1966. John Entenza, the publisher of the magazine, commissioned architects such as Pierre Koenig and Craig Ellwood to design houses, which were built as real life demonstrations of how modernist design could integrate technology, such as the steel frame, into buildings that accommodated contemporary life styles.

While in many cases this modernist morality was often an excuse to make design decisions that were actually based on formal preferences, it did provide a framework for tying buildings back to their means of production and to the ways people use them. This seems to be the only aspect of the modernist tradition that has survived, for the operative avant-garde imperative in much current Southern California avant-garde architecture is largely formal. Even when the avant-garde is concerned with issues of urban order, this urban order is often treated as large-scale sculpture or the formal resolution of latent site geometry, divorced from the complexity of actual site issues. This kind of divorce has been aided and abetted by the degree to which the art world has reinforced the solipsistic role played by many contemporary architects. It is not the devotion to or interest in formal or theoretical issues borrowed from the art world that is the problem. The problem is that the architect's freedom is often paid for by the loss of a larger consciousness of architecture's social role, some of the consequences of which are already clear. Avant-garde architecture has not been able to comment on or respond to the radical demographic transformation of Los Angeles into a substantially immigrant multicultural community, nor has it addressed many of the pressing social problems that the city faces.

As the archness and brittleness of postmodern irony and the anti-social abstraction for abstraction's sake of Decon wear thin, we need to explore approaches that reinforce likeness and communalities within the environment rather than fragment it further. If we are ever to have a segment of building production whose design intent can be clearly understood and appreciated by both the public and those inculcated in architectural culture, architectural cognoscenti will have to stop dismissing popular cultural values and find some common ground with the public. Stepping beyond the cult of the architect-as-artist/personality, acknowledging and chronicling the context and the vernacular that does exist in Southern California is a first step in that direction. If vernacular architecture can be judged and found lacking by the standards of formal purity associated with high-art architecture, then, perhaps by virtue of that lack and by constituting a call for architecture to communicate with a larger constituency, vernacular architecture also functions as a critique of high-art architecture. In this sense, it might be said that vernacular architecture performs the critical function absent from the contemporary architectural press.

Books such as *Experimental Architecture* are not bad because there is anything wrong with the individual designs they present. Rather, what is wrong is the way such books tend to present one category of building production as though it were the sum total or the apogee of all architectural production. This narrowness of focus and omission of other possibilities denies us all the possibility of asking primary and critical questions. How do those individuals already inculcated in architectural culture coexist with the world around them that largely ignores the values and rules of high-art architecture? What is the relationship of most people to the actual built environment? How do the buildings that we see from the freeway, the developer housing, and the blank-faced speculative office buildings and shopping malls get built and designed? How do they effect the quality of our lives? Architects and the media alike must become more preoccupied with these issues, even though they are precisely the issues that never get invited to architecture's beach party.

Editor's Note: A version of this essay was to have been included in *Experimental Architecture in Los Angeles*. Rizzoli declined to publish it.

Los Angeles and the L.A. School
Marco Cenzatti
1993

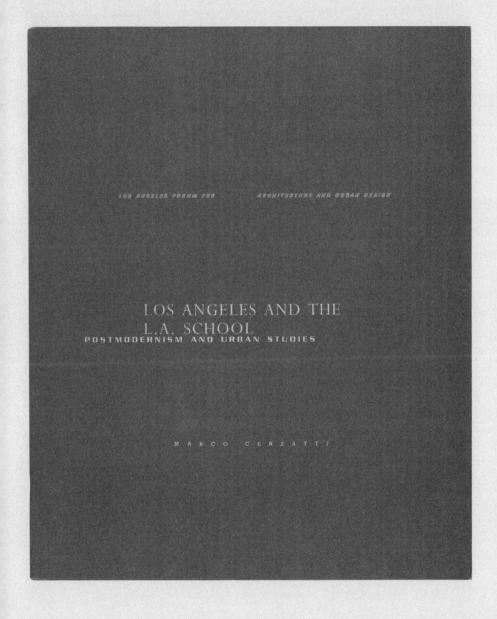

LOS ANGELES FORUM FOR ARCHITECTURE AND URBAN DESIGN

LOS ANGELES AND THE
L.A. SCHOOL
POSTMODERNISM AND URBAN STUDIES

MARCO CENZATTI

Experiments

LOS ANGELES FORUM FOR
ARCHITECTURE AND URBAN DESIGN

FORUM PUBLICATION NO. 10

"Skycam" Paintings by Peter Alexander 1992, courtesy James Corcoran Gallery

Designed by Christopher Vice

Special thanks to John Chase and Sylvia Lavin

This publication has been funded in part by grants from
the Design Arts Program of the National Endowment for the Arts and the Graham Foundation

LOS ANGELES FORUM FOR ARCHITECTURE AND URBAN DESIGN

835 North Kings Road

West Hollywood, California 90069

213 852 7145

U   <

LOS ANGELES AND THE L.A. SCHOOL

POSTMODERNISM AND URBAN STUDIES

M A R C O   C E N Z A T T I

LOS ANGELES AND THE
L.A. SCHOOL
POSTMODERNISM AND URBAN STUDIES

LOS ANGELES FORUM FOR   ARCHITECTURE AND URBAN DESIGN

1993

PETER ALEXANDER . SKYCAM
HOOPER , 1992 . ACRYLIC ON PANEL, 18" X 33".

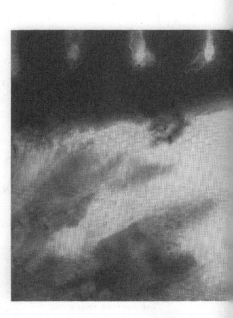

u   z

The Los Angeles School of Urban Studies

Very broadly defined, the name 'Los Angeles School' identifies the work of a group of local researchers who, from the early '80s onwards, discovered in Los Angeles a series of social, economic and spatial trends symptomatic of a general transformation currently taking place in the entire U.S. urban and social structure. Beyond these general statements, however, a more specific location and definition of the School is difficult to find. Its geographical 'centers' range from the U.C. campuses of Irvine and West L.A., to U.S.C. downtown and SCI-Arc in Santa Monica.[0] Equally difficult is to find the School's common conceptual denominator, given its focus on the empirical case of a specific city and its simultaneous assumption that Los Angeles exemplifies a more general dynamic. One, in fact, is left wondering whether the School's common project comes from a focus on Los Angeles—as the starting point of analysis from which a general model can be deduced—or from shared theoretical assumptions of individual studies. Mike Davis has summarized this ambiguity, pointing out that the Los Angeles School remains uncertain whether to model itself "after the 'Chicago School of Urban Sociology'

[0]   In addition to the authors discussed in this essay, other examples of the 'LA School' are R. Kling, D. Spencer, and M. Poster [1991]. Posturban California, Berkeley: University of California Press; M. Dear (1986). "Postmodernism and Planning," Environment and Planning D: Society and Space, 4, pp. 367-84; M. Davis (1987) "Chinatown Part Two? The Internationalization of Downtown Los Angeles," New Left Review, 164, pp. 65-86; M. Crawford (1992), "The Fifth Ecology: Fantasy, the Automobile and Los Angeles," in The Car and the City, M. Wachs and M. Crawford (eds.), Ann Arbor: The University of Michigan Press.

31

(named principally after its *object* of research) or the "Frankfurt School" (a philosophical current named after its *base*)."[6] Rather than eliminating this ambiguity, however, the School's identity can be better understood by clarifying its particular mix of the other two schools' approaches.

Both the Los Angeles and the Chicago Schools study cities that became important just as their respective schools were developing. During the twenties Chicago was rapidly becoming the American industrial city *par excellence*. In the following decades, much of the wide influence of the Chicago School came from the fact that its model exemplified better than any other the impact of changing economic and social conditions on urban form. The same is true of Los Angeles and its School: Los Angeles is exemplary of the new urban model currently emerging from a new round of economic and social changes taking place across the country.

However, there is also an important difference between the two schools that brings Los Angeles closer to Frankfurt than to Chicago. For the Chicago School the study of the city served as both point of departure and arrival. The studies of Park, Burgess, Wirth, and others were squarely focused on the urban as an independent object of analysis.[7] Their research created the foundations for an autonomous discipline (*urban sociology*) whose only goal and horizon was to analyze and understand the city as an autonomous organism.[8] By contrast, the Los Angeles School's empirical research focusing on Los Angeles belongs to a broader context which begins neither with Los Angeles nor with the specificity of the urban.

The element common to all the members of the School is, in fact, their adherence to the concept of restructuring, i.e., to the assumption that, following the crisis of the early '70s, a series of social and economic changes began to occur in most industrialized countries. This restructuring involves the city but does not begin there and is not limited to urban development. The empirical studies of the School are the result of a theoretical process that includes various aspects of restructuring, ranging from the changes taking place in industrial organizations (as in Susan Christopherson's, Allen Scott's, and Michael Storper's analyses, which are discussed in the following pages), to the emergence of new urban forms and social practices (such as Edward Soja's work described in the last section of this essay). Furthermore, the School's interest in restructuring lies not only in identifying the directions

[6] M. Davis (1991) City of Quartz. London: Verso. p. 84.

[7] See R. E. Park, E. W. Burgess and R. D. McKenzie (1925; rep. 1967) The City. Chicago: The University of Chicago Press.

[8] For a critique of the theoretical position of the Chicago School see Manuel Castells' essay *Theory and Ideology in Urban Sociology* (in C.G. Pickvance, ed. Urban Sociology, Critical Essays; London, 1976, Methuen) and The Urban Question (1977. Cambridge, The MIT Press, pp. 75-85) where the author criticizes the ideological character (i.e. the absence of theoretical validity) of urban sociology precisely for limiting its horizon to the city, with no consideration for broader social and economic dynamics which converge to determine the urban condition. Castells concludes that the mistake of the Chicago School was having considered the problem and its solution as identical; the description of the city and its explanation coincided.

6

in which industries or cities are evolving, but includes a shift in the theoretical perspective from which these changes are seen. As a result, Christopherson, Scott and Storper's studies of industrial restructuring reveal not only that one dynamic of industrial development is being replaced by another, but—perhaps more significantly—that different pathways of industrial evolution coexist. Similarly, Soja's work aims at showing that no single model of urban growth can explain the fundamental way in which all cities change. Instead, in one city many models overlap. Thus, understanding restructuring is not simply a question of identifying a new direction of urban or industrial development, but also implies the elaboration of a new theoretical perspective (a theoretical restructuring). This—to use postmodernist terms—begins with a critique of the totalizing and linear narratives of modernism, of its reliance on a center, and of its teleological search for a *causa prima*. The authors of the L.A. School attempt to uncover the existence of other narratives hidden by modernist logic: there are many routes to industrialization and to urban growth. In both cases many models coexist, overlap, and seem (and are) dominant according to the "center" chosen for consideration. Thus, the L.A. School, like the Frankfurt School, aims at proposing a new theoretical framework for interpreting contemporary society.

This parallel with Frankfurt has its limits, however. It can hardly be maintained that postmodernism (and restructuring studies) originated in Los Angeles. If we were to name a birth place for these ideas, we should talk perhaps of a French School, given the influence that such theoreticians as Foucault, Baudrillard, and Derrida have had on theoretical restructuring and Aglietta, Boyer, Lipietz etc. have had on industrial restructuring.

The definition of the Los Angeles School therefore cannot be exclusively based on either the empirical object of its studies or on the development of an 'original' theoretical framework. Rather, the School's strength lies in its location at the intersection between theoretical and empirical specificity. On the one hand, its strong theoretical orientation prevents interpretations of Los Angeles based simply on the empirical observation of one urban region, which would unproblematically accept Los Angeles as a universal template for a new urban form replacing the old (or, alternatively, which would portray Los Angeles as a marginal or exceptional case). On the other hand, these scholars do not use

1

Los Angeles simply as a case study of a fully-formed and pre-conceived view of the dynamic of urban restructuring. Following the postmodernist rejection of metanarrative and teleology, this implies the rejection of any theoretical model which, assuming universality, could be 'lowered down' to explain all other specific cases. Thus Los Angeles comes back into the picture not just as a blueprint or a finished paradigm of the new dynamics, but as a laboratory which is itself an integral component of the production of new modes of analysis of the urban. In this sense, Los Angeles is 'central' to the School. The very weakness of the city's 'modernist' development (indeed, its illegibility according to modernist canons), its growth at a time when both traditional cities and traditional models of urban explanation were in crisis, and its spatial and social fragmentation which echo in a physical form the multiple readings advocated by post-modernism, make it a particularly fertile environment for re-constructing urban theory.

8

Los Angeles from Exception to 'Model'

The recent emergence of the Los Angeles School does not mean that until the late 1970s Los Angeles (and California in general) was ignored. Beginning in the 1930s with Carey McWilliams' works a large literature has been devoted to the region. However, this increasing curiosity about Southern California was primarily informed by the conviction that the region was a special case, different from the rest of the country. Therefore, in order to identify the various causes that made it such a startling exception to the social, economic and urban norm of American development, Southern California needed to be explored and explained by itself. Even Reyner Banham's enthusiastic study of the city did not escape from this view:

"... Los Angeles, the uniquely mobile metropolis. Again the word 'uniquely' ... I make no apology for it. The splendours and miseries of Los Angeles, the graces and grotesqueries, appear to me as unrepeatable as they are unprecedented. ... Once the history of the city is brought under review, it is immediately apparent that no city has ever been produced by such an extraordinary mixture of geography, climate, economics, demography, mechanics and culture; nor is it likely that an even remotely similar mixture will ever occur again."[8]

[8]   R. Banham (1971) Los Angeles: The Architecture of Four Ecologies. New York: Penguin Books, pp. 23-24.

Even today the uniqueness of Los Angeles' geography, economics, politics, culture, etc. is still called upon to explain the development of the city.[2] To be sure, such a focus on the specificity of Los Angeles' features is a necessary ingredient to understand why the city grew the way it did. At the same time, however, too narrow a focus on the uniqueness of Los Angeles does not clarify why this 'exceptional' case has, over the last decade, steadily outperformed traditional metropolitan leaders such as New York or Chicago. Indeed, the continuing references to the uniqueness of Los Angeles' history and geography can actually hide similarities that, from Dallas and Phoenix to Atlanta and Silicon Valley, are emerging in the development of new metropolises, regardless of their different histories and geographies.

One reaction to the emphasis on the uniqueness of Los Angeles is the temptation to see Los Angeles as the new prototype of urban growth. Not only has its economic base continued to grow while other areas that traditionally led the country's economy declined (more on this in a moment), but its polycentric layout has become a firm point of reference in discussions of a new model of urban development—based on the center's loss of hierarchical importance in relation to the growth of "edge cities," exurbs or exopoles—which is becoming predominant across the U.S. In cases like Chicago or New York, the argument goes, this new urban form may be difficult to recognize, since it is masked by the pre-existence of earlier urban forms. Other cities, such as Dallas or Phoenix, with fewer leftovers from past periods of urbanization, resemble Los Angeles both in the physical form and chronology of their development. In still other cases, such as Orange County and Silicon Valley, where the presence of the past is even weaker, this model has taken even more extreme forms. If Los Angeles still retains a proto-center, Orange County and Silicon Valley have given up even the myth of a center as much in their names as in their physical form.

Between these two opposites, the Los Angeles School's emphasis on the concept of restructuring provides a more synthetic approach. If Los Angeles has shifted from the position of exception to that of model, one cannot discern the reasons for the shift by looking only at the region's internal history. One has to understand the economic and social changes that have been occurring in the larger American (and indeed global) context which have created the conditions for Los Angeles' new role. On the other hand,

---

[2] Among recent works, M. Davis (1991) *Do Cit* and K. Starr (1990) *Material Dreams - Southern California Through the 1920s* (New York: Oxford University Press) present vastly different views of Los Angeles' growth. They share, however, the same focus on the specificity of its history (histor fact, given their different perspectives) with interest in inserting Los Angeles in the broade text of changes on the national scene.

Los Angeles' leading role in contrast to the decline of other areas suggests that the new economic and social tendencies of restructuring have not developed evenly all over the U.S. In fact Los Angeles' 'unique' characteristics appear to be particularly hospitable to the new urban and industrial forms of development. Thus, restructuring poses itself as a concept bridging the specificity of the micro-histories internal to the area under study, and the larger-scale pathways of the macro-history of urbanization and economic development.

INDUSTRIAL RESTRUCTURING AND POSTFORDISM

In 1981 a Security Pacific Bank report loudly announced the end of the usual picture of Los Angeles as a marginal exception to the American economic landscape. The report recognized two major aspects of Los Angeles' growth. First, it acknowledged that traditional boundaries of Los Angeles—whether the City, the County or the metropolitan area—did not do justice to the kind of urban development taking place in the region. Instead, the report took as its area of study a sixty mile circle centered around downtown Los Angeles and including the entire Los Angeles and Orange Counties and the most populated parts of San Bernardino (76.8 % of its population), Riverside (56.3%), and Ventura (95.1 %). Secondly, it highlighted the exceptional rate of growth of this region between 1970 and 1980 and its new national preeminence:

The Sixty Mile Circle grew by more than 1,300,000
inhabitants (for a total of almost 11,000,000), well ahead of the Houston area, second with 932,000 new residents.
Greater Chicago(+ 137,000) and the New York area which actually lost 890,000 residents.

Even more significantly, in the same period, nonagricultural employment grew
by 1,315,000, four times the rate of Chicago's growth and 26 times Greater New York's. In particular, manufacturing
employment showed an increase of 23 percent in the Sixty Mile Circle (for a total of 1,205,000 jobs),
vis à vis decreases in the Chicago (916,000 jobs) and New York (1,397,000) areas respectively of 12.4 and 19.1 percent.

The gross product of the region (the total of goods and services produced),
following the Gross National Product of Poland and preceding Australia, was exceeded only by thirteen nations.
(The 1987 edition of the report situates the Sixty Mile Circle in eleventh position, having passed
Spain and the Netherlands)

II

The per capita gross product was higher only in Kuwait, Qatar, United Arab Emirates and Switzerland.
By 1987 the Los Angeles region was in third position, ahead of Switzerland and behind the three oil rich states (which
have a cumulative total of 1,800,000 residents).

The Sixty Mile Circle had the greatest concentration of mathematicians, scientists, engineers, skilled technicians, and
high technology industry in the U.S. The per capita income was 18% higher than the U.S. average.

The Los Angeles' twin ports of Long Beach and San Pedro have become the main gateway for trade
with Japan and the Pacific Basin. Los Angeles was the third center (after New York and New Orleans) of international
trade. It became the second center (passing New Orleans) by 1987.

The Security Pacific's data already signaled that
some form of industrial restructuring was taking place in the U.S. economy. The fact that Los
Angeles' growth over the last several years (following a period of slow growth and stagnation
in the late '60s and early '70s) came at the same time when the traditional industrial areas of
the Northeast (such as Chicago, New York, Detroit, Pittsburgh, Cleveland) were declining
suggested not only that Los Angeles was catching up with areas of older industrialization, but
that a major and generalized economic change was taking place in the country. This change has
been variously described as a geographical shift, with the industrial core of the country moving
from the Frostbelt to the Sunbelt,[7] or as a decline of 'smokestack' industries, replaced by
the emergence of new, 'clean' industries,[8] or as a mix of the two.

However, the Los Angeles case also shows that
industrial restructuring is more complicated than the Security Pacific report suggested. Hidden
in the aggregated employment growth of the report was also the loss of 75,000 jobs in the steel
industry (Fontana steel, the largest steel mill this side of the Rockies, closed in December 1983),
in the automobile industry (with the closure of Ford Pico Rivera and GM South Gate plant),[9]
and in tire manufacturing where, one after the other, Firestone, Goodyear, Goodrich, Uniroyal
have ceased operations. It is not just a question of smokestack versus clean industry either, since
some traditional industries, such as furniture and clothing, continued to expand in the region.
In the period between 1970 and 1978, for example, while New York lost 50,000 jobs in the
apparel industry, Los Angeles gained 30,000.[10] The concentration of skilled technicians and engineers was deceptive as well, since Los Angeles' economic growth is equally based on

[7]   E.g.: D.C. Perry and A.J. Watkins (1977). The
Rise of the Sunbelt Cities. Beverly Hills: Sage.

[8]   E.g.: J.I. Gershuny and J.D. Miles (1983). The
New Service Economy. New York: Praeger.

[9]   General Motors has announced the shut
down of the last auto plant in the Los Angeles region.
GM Van Nuys, for Summer 1992. For the history of
the rise and decline of the auto industry in L.A. see
R. Morales (1986) "The Los Angeles Automobile
Industry in Historical Perspective." Society and Space.
4, pp. 289-303.

[10]   M.C.D. Macdonald (1984). America's Cities: A
Report on the Myth of Urban Renaissance. New York:
Simon and Schuster. p. 178.

non-unionized[14] (and often below the minimum wage) work of illegal aliens in downtown sweatshops.[15] Nor should the high per capita income hide what several authors called the "third-worldization" of the region,[16] characterized by rampant unemployment among black and Chicano minorities (more than twice the white rate) and more than 500,000 people 'hotbedding' (sharing the same bed in turns) or living in refurbished garages or in cardboard boxes in the streets.[17]

        In brief, it is possible to isolate a specific dynamic for each facet of the industrial restructuring of Los Angeles: the geographical shift of industry to Sunbelt regions, the decline of traditional sectors and the emergence of high-tech industries, industrialization based on the low cost of labor, and even the deindustrialization of the region are all part of Los Angeles' economy. The problem is that these individual facets do not coalesce into an overall, unitary image; in fact, they contradict each other. Thus the kaleidoscopic image of Los Angeles' economy reintroduces the two aspects of restructuring previously discussed: it is not only necessary to understand how the new industrial dynamics are replacing established patterns of economic growth, but also to develop simultaneously an analytical framework able to comprehend the diversity of the new picture. As in Soja's postmodernist view, Los Angeles itself prevents the birth of a singular dominant narrative.

        To be sure, the Los Angeles School's industrial studies do not explicitly discuss postmodernism. However, it is easy to detect in Christopherson and Storper's study of the movie industry and in Scott's "Technopoles of Southern California" a preliminary critique of modernist metanarratives and teleology. Following the motto "bigger is better," in fact, the conventional wisdom posits that industries tend to concentrate production in a decreasing number of increasingly large firms while decentralizing production to increasingly peripheral locations. Product Cycle theory well summarizes this view of the trajectory of industrial evolution. According to this theory, the development of an industrial sector follows a well defined path: at first the sector is composed by a large number of small firms, which continuously introduce changes and improvements in their products. Later, as the product matures, the number of innovations decreases; as firms begin to standardize production, their number decreases while their size grows and many functions, previously fulfilled by external suppliers, become internalized to take advantage of economies of scale. Finally, with

[14]   The rate of unionization dropped, between 1970 and 1980, from 30 to 23 percent in Los Angeles County and from 26.4 to 10.5 in Orange County.

[15]   About 80 percent of the 125.000 jobs in the apparel industry are held by undocumented workers and more than 80 percent by women.

[16]   See E. Soja, R. Morales and G. Wolff (1983) "Urban Restructuring: an Analysis of Social and Spatial Change in Los Angeles." Economic Geography. 59. pp. 195-230; M. Davis (1987) "Chinatown Part Two?." Cit.

[17]   See E. Soja, A. Heskin and M. Cenzatti (1985) "Los Angeles nel Caleidoscopio della Ristrutturazione." Urbanistica. 80, pp. 55-60.

Experiments

fully mature products, innovations cease; once the standardization of the production process is complete, firms become fully integrated, eliminating the need for external suppliers altogether.[08]

Product Cycle theory also universalized a similar geographical pattern of firm location. This told us that firms in their first stage of development require the 'nurturing' environment of urban areas, where they can easily find the material inputs and services they need. However, once production becomes more standardized and economies of scale are internalized, firms tend to escape the high costs connected to urban areas. This leads them to move branch plants first towards the urban periphery and later, when their product is fully standardized, to green field locations.

As Christopherson and Storper have shown, the movie industry in Los Angeles followed this path from its birth to the 1950s, leading to the progressive formation of fewer and larger studios with production facilities located in what were (in the '20s) the urban fringes of Los Angeles: Hollywood, Westwood, Burbank, Studio City. Beginning in the early '60s, however, the story took a sudden and unforeseen turn that deviated from the Product Cycle theory's script. Rather than concentrating further, the industry moved towards increasing use of external suppliers; and spatially, rather than decentralizing further, firms have continued to locate in Hollywood and San Fernando Valley (which had become by then central locations).

Susan Christopherson and Michael Storper

THE CITY AS STUDIO: THE WORLD AS BACK LOT: THE IMPACT OF VERTICAL DISINTEGRATION ON THE LOCATION OF THE MOTION PICTURE INDUSTRY

Environment and Planning D: Society and Space
1986, Vol. 4, pp. 305-3

[08] Tellingly, the most famous example of this type of development is Ford's River Rouge plant, where raw material entered at one end of the plant and cars came out at the other.

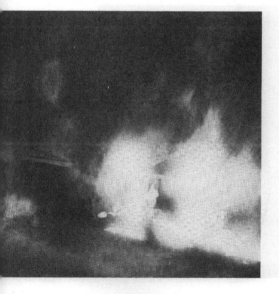

PETER ALEXANDER, JEFCAW
HOOVER, 1993; ACRYLIC ON PANEL, 18" X 12".

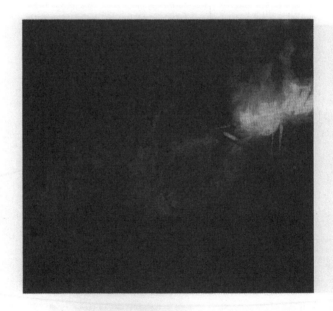

(OPPOSITE) PETER ALEXANDER, *SKYCAN GAGE*, 1993. ACRYLIC ON PANEL, 18" X 23".

PETER ALEXANDER, *SKYCAN CRENSHAW*, 1993. ACRYLIC ON PANEL, 18" X 23".

Christopherson and Storper's study deflated a primary assumption of modernist metanarratives. It rejected the notion that in industrial development there is continuous progress, a technologically determined teleology that guides production from one organizational form to the next, with the new form always inherently superior. The development of the movie industry shows that this path can reverse itself for a variety of reasons. Political conditions, labor markets, inter- and intra-sectoral competition, as well as technological changes, all play a role in the shift.

Scott's study of the Technopoles of Southern California chipped away at yet another aspect of the modernist industrial metanarrative. He showed that restructuring consists of more than changes of direction in mono-directional paths of development (even if these take unexpected turns). By focusing on industries whose development paths have always been at odds with the expected tendency towards standardization and ensuing locational patterns, he uncovered the co-existence of multiple paths of industrial development. Over time, the interaction of Southern California's high-tech industries and the characteristics of the region have created industrial complexes ("high-tech industrial districts") which have never gone through a phase of standardization and locational dispersion.

Allen Scott

THE TECHNOPOLES OF SOUTHERN CALIFORNI
Environment and Planning A, 1990, Vol. 22, pp. 1576-1605

* * *   Together, Christopherson, Storper and Scott have shown how some of Los Angeles' major industries did not follow the expected scripts. <u>Temporally</u>, Christopherson and Storper tell us that the same industry can take different developmental trajectories, suggesting that there is no technologically inevitable evolution of production systems. <u>Sectorally</u>, Scott points out alternative directions in which different industries can be organized and evolve. <u>Spatially</u>, both accounts show not only that the presence of particular economic activities in a region shape the development of the area, but also that the local characteristics, in a circular process, influence the organization of production. Thus the lack of a center for Los Angeles, or, better, the presence of many centers both shapes the locational patterns of its industries as well as is shaped by the characteristics of this industrial development.

        These studies of Los Angeles and its industries, however, are not enough to dispel objections that both the region and its industries are exceptions to 'normal' urban and industrial development. After all, it can be argued that the movie industry is not a 'real' industry and that aerospace is too tied to the ups and downs of government commissions to develop 'normally'. Christopherson, Scott and Storper address this difficulty by integrating their specific studies of the movie and high-tech industries in Southern California into a broader industrial dynamic that signals the passage from a Fordist to a post-fordist organization of production.

        This argument follows the work of the French Regulation School which identifies, after the economic crisis of the early '70s, the exhaustion of the dominant role that mass production and mass consumption played in Western society since the Great Depression.[12] For the Regulation School, Fordist production began with the advent of the assembly line, the use of single purpose machinery, and the increasing use of deskilled labor in repetitive tasks. This industrial arrangement led, between World War Two and the mid 1960s, to the standardization of production and to enormous productivity increases. Fordism depended more than just on mass production, however. It also required a continuous expansion of consumer markets as outlets for an increasing output of production. Thus, for the Regulation School, the second aspect of Fordism is the appearance of an array of mechanisms, from credit systems, to collective contracts for the workers, union recognition, and regulation

[12]   For a more complete discussion of the Fordist regime of accumulation and its crisis see M. Aglietta (1979) <u>A Theory of Capitalist Regulation</u>. London: Verso; R. Boyer (1990) <u>The Regulation School. A Critical Introduction</u>. New York: Columbia University Press; R. Boyer (1988) "Technical Change and the <u>Theory of Regulation</u>" in G. Dosi et Al., <u>Technical Change and Economic Theory</u>. London: Pinter; A. Lipietz (1987) <u>Miracles and Miracles</u>. London: Verso. For an excellent summary of Aglietta's work see M. Davis (1978) "Fordism in Crisis: a Review of Michel Aglietta's <u>Régulation et Crises: L' Expérience des Etats-Unis</u>." <u>Review</u>, II, No. 2, Fall, pp. 207-69.

19

of wage increases which fulfilled the twofold task of improving the economic conditions of the working class (therefore supplying a social expansion of the market) and offering a system of regulation for the relations between management and labor, therefore guaranteeing continuity of production.

By the early '70s Fordism was in crisis. The Regulation School explained this by identifying two limits in the Fordist system. The first limit was the rigidity of Fordist production methods, such as the assembly line, which severely hampered the manufacturer's ability to change rapidly the volume and type of products. Given the rapid changes in quantity and quality of consumer demand over the previous two decades, this posed serious problems. The second limit was the increasing difficulty of balancing the higher labor costs (necessary to expand the market) without a decline in profitability caused by increasing labor costs.

In the midst of the Fordist crisis, observers began to see signs of recovery in the appearance of new productive systems that bypassed the rigidities of mass production. A large number of studies identified the growing importance of forms of production that, instead of following the typical features of Fordist production (such as large firms, integrated production and output standardization) used various systems of flexible production.[20] Ways of increasing flexibility run the gamut from the introduction of new technologies that eliminate the rigidities of the assembly line in mass production, to the 'disintegration' of the Fordist integrated firm by expelling rigid departments of production, to the growth of interdependent systems of small and medium sized firms. The flexibility of these systems is predicated on two major elements. First, individual firms have relied on multipurpose machinery that allows them to change output without the costly and time consuming re-tooling necessary with the devoted machines of the assembly line and by employing a work force of skilled workers who can shift to different operations without re-training. The *system* of firms supplies a second form of flexibility, since by shifting linkages within the network of part suppliers and subcontractors the final products can be changed more rapidly than in an integrated firm. Flexible specialization studies have shown how, in different combinations, these elements are at the base of the recent industrial success of areas as different as Japan, Southern Germany and Central Italy.[21]

[20] It should be noted that these "Flexible Specialization" studies concentrate on production, leaving in the background the consumption side of Fordism. Among them, see in particular: M. J. Piore and C. F. Sabel (1984), The Second Industrial Divide. New York: Basic Books; P. Hirst and J. Zeitlin (1989), "Flexible Specialization and the Competitive Failure of U.K. Manufacturing," Political Quarterly, Vol. 60, No. 3, pp. 164-78; D. Leborgne and A. Lipietz, (1992), "Conceptual Fallacies and Open Issues on Post-Fordism," in Scott and Storper (eds.) Pathways to Industrialization and Regional Development, London and New york: Routledge.

[21] See Piore and Sabel, Op. Cit.

Here Christopherson, Storper and Scott's cases re-enter the picture as two other examples of successful restructuring, of growth along the flexible lines of postfordist production. Yet, they cannot be reduced to a mechanical result of the generalized crisis of Fordism. The movie industry, as we saw, began its own restructuring well before the advent of the Fordist crisis, while Southern California's high tech industry never went through a Fordist phase. This also allows Los Angeles to re-enter the picture in the double role it plays for the Los Angeles School: bridging the gap between specific examples of general dynamics and the uniqueness of an exceptional case.

The divergence of Los Angeles' development from the expected pattern is an indication of the double character of restructuring—as both material and theoretical shift. Fordism dominated not only as an organization of production that defined alternative forms as marginal or obsolete, but also as a theoretical position that assumed that the development of mass production posited general rules. Its crisis has allowed both 'other' organizations of production and 'other' theoretical explanations to enter the picture. In this changing situation, the recognition of the industrial 'Other' poses two theoretical problems. On the one hand, there is the danger of re-imposing yet another totalizing explanation, which simply seeks to replace Fordism with an alternative all-inclusive theory, rather than creating new ways of producing theory that encourage 'flexible' explanations equivalent to different and simultaneous patterns of development. On the other hand, Christopherson, Storper and Scott's case studies narrating specific micro-histories (almost Foucauldian genealogies), while respecting individual areas and sectors, remain as fragments. This suggests the possibility of constructing a more comprehensive framework without falling back into dominating master theories that neglect the meaning and importance of specificity and diversity.

POSTMODERNISM AND SOCIAL RESTRUCTURING

It is Soja in particular who has taken on this conceptual challenge. Beginning his theoretical restructuring by "reasserting spatiality," he has criticized modernism's systematic privileging of history, or better historicism, i.e. explanations of social phenomena solely based on temporal unfolding. In order to escape the totalizations of modernism and to bring other subjects and histories into focus Soja argues for a change of

21

theoretical perspective that will give equal relevance to time and space and that will balance history with geography. Historicism, by its very nature, privileges the sequentiality of events. Events are always presented in a linear fashion, inevitably following one another. Even if other subjects and histories are sought and found, each of them is exclusive of the others. If history-histories remain the only cornerstone of the social sciences, the sequentiality of narrative is unavoidable and the contradiction between what is chosen as central and what is marginalized or excluded persists.

For Soja spatiality offers the possibility of adding (rather than replacing) the linearity (or linearities) of history (-ies) to the simultaneity of geography (-ies), where many events take place at the same time in different places. Thus geography must be a necessary counterpart of attempts to re-found history on the basis of the 'otherness' that Foucault argues has always escaped the modernist picture. Space, however, is not just another ingredient that can be 'injected' into modernist analyses. Soja addresses the blindness to spatiality which has progressed with the evolution of modernism. In fact, he argues, modernist attempts to deal with spatiality have oscillated from a conception of space as totally opaque—a reification of space as a collection of measurable "things-in-themselves"—and space as perfectly transparent—its fetishization as "mental design."[10] In the first case space is seen as largely irrelevant to social and philosophical progress, and is reduced to a "thing" shaped by history. Space is equally unimportant in the second case, having retreated into an ideal realm of individual perception, where it can have little influence on social reality.

The spatial dynamics described in Product Cycle theory are an example of the passivity that geography retains in modernist views. It depicts industries that locate on a landscape in which urban centers, peripheries, and green field locations are universalized until only time is left. Space is reduced to the passive and measurable consequences of its historical evolution. The same banalization of space is recognizable in traditional models of urban growth—from Burgess' concentric city, to Hoyt's radial development and Harris and Ullman's system of satellite cities—which see the urban form simply as the spatial inscription of general (and temporal) rules of urban "ecological" growth.

The progressive annihilation of space continues in (late) modernist attempts to describe recent urban developments, such as the center's loss

[10]   E. Soja (1989) Postmodern Geographies. London: Verso. pp.124-127.

of importance and the proliferation of edge cities and exurbs, as a homogenized phenomenon repeating itself everywhere, creating modular and undifferentiated landscapes. Los Angeles is obviously not exempt from these interpretations. It has been variously described as a "hundred suburbs in search of a center" (Gunther, Pierce) or as an ensemble of "urban villages" (Leinberger and Lockwood) to indicate what these writers see as the endless repetition of its pattern of growth. Instead of a commercial center, a web of shopping malls covers the region. Although the Central Business District, the traditional urban center, still exists and contains the area's highest concentration of banks, offices and corporate headquarters, its form and functions are repeated in duplicate clusters, from Century City, Pasadena and Long Beach, to Costa Mesa and Irvine. Thus, they conclude, it is fruitless to look for hierarchy or differences between these centers.

Even the Security Pacific's Sixty Mile Circle is indicative of the progressive erasure of spatiality, hiding not only the contradictions internal to Los Angeles' industrial structure, but presenting the urban area, precisely, as a homogeneous circle. Against the risk of elevating the Sixty Mile Circle to a totalizing image of Los Angeles, Soja proceeds to deconstruct it. Drifting along the edges of the circle and shifting constantly between inner and outer cities, centers and peripheries, he has shown that in addition to the circle there are other geographies-histories to be discovered in their continuous evolution and interaction and that Los Angeles' absence of a hierarchical structure is not the end of spatial differentiation, but, on the contrary, the emergence of a new round of differentiations, of new centers and peripheries continuously produced and overlapping.

Edward Soja

AKING LOS ANGELES APART: TOWARDS A POSTMODERN GEOGRAPHY
From Postmodern Geographies—The Reassertion of Space in Critical Social Theory.
ondon: Verso Books, 1989. Chapter 9.

Deconstructing the Sixty Mile Circle is the first step in Soja's attempt at theoretical reconstitution. Pointing out the limits and biases of this text (ambiguously, the text is both the area included in the circle and the Security Pacific report), Soja reveals the multiplicity of stories and geographies that the Sixty Mile Circle hides. He also suggests that the space he is concerned with is not the physical and inert space endlessly measured by modernist geographers, but a space that is socially produced and reproduced. The new urban form, far from leading to homogeneity (or better, in addition to homogeneity), also continues to create spatial differentiation. Indeed, the current phase of urbanization, if anything, has made spatial differentiation more dramatic and important than ever.

Soja is not alone in arguing for the increasing importance of social space. Other writers have found that improved transportation and communication do not annihilate space, but, on the contrary, make it more relevant. David Harvey calls it a consequence of "time-space compression," with the decreasing importance of spatial barriers leading to greater sensitivity to "the variations of place within space."[58] Similarly, Gianni Vattimo points out that almost instantaneous information may be leading towards a transparent society, but transparency is characterized by chaos and difference, rather than by clarity and homogeneity, since we can now perceive local "dialects" of places previously hidden from us.[59] For Soja, however, the most important feature of postmodernity is the appearance of a different kind of social space.

Relying on a periodization that follows both the evolution of capitalism from its competitive phase, through Fordism and postfordism and the theoretical periods identified by postmodernists such as Foucault and Baudrillard, Soja distinguishes three periods of spatialization. The first is characterized by the dominance of physical space—the space which simply reflects a-spatial phenomena—inherited from from the Renaissance (i.e. from pre-industrial times when social life took place in a given and largely immutable spatial surface). Theoretically, this is the space perceived, measured and analyzed by traditional, mainstream science in an effort to understand external reality. Baudrillard uses the metaphor of the mirror to summarize the theoretical framework of this period: the purpose of knowledge is to accumulate accurate reflections of the real. The second type of space is shaped by man: it is the space of the uneven development produced by capitalism, shaping a landscape

[58] D. Harvey (1989). The Condition of Postmodernity. Oxford: Basil Blackwell, pp. 285-86.
[59] G. Vattimo (1988). The End of Modernity. Baltimore: The Johns Hopkins Press.

of centers and peripheries. At a theoretical level, the discovery of this space corresponds to what Baudrillard calls the period of the "mask," marked by the development of critical theories that question the belief that knowledge can appropriate reality by simply looking at its visible appearances. Instead, "the masters of suspicion," Marx, Freud, de Saussure, argued that appearances are deceptive and knowledge should unmask them, reaching under the surface of things to unearth the essence and deep structure of reality.

Soja argues that we are now entering a third period, in which the production of space is becoming increasingly independent from external reality. In fact reality itself appears as the result of the creation of space. This resembles Baudrillard's third phase of simulacra, where copies are made of originals that do not exist. Now, appearance no longer refers to an external, if hidden, reality, but only to itself. Therefore "true" and "false," "real" and "imaginary," "signifier" and "signified" have lost their meaning. Soja claims that this simulated social space is no longer produced by human adaptation to territory (as in the first period), nor by transforming it (as in the second period), but by imagining it, with the real territory only 'reflecting' an imagined one. This does not mean, as Baudrillard maintains, that reality has disappeared. For Soja these periods do not replace one another, but create successive layers each of which—as an order of appearance—constructs and reveals a specific type of urban space.

Orange County, even more than Los Angeles, demonstrates the increasing importance of these "hyperspaces." The absence of previous periods of urbanization provides an ideal ground to explore how the current layer evolved (Disneyland's simulacra offer a significant starting point). Orange County's *tabula rasa*, however, does not lead to a homogeneous landscape. On the contrary, the main characteristic of Orange County's urbanism is the differentiation and fragmentation of its elements. In fact, this differentiation is so extreme that the word 'fragmented', by implying a previous unity, does not do justice to the multiplicity of internally coherent and externally disconnected landscapes that compose Orange County. In this setting, a 'total' reading or a single formal 'model' becomes impossible. Far more than Los Angeles, Orange County presents in physical form a Derridean deconstruction where the appearance of any narrative can be immediately countered by alternative readings. Soja, recognizing this condition, has adjusted his mode of analysis and

presentation to this (these) new reality (-ies), creating a collage of quotations and snapshots where
the author imposes a narrative only to present a simultaneous collection of images.

Edward Soja

INSIDE EXOPOLIS: THEMES SCREENED IN ORANGE COUNT
From Variations on a Theme Park—The New American City and the End of Public Spac
M. Sorkin, ed., 1992. New York: Hill and Wang, pp. 94-12

The City as Text

In postmodernist parlance, "text" has become a key word to indicate how reality is both socially constructed ("written") and interpreted ("read"). In books, speeches, paintings, or music, not only the subject matter changes from one text to another, but also the interpretations of each text change, depending on the interests and perspective of the reader. From Roland Barthes' "death of the author" to Jaques Derrida's deconstruction, we have been made increasingly aware of the importance of our own reading(s) over any stable interpretation of meaning. Within the text, we may privilege a specific discourse in which we are particularly interested; or we discover a hidden narrative, a particular sequence of events or concepts of which perhaps even the author was unaware, but that for us becomes the leading thread of the discourse and of the text. Conversely, the most important aspect of a text may be its silence in relation to a specific topic or discourse. Paralleling Baudrillard's and Soja's three phases of knowledge, postmodernism tells us that—rather than a mirror of the author's ideas, or an encoded appearance from which the true message should be extracted—the reading of a text is a reflection of the reader.[56] However, this does not mean that a text is open to any interpretation and the reader is free to chose any meaning (which would imply that any text is the same as any other). Rather, it means that the specificity of a text cannot be established in isolation. The privilege we attribute to a particular aspect of the text does not follow from an intrinsic superiority discovered within the specific text or from the whim of the reader. A text is always part of a web of other texts; it is connected to other works of the same author, or related to other works on the same topics, or linked to our own previous readings, etc., and its specificity thus derives from its positioning in relation to other texts. A text is, in other words, always immersed in a context that directs our reading.

From this perspective the importance of the Los Angeles School, and the possibility of identifying what unites its participants, more than in the specific stories they tell us, lies in the mode of reading the text of Los Angeles that they suggest. To be sure, their focus on Los Angeles' industries and spatial differentiation does not exhaust the narratives of the text. Even within their own narratives, other stories can be found. The growth of the Technopoles or the 'Disneylandization' of Orange County can be easily matched, for example, by the decline of the old "poles" of South Gate or Vernon or by other productions of space (such as the appropriation of roadsides and street corners by the homeless, or the struggles over the gentrification of downtown). What makes the work of the Los Angeles School relevant and confers its products a unity is the context that shapes its stories. The concept of restructuring, in fact, orients not only the understanding of industrial development (via postfordism) and of space (via hyperspace), but, with its epistemological implications for how theory itself is constructed, also indicates how various narratives coexist in the text .

At the same time, if a text cannot be read in isolation, neither is the context established *a priori* of the text. In fact, as much as the reader is responsible for the reading(s) of a text, the text itself remains the focal point to which the other texts refer. The destabilization of the relationship between author, text, and reader that postmodernism suggests denies the possibility of establishing a priority between text and context, and replaces it with the simultaneity of the two. In this sense the theoretical perspective from which any text is interpreted is included in the object studied. Just as we cannot learn to read without rules that allow an interpretation of the text, the text itself is equally central

[56] See R. Barthes (1971) "From Work to Text." *Image-Music-Text*, New York: Hill and Wangs. p. 158.

28

in suggesting the rules for its interpretation. The urban text compounds this oscillation between text and context. Daily, countless authors/readers/actors intervene on this text, reading it from their particular perspective and adding or changing its parts. Industrial firms, workers, policy makers, real estate developers, ethnic communities, neighborhood associations, illegal immigrants and homeless, each of these social actors lives a different city and intervenes on it in a different way. If the meaning of a literary text floats according to the reader, the urban text is doubly floating, for the reading affects the production of the text. The city talks back in a way in which no book or painting can and the L.A. School has demonstrated that Los Angeles speaks, to use Vattimo's phrase, in a multitude of different "dialects." Los Angeles, like Chicago in the thirties, may be exemplary of a new urban model, but the most important aspect of its exemplariness relies on our realization of the fact that the model is always partial.

ISBN: 978-0-9763166-8-4

Gehry:
In His Own
Theme

An Interview with
Frank O. Gehry

Sylvia Lavin

LA Forum Newsletter
February 1993

SL: Do you agree with most of the architectural press's assertion that only your Entertainment Center escaped Disney-itis because it is the only un-themed building at EuroDisneyland?

FOG: In before-the-opening views, the building seems to have escaped, but in after-the-opening views, it looks caught. I didn't want to go to the opening because I was worried I might not like it and even when I accepted the job I knew it was going to be precarious. But I didn't want to be holier-than-thou about what I coined "entertainment architecture," which is not architecture, but which is also not non-architecture. Even though journalists shouldn't be talking about it in columns devoted to Architecture with a capital "A," if you think of the Columbian Exposition of 1893, some important things did develop from that "entertainment architecture." In fact, initially I was very interested in the relationship between these two kinds of architecture and it gave me some hope about what the whole place might be like. I had asked the Disney people to bring in Rem Koolhaas, Jean Nouvel, Hans Hollein, Arata Isozaki, Peter Eisenman, Christian de Portzamparc—and some of these architects were even hired to do studies. I thought there was a growing interest in European architects; the project was in Europe, they already had all the Americans on their list, and since the whole thing could have been an experiment of sorts, I thought they should have a variety of people. When I was asked who my choices were, I suggested tough guys, not push-over postmodernists. Then they cancelled all these people who had been hired to do studies—in a single meeting Disney shifted against the tough guys.

SL: How dependent did you feel your ability to be a tough guy was on not having a theme? Would you have accepted the job had it come with a theme and would you accept another Disney job even if it was un-themed?

FOG: No and never. Disney suggested I might do a huge hotel. They didn't know what the hotel's theme was yet, but it would have had a theme and I couldn't do the project. In the end, however, I found that I had become guilty by association. The entertainment center, in the context of all the other stuff, became a theme building anyway. The building became a Frank Gehry–themed building.

SL: Do you think that Frank Gehry architecture is particularly susceptible to becoming its own theme?

FOG: I think it would have happened to anybody. It might even have been worse for some others. Think what would have happened to Rem Koolhaas. Since he tends toward stylization—he plays around with the styles of the 1940s and 1950s and uses a kind of Harrison/Abramowitz language—in some ways he gets close to being themed already.

SL: What constitutes a theme?

FOG: Michael Graves was given New York or "Metropolis" as a theme and he took theming very seriously. But if no one had said anything, I can imagine that he might have evolved from nowhere the idea of a hotel with towers and turrets representing some urban downtown. If you did a huge hotel in France on the banks of a lake, a reasonable strategy would be to make towers and turrets like those at Chambord or a million other places. That strategy could develop toward an urban idea with connotations of downtown cities that could end up looking like New York, but it would not be themed by Disney and would stand some chance of being honest. The architect could have evolved his own theme without realizing that he was being themed. It's the context of Mickey Mouse and Disneyland itself, where everything from Main Street to the Magic Castle is already ersatz, that changes everything. Claes Oldenburg wouldn't do anything there. He felt that no matter how tough something he did might be, in that context, it would be co-opted by the real thing, which is the ersatz thing. The force—to sell trinkets and rides and ersatz experience—is powerful enough to co-opt anything. If Le Corbusier had built Romchamp at EuroDisneyland, it would have been a themed church. I don't think anyone can survive. That's the lesson of EuroDisney—you can't win and you can't survive. A pound of Mickey is worth a hundred pounds of everything else.

SL: What does the EuroDisneyland phenomenon have of significance to say to architecture?

FOG: In the last analysis, I don't think EuroDisney is about architecture, even though I think we all believe that Michael Eisner is brilliant and that he is genuinely interested in architecture. In many regards it's thanks to Eisner that Michael Graves has done really interesting work for Disney—with about another $10 a square foot, his buildings could have been really great. We believed in Eisner's struggle to prove to his partners that they could do good architecture at even the cheapest level. But the truth is that everybody understands architecture in different ways, and I think that Eisner's conception is closer to Robert Stern, Michael Graves, and Prince Charles' understanding than it is to my own. All during our design process there was another architect doing the same building only with a theme—he was being paid a parallel fee to do parallel work all the way through design development. If at any moment they had decided to dump us, they wouldn't have lost any time. I was reasonably prepared for that, since it's the way Hollywood works. Several screenwriters work on the same script simultaneously. From Eisner's standpoint, this represented a commitment to architecture. Ironically, when they finally saw the festival hall designs, they were ecstatic—our project is pretty theatrical and we had tried to make a good shopping center. But that's before Mickey Mouse got at it.

SL: Can and should an architect make a good piece of architecture that is also a successful shopping center? Is there a difference between accommodating and facilitating shopping?

FOG: In my opinion the question is not whether we can but the fact that we must be able to make shopping centers. I've always complained that architects like me don't do shopping centers. That's why I did Santa Monica Place. But, just like at EuroDisney, something got lost there, too—they came in with all their stuff and it's overwhelming. I've seen Roosevelt Fields, a shopping center in New York that I. M. Pei did—it's very Miesian and it looked like IIT. Pei controlled every detail, but it failed miserably because it was too sophisticated. It was a bad shopping center. So, how do you make a good shopping center? I made Disney stronger than Santa Monica Place—its image was stronger—and the goal was not just to allow people to shop, but to actually encourage them to shop. The idea was that during the day the building would be fairly benign, but then, after 4:00 p.m. in the dull Paris sky, it would come to life and it would become irresistible. I accepted that as part of the program and I didn't feel that I was selling out just by accepting the program. My concern was how to make architecture, instead of just *building*, that people would respond to and use and that would enrich their experience. Had I pushed a little harder and gotten more involved in the design of all the elements, I think it could have been different—that was my miscalculation. I thought the strength of the building's image could hold the stuff Disney pasted on to it, and by the time I realized it couldn't, it was too late. In the context of Disneyland, you can't escape. But if I took this same building and put it somewhere else, including the barrage of graphics, it would be sustainable. One would have to be involved at an extreme level of detail and avoiding Disney's tendency to homogenize everything might even require collaboration. If Koolhaas, Eisenman, Venturi, and Hollein had been building EuroDisney, I can imagine us ending up with a better thing. Not a better Disneyland. At the end of the day, I think maybe architecture and Disney don't mix.

SL: You place a great deal of emphasis on Disney's capacity to negate truthfulness. Is the rest of the world "outside Disney" so much more innocent?

FOG: There is a question of critical mass. Two Rodeo Drive is Disney outside of Disneyland. But then there's Wilshire Boulevard, which is simply more honest— there is a toughness about reality that you can't fake. Some pieces along Wilshire Boulevard may be contrived, but Wilshire itself was not contrived in total. The whole is bigger than any of its parts. Disney is all chocolate sundaes and the whole simply overwhelming. Simply by being there you get covered in whipped cream. I believe in the difference between reality and illusion. To be overpowered by the real is one thing; to be overpowered by the ersatz is something else.

Disney needs illusion to sell, and theirs is a seduction that uses nostalgia, but, in the end, they too are overpowered by their own images. Eisner really wants to be a patron of architecture—he would like to be a Medici, but since he exists as part of a corporate structure, defined by the bottom line, his engine can't really be fueled by architecture. He can't escape his own context any more than architecture can. But Eisner still represents a ray of hope—he's a major client, he's very smart, and he's already taken a long shot for which he should be congratulated. But what he could still do is take a leading role in getting the movie industry involved in city building. If you think of how important something like Fritz Lang's *Metropolis* has been to our understanding of cities, think what it might be like if architects were encouraged to develop a three-dimensional Metropolis, if they were given a chance to update that image and find a new model appropriate to our own time. That could be exciting and Eisner could help get us there. As it stands now, Disney's job is to always look good in contrast to society's degeneration. Given the rate of our social disintegration, maybe Disney will look even better in 300 years. Maybe in that context, Eisner will seem like the Medici and Disney will look like Florence.

Interlude: Art and Architecture

Art and Architecture: A Discussion

Margaret Crawford, Chava Danielson, and Christopher Tandon

LA Forum Newsletter, October 1994

This conversation took place against the background of a recent redefining of the funding process for public art projects in the local municipality of Culver City. A great deal of press time and public energy has gone into arguing exactly what the parameters of both the selection process and the allocation of funds should be. Specifically, the question was asked, are there conditions under which the funds set aside for a public art project should be returned to the developer and invested in the architecture? More simply, can the architecture itself be considered art?

Three members of the Forum—Margaret Crawford, Chair of the Department of History/Theory at SCI-Arc, and Christopher Tandon and myself, both more recently graduated from architecture school and entered into design professions— came together to discuss what we found to be a striking subtext to the entire debate. That is, a rampant confusion and disagreement about what it is that architects practice and how you might begin to define architecture itself.

— Chava Danielson, editor

CT: I think the reason that so many in this debate are quick to say that architecture is not art arises from the fact that in the 20th century, architects themselves, in defining the profession, have downplayed their role as artists. Do you think that's true?

MC: It didn't happen in this century. It happened with the professionalization of architecture and the codification of architectural qualifications.

CT: I was thinking more of late modernism. Prior to that, at least through expressionism, architecture was still considered art, and if—only by architects—considered one of the highest forms of art.

MC: It doesn't really have to do with modernism; it has to do with professionalization, which came before modernism.

CT: But in continuing to define the profession, one of the claims of modernism was that architecture is about function and economy. Architects then excluded the idea, or didn't talk about the fact that part of what we do is make works of art. That buildings are art. We look at buildings as art.

MC: But this is the wrong definition of art. You have to look at these things objectively. In the way that they're actually constructed and practiced in society and the economy. And I will tell you that architects are licensed by the state, they undergo a very particular kind of education, and they are hired by clients to perform certain duties that are spelled out in a contract. That is how they perform whatever it is that they do. Artists on the other hand, operate in a free market situation; they are unlicensed. Anyone can wake up in the morning and say, "I am an artist," and the market and history will prove or disprove that statement. The artist rarely—and here's where public art gets a little less clearly defined—but the artist does not work on commission. An artist would be unlikely to even get a public art commission unless they had a previous body of work that was simply produced and then sold on the open market. This is a completely different type of activity, and a completely different way of performing work than the architect. And that's an objective definition of these activities.

MC: The confusion here is between visual art and architecture. And the question here is that, is there some miracle that occurs at a certain level of quality in architecture where, like transubstantiation, architecture miraculously becomes art?

CD: You mean, becomes other than just a service to the developer, helping him subdivide his property in a profitable way, so that he can be taxed the 1%, and the city can then buy some art?

MC: No ... no, it's actually that a miracle occurs, and one practice is miraculously transformed into another practice. I think that's a little, well, miraculous is the only word one could use for it. I would say that this is trying to redefine something on the basis of quality rather than on the basis of the nature of the practice. And I think that's misconceived. This doesn't have anything to do with the actual subject at hand (the current controversy in Culver City), which one could think about in a different way, that might allow architects to actually participate in these programs.

CD: Somebody made the point that the underlying motivation of percent for art programs was to improve the quality of civic life, and a well-thought-out building with intelligence and artistic "transubstantiation" improves the quality of civic life in a way that a developer-designed building doesn't. And so the difference between one and the other is that one has a civic value...

MC: But, you see, that's not the issue again. The fundamental point of percent for art programs is acknowledging public responsibility. That is what it's about. It's that developers and architects, civic leaders, zoners, planners, everyone, users, must acknowledge that there is public responsibility in building. It's not about improving the landscape or anything like that; fundamentally it's about acknowledging public responsibility. So, how then is public responsibility constructed? Is it constructed aesthetically, is it constructed in terms of amenities, is it constructed in many other ways? This is my objection to the whole debate— the right questions aren't really being asked.

CD: If you are trying to define architecture by its role in the marketplace, my question is, then, what are the complications that arise from the fact that architects, I think, now believe that the artistic merit or the artistic value of the architecture they produce is conceptual, and not commodifiable. And also, that art, that the boundaries of what it is to produce art, have been expanded in this century...

MC: This is still a subjective point of view, and in this discussion, it's simply the architect's self-definition. We can't accept that. That is not an objective definition that can operate in making an argument to the world at large.

CD: But, don't public artists have the same problem?

MC: Same thing for artists. Both of these professions do, I agree. They claim certain things, but both of these are inappropriate bases for even discussing this issue. If you want to re-conceptualize the nature of public responsibility in building, you need to start with that, and as far as I can tell, no one has actually done it. The arguments are all based on their own internal self-definition of their activity, and I don't think that's useful.

CD: But I think this is an important point in understanding some of the contention. The fact is that art has evolved into something that is not as commodity-based as it used to be, and architecture has evolved into something that is not as commodity or decoratively based as it used to be. The problem becomes one of taking the excess value of what each of these professions produce—that part outside its market value that educates, that is artistic, that frankly transcends everyday life—and defining it in a way that is useful to a bureaucracy and can have a budget, in this case a percent of construction cost, assigned to it by that bureaucracy.

CT: What would you say the basis for the animosity is, then?

MC: In the course of the development of both of these activities, and probably based on the kind of self-definition that both of these activities aspire to, they are coming into conflict, because the world of non-commodified operations is minuscule. Ironically, to me what they're both doing is seeking a kind of public commodification, in which they're getting paid not by the client, but by the state or the public. They're actually seeking some kind of legitimating public commodification. Since they don't want to accept market commodification, they are both aspiring to a kind of transcendence from the marketplace. Obviously they're going to come into conflict, because they are unwilling to accept that we live in a capitalist society. That's why they're seeking what I would call miraculous solutions based on, again, this transubstantiation. And so, I mean, it's actually kind of ironic. They're seeking miracles really, both of them, to escape what they see as the confinements of commodification.

CD: Right, they don't want to accept it.

MC: They don't want to accept it, you see. And I would argue this is the wrong thing to do.

CT: And what's the right thing to do?

MC: I think you have to acknowledge the fact that you live in a capitalist society, and that both of these activities are fundamentally marketplace activities. They are different marketplaces clearly, and so looking to the state as a solution doesn't actually offer transubstantiation or transcendence or miraculous freedom. It actually offers a completely different set of conditions that in their own way are as confining as the conditions of the marketplace—because they actually involve a responsibility to the public, which still has not been adequately defined. But that's what it's all about. I would say both artists and architects have proven pretty reluctant to accept this.

CD: Sure, it is very confining.

MC: Because, you mean that the public is basically not really very interested in what they do.

CD: And also there is no such thing as "the public."

MC: Well, right, there are "publics" ... that's true. There is no public and then, instead of this ideal, wonderful kind of world of the public supporting you, what you actually get is what we see happening here in Culver City—entrenched political interests, political favors owed, etc.—I would say unrepresentative members of the "public" and interest groups fighting for themselves. And so is this the public? Is this better than marketplace? I think many people working in public art would probably say no. So, again, I think that the mistake is that both architects and artists want to escape the conditions that their particular activities are constructed under, and achieve some kind of transcendental freedom. I would say that that's impossible, and that the whole aspiration of doing this is misconceived from the get-go.

CT: So, architects are seeking recognition of the value of architecture, as opposed to building, from the state. Because they aspire to create art, which rarely happens when one is providing a service to and meeting the economic interests of a developer. But in turning to the state you then have to deal with some kind of public policy, often in the form of zoning restrictions, design review, and all those other things architects also complain about.

MC: All those terrible things.

CT: But those things are the public's defense against, not specifically architecture, but against development and the marketplace, which architects are perceived as being part of. Consequently, it's unlikely that architects will find freedom by turning to the public or, really, the state.

MC: Right, and I hate to say it, but there is no transcendence. There is only one or the other.

CD: So, what do you think? Do you think there's a place for an architect to think about what they do as being more than just what they have been hired to do?

MC: Yeah, it could be, but l would say that in order to do that architects actually have to accept the conditions under which they work, and within those conditions try to develop modes of working that accomplish other things. This is very different from aspiring towards a kind of miraculous condition, which doesn't actually exist. And to me there are actually a lot of really exciting possibilities in doing that. I would be interested in seeing architects focus on the nature of the constraints they encounter instead of dreaming their way out of them. They could focus on the ways in which these constraints are constructed, and possibly come up with ways in which to restructure those constraints. I think you actually really need to look at how things operate in the professional world of building, and then you could come up with some fantastic solutions. But no one wants to touch it because it's too alarming.

CT: In the practice of making art, there is a reluctance to define one's activity: in a sense, you can leave it to the marketplace. But then you have institutions like the NEA giving money and trying to define or set criteria. This is a lot of what happens in public art as well, but that debate hasn't come up yet: who curates it, who decides.

MC: Because it's very cut and dry, actually ... who does it? These various public agencies decide.

CT: But these are public agencies that are commissioning, in fact, as opposed to the NEA, which is giving funding to artists in a broader sense. The NEA doesn't take possession or purchase anything. Its purpose isn't acquisition, it's to support artists. Public art programs are about improving the public realm in whatever city you happen to be in. It is a commission, or at least the acquisition, of an art piece. It is about the art, or the object, not the artists, which actually makes it more difficult.

MC: I think also that public art is extremely under-theorized, under-examined. Because it isn't about improving the way the world looks, it really has to do with debate in the public realm. And that's the reason it's been so troubled: it's very difficult to think of virtually any public art that hasn't been controversial. The battle record of public art is horrendous and that's because it's an inherently conflictual field. What is the nature of public, and what does that mean? Does that mean the common good? In the 1930s, people were willing, for example, to accept the idea of massive infrastructure, like dams, as something that represented the common good. Try to get a dam built today. You cannot do it. There have been virtually no dams built, and they are even thinking of removing dams. Part of the reason for that is there is no consensus about a common good. I would say that there is no common good. In order to discuss this you have to really discuss the nature of democracy and how it operates in a specific kind of state, like the United States. I think now there is no public sphere: there are multiple public spheres and they are all fighting it out. And so the idea that you can achieve consensus in this way is absurd.

The whole battle in a way to me is what public art should be about. It shouldn't be about producing, it should create an arena where you can struggle about meaning. It is about the very nature of public discussion and competing interests claiming this kind of territory of the public.

CD: So how does that fit into your idea of the marketplace?

MC: Again, that's the idiotic thing. In Culver City it's absurd. Because we are talking about the nature of the local state. How does a local state, the Culver City government, operate, what interests is it beholden to, who are the participants in Culver City politics, who are the economic powers in Culver City, and who are the people who actually live in Culver City? Basically the people who live in Culver City and what they want—no one is even paying attention to them in this discussion. It's turned into a discussion of the nature of the state, not about the nature of the public.

I think everybody's heart is in the right place in public art. They really are less self-interested than a lot of other people. At the same time, they're really blind to bigger issues. Because they want to do something positive, they find it difficult to acknowledge the contested-ness of the territory. That basically it's a struggle. That every inch of the territory is completely contested. Of course, why would anyone want to do anything like that? Instead of doing something great, and expecting that it's going to happen, it never happens, almost never. I started teaching a course in public art, and we continually looked at public art situations that ended in controversy and fights. That's the history of public art.

MC: Collaboration is another issue, I think, in a sense that's part of the issue here. Architects don't want to collaborate here because they collaborate so much in getting a building built. What's left for them to do is already small enough, it's understandable.

CT: And from the other side, architects have to take responsibility for the fact that so much of the architecture they are doing is not being accepted by the public, perceived as bad, and somehow needs to be spruced up with art.

MC: Do you think that's true?

CT: Well, it's certainly something that I came across. The origins of a lot of public art programs were, in part, this perceived deficiency in buildings, or the built environment.

MC: I would say that architects and public art people would both agree that the built environment stinks. They just have really different ways to address the problem. But they never really address the issue properly. If it sucks, why? It doesn't go back to the source of the problem. The problem with all these debates is that they are really superficial, I think.

CT: Is the 1% allotment for public art just superficial, too?

MC: I think that it doesn't address this larger issue of democracy, fundamentally. There are two issues here: one is capitalism, one is democracy, and to me this whole thing raises issues about the interrelation of one to the other. This is sort of happening in the slippage between capitalism and democracy, and that's where public art finds its niche. I don't think that it has theorized capitalism or democracy in any kind of significant way, and that's the problem. It's trying to find space ... that's sort of between the two, and it hasn't.

CD: There is also a difference between a voice of the public, which is perceived as valuable and good, and the fact that the will of the public is being carried out by a government agency, which we don't like involved in artistic decisions.

MC: But that's actually another issue of professions. There is a third profession involved, which are the bureaucrats, who everybody hates. But they are actually convinced that they are the only ones doing the right thing.

CT: They have a mandate.

MC: Because, in a sense, they are the official bearers of the public mandate. I think there is a lot of difference in that camp, because some of them are actual representatives of the public. Others are people from the art world who have moved into public art, and are actually trying to balance the two. But nobody involved is the public.

CD: I don't know how you decide which public gets a voice.

MC: That's the interesting question, I think, about public art. That is the question that is totally unaddressed by this controversy in Culver City. The public, as always, are the last people to be brought into it, or even considered. That is ironic.

CT: Would you trust it to put it to a vote of the populace of Culver City? They could all decide, this is art, this is not art.

MC: Hey, that's democracy.

CT: And we can all live with that decision, then.

MC: Sure. Like four people would vote. The problem with this is that it raises questions about the way democracy operates and, on the other hand, it raises questions about the way in which capitalism operates. If there were actually a vote for every painting, that would be kind of fun. Then you could talk about this as being democratic. But it isn't, because value and quality are established by the marketplace.

When you discuss these issues of the public and democracy, it necessarily brings up the issue of taste. Public taste and professional taste, either in the case of architects or artists, have no connection. And in a way I think this is a challenge, a massive challenge for both artists and architects. The fact is, the way that art and architecture draw boundaries around themselves is all about separating yourself from the public through taste—that's how you get cultural capital. We all know that both architects and artists possess virtually no economic capital, but tons of cultural capital, and their whole image of themselves, and their image of their profession is based on this idea of possessing cultural capital. Cultural capital, virtually by definition, means the high versus the low, the abstract versus representation. That's a kind of boundary, and a kind of line that's separating them from the public, because once they remove that line, they actually become the public. And that's pretty alarming because their whole self-definition, and the definition of these arts in capitalist society, is distinct from the popular or the public.

CD: I'm just not sure how you do that. I know that when architects design things to please the design review boards that communities confront us with, the results aren't particularly interesting. I'm not convinced about who benefits.

MC: This isn't simply a populist issue of doing what a self-appointed public demands. I don't think that's the answer.

CD: Calling yourself a design review board, and announcing yourself as the voice of the community is just as much a self-definition as the architect's self-defining...

MC: Yes, of course. And the idea of a representative public is non-existent. So, I don't think it comes down to this...

CT: The architect does need to be able to say, "I do have a certain expertise," otherwise there is no profession. What do you think of the oft-stated idea that part of the job of the architect is to educate the client to the value of innovative or new design?

MC: Whenever anyone says education that means force my ideas on someone else. They always say, "Oh, this is a problem of education." That means: "I know and you don't." That's totally deceptive. I don't think it's a problem of education. I think that right now in the United States, popular culture is a thousand times richer than architectural culture. There is just no escaping it. It has so much more creativity and vitality, and yet architects can't really tap into that, at all. At the same time, if architects start really incorporating popular culture in their work, they are going to lose their cultural capital, which is based on totally monopolizing the category of the high. The risk on the other end, of course, is becoming completely irrelevant to anybody who's not in your profession and becoming part of a niche market. It's really a question of how to operate: is there a transgressive way of operating within a capitalist culture? That's what it comes down to.

II.
Detours

On Detours
Victor Jones

"Jumbo Size Architecture," "The Giant Revolving (Winking) Chicken Head and the Doggie Drinking Fountain," "The Ecology of Fantasy," "Lesbian Domesticity," and "Taco Trucks?"

To the casual eye these titles could be easily dismissed as a mishmash of topics. The seemingly disassociated nature between gender, street life, and themed environments is compounded by their generally accepted outlier status within design discussions. With no common ground in sight, their messages are destined to this repository of misfit ideas. Ironically, much the same has been said about Los Angeles and its struggle to be recognized as a bona fide urban experience. Like the writings in this section, Los Angeles lays further than most architects, historians, and urban designers have been willing to travel. And yet, this collection of writings entitled "On Detours" traces an alternative path. In this sense, the words "Los Angeles" and "Detours" consort agreeably. The essays and interview that follow offer other ways of seeing, thinking about, and experiencing the built environment while touching on constraining biases within contemporary architectural discourse and practice. Subject matter often excluded from design conversations find traction thanks to novel analytical methods and modes of exploration. Together, these transgressive inquiries register a push back against what were and in some instances continue to be questionable limits within the various design disciplines

In Alan Hess's probing essay, "Jumbo Size Architecture," the architect-cum-critic exposes the elusive nature of big box retail architecture and its dominion over the Southern Californian suburban landscape. Searching for untapped potential to inform contemporary architectural practice, Hess's investigation is as much about how these complex systems function as it is about what they look like. Rather than fixate on the topic of "Bigness," Hess delves into the organizational patterns and inner-workings of these behemoth enterprises. Moving 20 years forward, it is difficult to imagine Jessie LeCavalier's book *The Rule of Logistics: Walmart and the Architecture of Fulfillment* not having been influenced in some way by this original work.

When Margaret Crawford wrote "The Ecology of Fantasy" in the late 1980s, there was widespread cultural panic in academic circles about the relationship between theme parks and modern American urbanism. The essay skillfully entwines Reyner Banham's autopia and Jean Baudrillard's hyper-reality with themed environments such as Disneyland's Main Street. The essay was originally written for a symposium Crawford and transportation planner Martin Wachs organized at the University of California, Los Angeles (UCLA). Later published by the LA Forum, the essay also appears in two books: *The Car and the City* and *Variations on a Theme Park*. Crawford, looking back, criticizes the triviality surrounding themed environments in the face of the civil unrest that plagued Los Angeles in the early 1990s. Nonetheless, the essay remains a cornerstone in the education of architects and urban planners.

Urban designer John Chase was one interested in dingbat apartment buildings and strip malls. Gleaning poetic insight from unremarkable architecture was Chase's passion during his short life. "The Giant Revolving (Winking) Chicken Head and the Doggie Drinking Fountain" serves as a lesson in appreciation for the "as-is" character of cities. The essay (also published in the revered book *Everyday Urbanism*) catapulted his involvement in larger planning projects, defining an era of building and development in West Hollywood and greater Los Angeles. Admired and despised, relished and repudiated, Chase's essay is a key reference for recognizing quotidian architecture and experiences in the city.

Catherine Opie's photographs of freeways and mini-malls were on view at the Museum of Contemporary Art (MOCA) when Rachel Allen interviewed the artist. Allen and Opie's conversation penetrates the surface to discuss what is behind the masterful pictures of planned residential communities in Valencia, dilapidated Victorians in MacArthur Park, and mansions in Bel Air or Beverly Hills. A rare glimpse into the artist's personal stance towards politics, gender, and space craft a deeper appreciation for the work. Originally published in 1990, this transcript continues to highlight ongoing struggles with gender equality, creative practice, and the built environment.

Ted Kane, like Sylvia Lavin, imagines Los Angeles as "a cultural ecology organized around traffic flows and media environments rather than grids and monuments, more interested in cross pollination than hierarchy." During a brief period after graduate school, Kane began to question the dearth of identifiable landmarks in Los Angeles' endless horizontal extension. His inquiry led him to invisible systems that were either unrecorded or so obscure they were effectively imperceptible. "Taco Trucks" tracks mobile food units and their daily routes across Los Angeles' vast and center-less expanse to record the invisible forces of urban economics, regulations, and politics. Michael Dear would likely describe the essay as "culinary mapping"—a novel approach to empirical analysis that exposes unanticipated governing logics within the city.

Since no one viewpoint can substantiate this ensemble of text, the question of what connects this apparent wabi sabi requires a deeper appreciation for all things unfamiliar. The red thread linking each piece is their shared vigor for discovery as opposed to reinforcing established myths. But, if these corralling voices help to diminish the cultural divide that relegated Los Angeles to the fringes of architectural discourse, this ensemble of written material continues to point out other divisions embedded in the spatial practices. More than 20 years after they were first published, their messages remain timely, underscoring the necessity for discussions about difference and inclusion—whether that be about gender, culture, socio-economics, race, or aesthetics. With that in mind, it might explain why this section about Los Angeles also manages to *feel* acutely like Los Angeles—messy, loose, unpredictable, but also a place where supposedly unrelated things, are revealed, in their truer form, inseparably intertwined.

Jumbo Size Architecture

Alan Hess

LA Forum Newsletter
October / November 1990

If an unexpected volcano out at Mammoth suddenly turned California into a huge, gooey papier-mâché snapshot, where should 21st-century archaeologists start digging to figure us out? What one location will tell them the most about how we lived?

I'd tell them to find the remains of a Price Club membership warehouse store. Scraping away at the goo, these archaeologists would find the bare bones of the 1990s preserved more thoroughly than any museum ever could.

A Costco or a Home Club would do just as well. Buying in brain-boggling bulk, these immense emporia offer almost everything anyone would need for a well-stocked household—food, VCRs, tools, diapers, tires, ground tillers, industrial strength cleaners, restaurant packs of napkins and catsup, clothes, toilet paper, tires, Coke, umbrellas, office supplies. It is a survivalist's Disneyland. Limiting entry to a paid membership drawn from associations, credit unions, savings and loans and professions, they keep prices down.

But just as important as the stuff inside is the building these goodies are wrapped up in.

These are mean, lean selling machines. They strip the capitalist distribution system down to its raw bones. No skyscraper, no corporate headquarters, no band building conveys the nature and guts of our economic system more effectively than a single Price Club.

The tradeoffs in the design reflect the belt-tightening of the 1980s and 1990s based on the warehouse-selling model of Toys-R-Us. Warehouse stores don't sell 7-Eleven corner close convenience. Located in mammoth warehouse buildings on the edge of town where land is less expensive, you have to drive to them. They dispense with the departments, salesclerks (a dying breed anyway), fancy displays, mannequins, ceilings, paint, and mood lighting of frou-frou stores like K-mart. All that's left are bare walls of unpainted concrete block, the bare roof structure of laminated wood beams, and the loot of the consumer culture spread out like a starry firmament before your dazzled eyes.

Economic necessity is always the mother of architectural invention. Today's warehouse stores have direct ancestors in Macy's and Marshall Field's, where several small shops were first successfully combined under one roof to create department stores.

Gone was the homey friendliness of visiting the local milliner, shoemaker, or dressmaker on Main Street. All were available under the roof of one efficient multi-storied block—"World's Largest Store," Sears called itself. You had to go all the way downtown to shop there, but it was worth it. These emporia were progressive steel-framed architecture, too, with vast light wells cutting through the center of the block to bring natural light to all departments.

Such features, inspired only by efficiency, rose into great architecture in the hands of Louis Sullivan in his 1901 Carson, Pirie, Scott & Co. department store on State Street, Chicago. He exploited the eye-catching advertising potential of window displays by surrounding them with his trademark organic ornament. He raised merchandising necessity into expressive architecture.

No one has taken a Price Club that far yet. But the raw ingredients are all there.

For one thing, warehouse stores are evolving as proto-community centers. Social centers historically develop around shops, on Italian piazzas, or by Egyptian bazaars. Malls have made limp attempts to create public gathering spaces with sculpture, fountains, fashion shows, and food courts. None of them quite work. Warehouse stores' windowless walls and vast parking lots make absolutely no attempt to be a welcoming place for people to sit and gather. But without trying, they've become the place to be on Saturday mornings.

Clustered around the entry are ice cream pushcarts and hot dog stands—festive accents for the otherwise nondescript entry through roll-up overhead doors. A few redwood picnic tables shoved against the tilt-up concrete walls are all that's needed. Later generations of Price Clubs may pull these pieces together to capitalize on the energy of gathering people.

Inside, the central space stretches almost 400 feet to the rear of the building, its floor filled with merchandise. At each side, steel frame warehouse shelving extends to the high ceiling. Most of the inventory is stored overhead—no niceties of hiding cartons behind the scenes as at Bullock's or the Broadway. At eye level are the open boxes or bins from which shoppers can pick. Hawkers tempt you with samples of food and drink.

Without the usual grocery store displays, the colored logos on unopened pasteboard boxes are the only notes of decoration. But they are surprisingly effective. Against the gray concrete floors and seemingly endless space, neatly stacked boxes of Brillo pads, Clorox bleach, and tomato soup turn each aisle into a mini Andy Warhol retrospective. Life mirrors art mirroring life.

Echoing the small brown pasteboard boxes at another scale are gargantuan cubic industrial freezer units, extending just shy of the ceiling beams. Their titanic bulk and glittering galvanized sides match the scale of this mammoth functional architecture.

If the aisles feel too wide, they are. This store is designed for forklift trucks, not for people. After customer hours, trucks scurry around, replenishing shelves and bringing in new deliveries.

At the end of this Alice's Wonderland is the checkout line—a couple dozen cash registers chiming away in computerized beeps. Nearby, as at any supermarket, stands the candy display. But stretching at least 50 feet, this one is the ultimate checkout counter candy display.

This is true American design. Membership warehouse stores are an anti-mall where the irrelevant frills and petty distractions of mall architecture are edited out. All that remains is the soul of consumerism.

Here is a raw architecture, but it has a raw clarity about it that gives it a raw beauty. It feels good to shop here because it has not style but is a celebration of the act of economic distribution itself. Your family station wagon is one more link from the factory and farm field to the store to your kitchen shelf.

What it lacks in grace it makes up in muscle. This is no effete prissy namby-pamby high-tech boutique with bumpy rubber flooring and a few exposed light bulbs. This is real utilitarianism.

And in its bare-boned glory, it is magnificently beautiful, a thing of awe and splendor as hundreds of people go about the business of buying. Price Club is a museum of American Culture, displaying everything from the no-calorie, no-sugar, no-caffeine beverage-like substances we slurp to the pre-sliced, pre-packaged, pre-buttered slices of cheese we munch, to the electronics wizardry we rely on for entertainment and keeping in touch with each other.

If Mammoth blows, somebody save it.

The Giant
Revolving
(Winking) Chicken
Head and
the Doggie
Drinking Fountain

John Chase

Everyday Urbanism
Monacelli Press, 1999

As the home of the Sunset Strip and a regional mecca for gays and lesbians, West Hollywood is hardly an average small town. But even in this two-square-mile area sandwiched between Beverly Hills and Hollywood, with a population of only 36,000, responding to and accommodating everyday life is an important objective for urban design. Because of West Hollywood's location and heavy traffic—both automotive and pedestrian—new development projects often include modest amenities that enhance the everyday life of the pedestrian as well as theatrical, expressive, or dramatic ornaments that register from passing automobiles.

In stark contrast to other areas in Southern California, one of the city's chief urban design goals is to make it easier and more pleasant for people to be on the streets. West Hollywood's urban-design policies attempt to encourage the relationships that flourish between pedestrians on the street, relationships that are virtually impossible between motorists. In an urban environment dominated by commercial strips developed along heavily trafficked major boulevards, it is neither possible nor desirable to make the cars disappear; they are an essential part of any vital Southern California cityscape. It is feasible, however, to promote sidewalk activity that is strong enough to compete with automotive activity. The aspects of everyday life that can be incorporated into the public sidewalk— from bus-bench advertising to parking lot landscaping—ideally function as development details that make the street habitable. These small-scale features complement the more spectacular urban-design elements that are oriented toward the automobile.

Pedestrian amenities make sense only if someone is on the sidewalk to use them. Again, in contrast to other areas in Southern California, in West Hollywood at least three distinct groups experience their community on foot. These inveterate walkers include the city's Russian immigrants (approximately 13% of the population); gay and lesbian residents (approximately 30% of the population); and patrons visiting Sunset Strip rock clubs, gay establishmentson Santa Monica Boulevard, and West Hollywood's other hotels, restaurants, and bars. Improving everyday pedestrian life entails installing a diversity of features and activities that people can use on a regular basis. Motorists whiz past the sidewalks—they cannot interact tangibly with the streetscape as they speed by. Pedestrians can participate in their environment on a moment-by-moment basis—ancillary activities can be easily incorporated into a journey on foot. Well-equipped public pavements can be as hospitable to human beings as good interior public spaces. Common street objects such as bus shelters, drinking fountains, mailboxes, pay phones, newspaper vending machines, and dog-walking amenities give pedestrians a richer program of possible activities for a sidewalk sojourn and strengthen the bond between strollers and the streetscape. West Hollywood is a valuable location for businesses because of its lively mix of residential and commercial use. The area's adjacency to Beverly Hills and a high concentration of design showrooms, hotels, nightclubs, bars, and restaurants make it a vital urban center. Because of this desirability, the city is able to ask for public improvements in exchange for granting developers the right to locate their projects in West Hollywood. The city's urban-design policies are focused on strengthening the relationships between development projects and their surroundings. Buildings in West Hollywood must have front entrances that face the street rather than rear entrances that head to the parking lot. Facades must have enough windows so that passersby can get a sense of interior activity.

At the city's behest, developers have recently begun to provide tiny plazas adjacent to the public sidewalk as a benefit to walkers. These miniature parks, accessible to all, effectively extend the public space of the sidewalk. They are often carved out of the mandatory landscaped buffer around parking lots, a perimeter that is legally required to be at least five feet wide. In some cases, these plazas also respond to the automobile with the inclusion of bold, large-scale elements that read clearly at 20 or 30 miles per hour. These elements often reflect the glamour, excitement, and creativity that residents and tourists alike expect from businesses in a community distinguished by the strong presence of both the entertainment and design trades, incorporating the spectacular into signage or architectural elements vitalizes a project's relationship with motorists. And because car accommodations are always required for new developments, parking lots and their required buffering strips of landscaping offer an ideal opportunity to insert on private and public areas for pedestrians.

Koo Koo Roo

There are no better bodies than those to be found in West Hollywood. The demands of the marketplace, both romantic and industrial, keep West Hollywood's gay men, single women, actors, and actresses buff and trim. Low-fat diets and high-intensity exercise are the standard doctrine. Many West Hollywoodites exercise at one of two large gyms, both on Santa Monica Boulevard east of La Cienega. Just across the street, at the corner of West Knoll and Santa Monica, gym-goers dine post-workout at Koo Koo Roo, a chain restaurant for the health-conscious that specializes in skinless chicken and plenty of vegetables, both raw and cooked.

There was room in the restaurant's required parking lot landscaping to develop a small, partially paved area next to the sidewalk, the logical place to situate the phone booths, a drinking fountain, a bicycle rack, and seating, all set beneath a row of shade trees. Because most of the neighborhood exercisers walk to their workouts several times a week, this has become a see-and-be-seen section of the boulevard.

When Koo Koo Roo decided to open a location in West Hollywood, one of the chief problems was how to reconcile the chain's need for a consistent corporate identity—as represented by the Koo Koo Roo chicken emblem—with the city's policy of discouraging new buildings on Santa Monica Boulevard that are cookie-cutter franchise clones. Fast-food restaurants that are aesthetic clones of their sibling restaurants across the country weaken the eclectic, distinctive urban character of the town.

Koo Koo Roo first proposed the installation of an enclosed corner tower bearing its standard two-dimensional chicken-head logo. To Koo Koo Roo, this logo represents a dependable standard of quality. The city asked the company to create a more original version of the logo, one that reflected the inventive design atmosphere of West Hollywood. Koo Koo Roo responded with a three-dimensional, revolving, and winking chicken head that looks like a giant toy. A generic piece of corporate signage thus became memorable and unique to the area. The readily recognizable image of the winking chicken takes on greater power as a symbol, strong enough to take its place alongside other unforgettable media symbols such as the Michelin Man or the RCA Victor dog. Because it is exclusive to West Hollywood, the winking chicken assumes the informal landmark status that frequently characterizes Southern California promotional installations, as exemplified by such famous beacons as the Sunset Strip's giant Marlboro man and the now demolished whirling Sahara showgirl. The three-dimensional logo speaks to the passing motorist, while Koo Koo Roo's plaza becomes part of the activity pattern and life of the passing pedestrian.

Gelson's Market

Gelson's Market is a neighborhood supermarket at the corner of Kings Road and Santa Monica Boulevard. The area it serves, a densely developed residential section of West Hollywood, has more condominiums and elderly residents than any other neighborhood in West Hollywood, and is unusually genteel. Residents walk their visibly well-loved dogs beneath the shady canopy of the mature oak and camphor trees on Kings Road. In the corner of the Gelson's parking lot, next to the sidewalk, a tiny public area has been created for these citizens to enjoy. The small plaza is nestled into a gap created by the layout of the angled parking spaces. Rather than absorbing the extra area into merely ornamental parking lot landscaping, however, the designers chose to complement and extend the public space of the sidewalk. Two seats flank a drinking fountain with individual spigots for adults, children, and dogs. The little plaza is a destination point for local walkers, marking the heavily trafficked crossroads of quiet, dignified Kings Road and busy Santa Monica Boulevard. An overhead trellis defines the space and relates it to the trellis that shields Gelson's main entry. Landscaping rounds out the sense of enclosure and welcome. The plaza is just large enough to be habitable, the equivalent of setting a sofa on the front porch to take in the passing scene. Focused by an unusual feature, the canine drinking fountain, the space enlivens the quotidian activity of walking the dog and becomes a social gathering point.

Sheriff Plaza

I would like to suggest the possibility for one more of these small but eminently amenable public spaces, at the corner of Santa Monica and San Vicente boulevards. This intersection is already one of the world's great gay intersections. When the AIDS Ride bicycle tour returns from San Francisco to West Hollywood, the crowd gathers at this corner. People assemble here in protest when yet another bill is introduced to limit rights according to sexual orientation. This stretch of Santa Monica Boulevard is one of the few places in Los Angeles where the nighttime foot traffic is so dense that pedestrians actually have to slow down to avoid bumping into each other.

On the southeast corner of this intersection sits the West Hollywood station of the Los Angeles County Sheriff's Department, which has traditionally been more tolerant toward gays than the LAPD—the city police department. Because there are no windows in either of the station's two street facades, however, many passersby had no idea the station was there. In order to call attention to the building and its purpose, the city raised onto a pole a three-by-three-foot neon sign created in the form of a sheriff's badge. (The sign is a duplicate of one erected at Universal Studio's CityWalk, an urban entertainment center.) The icon stands on a small, triangular landscaped area left over by a corner indentation in the station's brick walls. The star-shaped sign is a spectacular object that changes the corner dramatically, communicating a sense of public security with its neon symbolism. It reminds pedestrians how close they are to the station's protection.

The sign points to a perfect and untapped opportunity for public space; if a little bit of the area around the sign were to be paved, the site could accommodate such amenities as a bulletin board for communication between the sheriff's department and local residents, a drinking fountain, seats, and telephone booths, all of which would facilitate casual use of the space. Strollers could reconnoiter and take stock here on the way to or from the area's stores, bars, and restaurants. By providing a spot to linger, the space would acknowledge the importance of being out in the public world. It is especially desirable to create this kind of corner pedestrian oasis here, since the two intersecting boulevards are so wide, and intervals between changes in the traffic signals so long, that crossing can be quite daunting.

Billboard Gardens

Billboard Gardens is a project currently under development that has the potential to incorporate both everyday and spectacular elements. The proposed complex will be built on a narrow lot that slopes from Sunset Boulevard to a residential Street below. As presently constituted, Billboard Gardens would split the site into three zones. Apartment housing would take up the southernmost zone, along the residential street. Private gardens for the apartment dwellers would abut the building, with public gardens above; this landscape would be designed according to a strong theme or central concept, such as a Persian garden or a scented or hanging garden.

Above the gardens to the north would be a commercial plaza facing Sunset Boulevard, the entrance flanked by billboards incorporated into a triumphal arch; from the inside, the arch would frame a view of the city below. Extending from the outside sidewalk, the plaza would have such space efficient amenities as a newsstand, a small restaurant, and coffee and ice cream stands. People who did not patronize the stands could nonetheless visit the plaza's terrace, making it a truly public space. Citizens could come here to take in the view (the only public space on the entire strip where one might do so), play cards, checkers, or chess, read the newspaper, or perhaps watch an outdoor television set tuned to the city's cable channel. Billboard Gardens would simultaneously serve as housing, pedestrian amenity, and public spectacle for the motorist.

Top Ten Reasons Why Little Tiny Spaces On Great Big Boulevards Are A Good Idea

1. They slow down the urban pace. Commercial strips are all about getting from one destination to another in a car. Liberating various nooks and crannies to the public gives pedestrians a spot to stop and linger.

2. They don't charge admission. Anybody is free to use these spaces, even without patronizing the sponsoring store or restaurant. They really are public spaces, even if they sit on private land.

3. They are infinitely flexible. These spaces are created as the opportunity arises, and they can be readily altered to fit changing circumstances. They are part of developments created to accommodate particular businesses, but they can be remodeled or replaced to suit new establishments or needs. In that sense, they provide ad hoc situational opportunities for businesses responding to consumers' desires for novelty and innovation.

4. They're cheap, at least in comparison to other kinds of development. There is no land cost, normally one of the greatest expenses in the provision of public amenities, because these areas are located on a portion of the site that must already be set aside for the legally required parking lot landscaping.

Detours

Features such as small, paved patios, benches, and special lighting are relatively minor capital improvements. Finally, because the areas themselves are quite small—sometimes as tiny as a standard parking space—their cost per square foot is not multiplied by a high number.

5. They benefit everyone, private interests included. The tiny public pedestrian spaces, civic improvements that clearly encourage people to explore and enjoy a neighborhood, enhance the overall perceived value of a street. The private sphere indirectly benefits from this enriched value but also reaps tangible reward from increased patronage.

6. They make neighborhood residents more amenable to commercial development. In densely populated areas of Los Angeles such as West Hollywood, where commercial and residential uses cohabitate, new development virtually always backs up against residentially zoned land. Whether or not it is within legal zoning rights, new development is often unwelcome to residents. They fear the attendant increase in noise, traffic, and scarcity of parking. Such protests can delay, amend, or prevent proposed developments. Creating these miniature spaces might not answer primary quality-of-life concerns, but they can provide some benefit to a densely developed urban area.

7. They humanize the street. Thoroughfares with heavy vehicular traffic often become a no-man's land. Residents feel neither attached to nor responsible for this indifferent, disposable environment. Public amenities associated with private establishments and situated next to sidewalks make sections of the street seem more occupiable. These bits of pavement become an extension of the walkers' home territory.

8. They involve the private sector in the public good. There are few ways to induce private businesses and their architects to think about and provide for the general public. This is one of them, and it is relatively painless.

9. They accommodate equal opportunity aesthetics. The pedestrian nook tinkers with land use rather than with architectural style. Communities such as West Hollywood base their identities on the free and energetic expression of individual people, businesses, and organizations. That is why West Hollywood was never swallowed up by Los Angeles, and why for many years it was reluctant to incorporate as a city. Just as it is impossible to imagine literature without a variety of characters, so is it difficult to conceive of a city like West Hollywood without both architectural hetero- and homogeneity. Pedestrian amenities do not impose a particular style or aesthetic on a sponsoring project. And regardless of the affinity any one passerby feels for the architectural vocabulary of a project, that passerby can still benefit from its pedestrian relationships and amenities.

10. They encourage diverse social encounters and help attract tourism. West Hollywood is home to two completely different cultures that are well versed in pedestrian life. Both the gay and lesbian and the Russian immigrant communities are experienced at creating vibrant street life, even under difficult circumstances. The city has the potential to help develop a third category of pedestrians— tourists. The increasing prominence of clubs, restaurants, and hotels in West Hollywood has great potential to contribute to a lively pedestrian environment.

The Ecology of Fantasy

Margaret Crawford

Forum Publication No. 3

published by

**the Los Angeles Forum
for Architecture
and Urban Design**

Detours

The Ecology of Fantasy
Margaret Crawford

published by
the Los Angeles Forum
for Architecture
and Urban Design Editorial Committee

Aaron Betsky
Christian Hubert
John Kaliski
Gary Paige
Natalie Shivers

3454 West First Street
Los Angeles, California
90004

(213) 389 6730

With the opening of
Disneyland
in *1955*, an environmental
paradigm emerged which was
to haunt the ecological,
cultural and psychological
landscapes of Southern
California. By organizing his
amusement park around
thematic zones based on
fictional environments,
Walt Disney replaced the
squalid ambience of the
carnival with conceptual
models of American
mythology at two-thirds scale.
Main Street · equals
Small Town America,
Frontierland, the myth of
the Western Frontier,
Tomorrowland, the corporate
and technological promise of
the future. These myths were
packaged for immediate
consumption and soon made
Disneyland the most
visited attraction in Southern
California.

3

In spite of its incredible success, Disneyland itself was only good for one afternoon, not for life; physically it was too limited, and its technology too complete to be directly adopted as a model for environmental planning. At the same time, its reduction of a complex and debatable reality to a single, agreed-upon theme- a theme which could be both cliche and archetype-suggested that environmental reality could be replaced by a focused thematic irreality at a larger scale.

This offered a way out of the ecological impasse facing Los Angeles in the late Fifties. Although the city had long generated fantasy commercial architecture, such as Tail o' the Pup, a hot dog stand shaped like a hot dog, or The Brown Derby, a restaurant built as a hat, these buildings existed as isolated elements, based on limited images, in a larger environment dominated by powerful geographic features. In the early Sixties, Reyner Banham classified these into four ecologies; three natural systems– the beach, the foothills and the basin– connected by Autopia, an artifical network of roads and freeways.[1] Fantasy architecture, confined to a setting of palm trees, orange groves and snow-capped mountains, had no room to expand.

By introducing the concept of the theme environment, Disneyland allowed a new system of land use to emerge, liberated from the actual physical setting of the city, and based on a landscape of the imagination. Like Disney's "lands", theme environments consist of controllable settings designed to convey a unified image. Based on a limited set of themes, presented with a consistency and coherence not found in everyday life, they offer a reduced experience of a more complex reality, whether historical, geographic or cultural. The underlying theme of Disneyland, of course, is consumption. Although Disneyland

1. Reyner Banham, Los Angeles, The Architecture of Four Ecologies, (Harper and Row, New York, 1971)

functions efficiently as a disguised shopping
center providing thematic arenas for consumption,
Disney's most profound innovation was to transform public space and the built
environment into a
commodity.   The success of packaged environments at scales ranging from the
reconstitution of several city blocks into South
Street Seaport's shopping and food zone to
small single buildings testifies to the accuracy
of Disney's insight. Theme environments offer
entertainment and escape as increasingly necessary elements of leisure time. The ultimate
expansion of Disneyland beyond the boundaries
of the theme park into daily life is indicated by
Disney Enterprises' most recent project– a
hotel, entertainment and shopping complex to
be built in Burbank which will feature a steak-
house in a boat that appears to be teetering on
the edge of a waterfall, a seafood restaurant
where diners will have the illusion of eating
underwater, and a nightclub hosted by holographic images of celebrities of the past. [2]
Although it might be amusing to regard this as
simply as an extreme example of kitsch, these
environments represent a broader tendency
toward fantasy images with important cultural
implications. Theme environments can be seen
as particularly visible examples of a hyper-real-
ism increasingly present in contemporary life.
As defined by the post-structuralist philospher
Jean Baudrillard, hyper-realilty is a condition in
which "simulation" effaces and replaces
reality.[3] Hyper-real representation produces
an imitation that becomes more real than reality itself. One effect of the hyper-real is to
impoverish reality. An actual small town can
never be as perfect as Main Street in
Disneyland just as Fifth avenue can never be as
clean or well-organized as a shopping mall.

Detours

2. "Next Stop Wolfgangland" Los
Angeles Times, Calender section,
Sept. 20, 1987

3. Jean Baudrillard, Simulations
(Semiotexte, New York, 1983.)

Theme environments are not unique to Southern California. Train restaurants made of box cars and newly-built New England fishing villages which are actually shopping malls have become a cliche of the American environment. However, only in their point of origin, Southern California, with its constant stream of immigrants, absence of conventionally percievable history and lack of urban self-definition, have they become the dominant realm of spatial and social experience. As in Hollywood films, also clearly a significant cultural influence in the local acceptance of theme environments, fiction vanquishes the real.

The means for achieving this was the subsumption of the region's three natural ecologies by the fourth, Autopia. The triumph of the automobile and its roadway network allowed another, latent ecology to emerge- the ecology of fantasy. Fifteen years later, Banham's original taxonomy, still tied to natural processes, is no longer valid. The automobile severed the links between Los Angeles' culture and its natural setting. The increasing contradiction between the automobile and the basin's natural limitations, which produced environmental damage from smog, ruptures of urban pattern, and destruction of landscape features, was thus resolved. In the new ecology of fantasy, the car is no longer an ecological villain, but a means of liberation, providing---

The automobile connects individual circuits of theme environments, a coherent conceptual grid overlaid on the real economic and topographic surface of the city. Driving from one theme environment to another, the endless, nondescript blocks of the city disappear. Robbed of conceptual validity, they become neutral filler between a set of points which constructs a coherent thematic reality,

physically discontinuous but conceptually integrated. Thus, although individual themes have coherence, serial themes can only become dominant in a setting of disjointed context.
Disneyland radically compressed sites remote in space and time. Looking from 19th century New Orleans across an African jungle and into the future accustomed us to accepting juxtapostion, but the automobile has made it possible to extend the principle of fragmented environments into daily life. More than just transport from one fragment to the next, the automobile functions as a medium, transforming our experience of the city we are travelling through. In the car, we move through the city without disturbing it or it disturbing us. Like television, another individualized medium, the automobile distances us from the world outside our sealed capsule while restructuring and abstracting it. The world, through a tv screen or a windshield, is reduced to an two-dimensional image, a visual event that does not invite participation.
Moving through space in an automobile is a televisual experience, a sucession of quick cuts and rapidly edited fragments unified by the medium of the automobile. Jean Baudrillard has observed that increasingly fluid and automated vehicles produce fluid and

access to an unlimited and constantly changing set of theme environments.

4. Jean Baudrillard, Amerique,
Bernard Grasset, Paris, 1986

automated spaces in which we can let ourselves go, tuning in to them like we tune into a television set. This promotes a flattening of affect, erasing the fragmentation of time and space, homogenizing everything to the absolute present. The continuous bombardment of people, places and things, once driven past, are quickly be forgotten. Driving erases memory. [4]

7

The physical environment soon acknowledged the perceptual changes introduced by the automobile. The spread of valet parking, a central element in the ecology of fantasy, can be seen as a response to the replacement of place by image. Now offered by supermarkets, art galleries, and shops, as well as restaurants, valet parking reduces the need to physcially interact with the social reality of the city to the six feet of sidewalk between the car door and the entrance. This allows an existence consisting totally of theme environments to become concievable. So far, this degree of selectivity over one's surroundings made possible by avoiding city streets and urban reality is unique to Los Angeles. Unlike the structural layers of Fritz Lang's **Metropolis**. which separate the workers from the owners' skyscraper city, the automobile permits a synchronic organization, where, without physical barriers, consumers of theme environments are equally well protected from the unwelcome realities of class and ethnic differences. The counterpoint of the automobile's reduction of experience is the increased need for the stimulation provided by theme environments. In order to entertain, shopping and eating have become increasingly theatricalized. Theme environments have even begun to penetrate daily activities, such as food shopping. In West Hollywood, for example, a Sushi bar, selling raw fish expertly trimmed by costumed Japanese chefs, has been inserted into an otherwise normal Safeway supermarket. An increasingly pluralistic and eclectic selection of themes is now available. Mass consumers are limited to intineraries of shopping malls, chain restaurants, and purpose-built tourist attractions, but Los Angeles has also generated permutations of increasingly specialized and sophisticated theme circuits. These rely on more abstract imagery. Punk, new-wave and yuppie themes are obvious; art and gay themes less so. Even recent immigrant

groups, such as Koreans and Japanese, have
created distinctive theme environments along
Olympic Boulevard and in Little Tokyo, with
images derived from Buddist temples and zen
gardens, now used on restaurants, hotels and
shopping centers. In a city of endless atomiza-
tion, infinite individual ecologies are available.
Two groups, however,
are excluded from the consumption of fantasy
themes. These are Hispanic immigrants and the
homeless, present in increasing numbers in the
city. These groups have inherited the physcial
city of pre-Disneyland Los Angeles. They lead
urban lives familiar to the inhabitants of many
cities– walking through crowded downtown
streets, using public transportation and gathering in public parks. These activities are pur-
sued in the course of lives based on a set of
unchanging themes: physical and economic sur-
vival and the maintenance of the family. Their
lives form a major barrier to the total incursion
of the ecology of fantasy. They exist as visible
reminders of irreducable reality, posing a challenge to the spread of hyper-reality.
Rather than consuming
pre-packaged environments, these groups are
forced to produce their own. The homeless, put
on the streets by the shutdown of mental hospitals, the disappearance of family assistance
programs, and the contraction of blue-collar
industries, must claim whatever marginal territory is available for living space– cars, sidewalks,
or vacant lots. They improvise provisional shelters from whatever materials are at hand, and
gather into temporary communities for safety,
for shelter, and to obtain services. Their spontaneous
creation of living environments from virtually nothing calls into question the calculated
construction of the theme environment. Skid
row, seen from a passing car, can be read as
an image, but the spread of homelessness has
begun to affect many other parts of the city.

9

In a place devoted to the search for increasingly esoteric individual themes, Hispanic immigrants establish community against great odds.. All over the city, newcomers have reclamed public places such as streets, parks, and markets, and transformed them into functioning social spaces. Broadway, between 3rd and 8th streets, has the most intense street life in the city, with pedestrian numbers far exceeding those of vehicles. Olvera Street, the original plaza of Los Angeles, turned into an ersatz tourist attraction in the 1940s, has now come full circle, used once again an authentic public square for a *passigiata* of families and couples.   More and more, these realities intrude on the neutrality of the street, making it difficult to maintain an unin terrupted circuit of theme environments.   Unemployed immigrants sell oranges and peanuts at stoplights and gather at designated corners for the "shape-up", an informal labor market, where they announce their availability for any kind of manual work. When they do find employement, it is often as the service workers, waiters, busboys, and valet parkers on whom theme environments depend. As silent observors, their presence implies another, as yet unrealized ecology, presently submerged, but likely to become dominant given the fact that, according to demographic projections, Latin Americans will consitute forty percent of Los Angeles' population by the year 2000.

What will be the result
of the inevitable collision of these disparate
ecologies? One possibility is suggested by the
science fiction film, **Blade Runner** (regarded
by many as an accurate projection of Los
Angeles' future), where everyone who can afford
to has moved off-world, leaving the city to its
third-world inhabitants. Off-world is not yet available, but outlying privately-developed new
towns, such as   Mission Viejo
Westlake Village,   whose physical and social coherence
are maintained by deed restrictions and security
guards, address the same needs. Another sce-
nario is the expansion of theme environments to
include "melting-pot" content, with non-Spanish
speaking second generation Mexicans happily
dining in Hispanic-theme resturants.   Less likely, given the
constraints of consumer economics and class
and ethnic division, is the possiblilty of synthesis. One can, however, still imagine a future in
which environments which do not orchestrate
escape from daily life would include an aware-
ness of multiple realities. **Although we cannot
expect Los Angeles to become less fragmented or less decentered,
or expect the private automobile to disappear, perhaps the best we
can hope for is that the
theme circuits
we endlessly create may become
inclusive rather than exclusive,
expansive rather than reductive
and that the principle
of mobility
might be used to cross
boundaries**

rather than to construct them.

11

Lesbian Domesticity

An Interview with Catherine Opie

Rachel Allen

LA Forum Newsletter
Late Spring 1998

Funded by the museum's first emerging artists award, Catherine Opie's photographs of freeways and mini-malls were on view at MOCA this winter. While her portraits of queers in the 1995 Whitney Biennial established Opie's international reputation, she has a pointedly photographed architectural subject, including master-planned residential communities in Valencia, mansions in Bel Air and Beverly Hills, and dilapidated Victorians in MacArthur Park. Recently, she participated in the LA Forum's "Fake Estate" lectures series, which investigated uses of architecture by L.A. artists.

RA: The first thing I want to ask you about is the photograph of yours that I like the most: the self-portrait "Cutting" from 1993. Did you draw it first on paper?

CO: Yes—over and over again for about a year. I knew that I wanted to do a cutting on my back of it after a relationship had broken up. When I talk on the phone I doodle the whole time and for a year that was the doodle that just kept coming out.

RA: What I noticed, when I looked at the image again recently, was the house with the smoke coming out of the chimney.

CO: That's because my dream house will have a fireplace in it.

RA: It's your dream house?

CO: It is. It's about an idealistic view of what domesticity is, and what I want from it. It is tied up with wanting that relationship where you grow old with someone and you have this really nice house with a fireplace and I go out and mow the lawn. One of those stick-figure girls would be me. Usually I wouldn't wear a skirt, but the only way to make it lesbian in stick figures is to have them both wear triangular skirts. I don't necessarily think that girls have to wear skirts.

RA: If you drew a butch-femme couple...

CO: ...it would look just like a straight couple. Right.

RA: In your lecture you showed a few photographs from a series you are currently working on, but have yet to show, "Lesbian Domestic." Is "Cutting" the first image in that series?

CO: Yes, exactly. That was the catalyst. I've been working on the Domestic series since 1993. It's a really difficult series because I photograph people and then they break up. Then I begin to question this ideal of longevity and domesticity.

RA: I suspect that a lot of people will stress the "Lesbian" half of that title. I'd like to look at "Domestic" for a moment. What is it about a house that you are idealizing? Is it the same as idealizing the relationship?

CO: Maybe it is. There is an idealization of family and what constitutes family in the American dream. What I was told growing up was, "You work hard, you buy a house." Working hard equals home ownership in my family. The idea is that if you own your own home, you've made it somehow. But then the American dream is such a joke, and throws in homosexuality on top of it, which is not supposed to be a part of the American dream, and it all ends up getting really mixed up.

RA: On the one hand, it is a paradox because it's an American dream to which lesbians aren't supposed to have access. On the other hand, it seems like a perfect fit. I'm thinking of the way women have been historically associated with houses while men are associated with the public sphere.

CO: But still, "A man's home is his castle." It's never "A woman's home is her castle" because she's not supposed to be the homeowner.

RA: She's the homemaker. She's at home waiting for him. So if there are two women there then they're not waiting?

CO: They're not waiting. Neither of them are waiting. And then, who knows whose castle it is?

RA: When you first showed "Houses and Landscapes," the work seemed to have shifted suddenly from people to buildings. You were already recognized as a portraitist, and some critics proposed that your pictures of houses are also portraits. Is that how you think of them?

CO: The houses are portraits in that they're not architectural photographs. They certainly talk about style in terms of architecture, but as far as the history of photography representing architecture goes, these break all those rules because they're so flat. They're straight on and they're not about shape, which is the way in which one would usually describe architecture. They are portraits in the same way that I make portraits in the studio. So they were right in thinking about it in that way. It's about the facade and how communities develop and how we look in terms of language. The thing that I find fascinating about these homes is their awkwardness visually. Architecturally, they are phenomenal because they're trying to be all these different things, all these different identities. And I find that just as interesting as my own community in how they construct the outside appearance of their facades and what they try to be.

RA: Is there an analogy between series, where the façade of a building is like the façade of a person? The architectural ornament...

CO: ...is like the tattooing. Exactly. I think that it's about signage, it's all about a certain kind of signage throughout my work. All of this work has to do with how powerful I think images are in preserving history or in the construction of history as signage. One of the reasons I switched from documenting communities outside of my own to my own community was that, politically, it was really important at that time period. I can't say this for sure, but if it had been a different climate politically, if AIDS wasn't around, if there wasn't a huge right-wing agenda attacking homosexuality, I'd have still been roaming around in my car looking at other communities like I was.

RA: The other series don't have the same political impetus?

CO: Not the houses and not the freeways, but the mini-malls do. The mini-malls are about immigration and about the fact that we're now in the 1990s in a corporate culture, and these mini-malls—these bizarre, stupid, ugly structures— exist as a central meeting place in the community. Beyond the church, the mini-mall is a family meeting ground where all these families come to have lunch every day. It's away from the Starbucks, the Noah's Bagels, the Jamba Juice, the Koo Koo Roo. The mall is about how, in a huge gigantic place like Los Angeles, we can still have this idea of the small shop owner. They are town squares. And they're weird. They're so great. The sign age is so important because when you're wandering, you know exactly what community you've arrived at in L.A. because of the signage on the mini-malls.

RA: Some architects would say that the buildings you choose to photograph are examples of bad design. Either they make stylistic mistakes, like the mansions, or they are unplanned, like the mini-malls. What do you think of that standard of judgment about what makes good architecture?

CO: There are always huge mistakes in the houses. They're a postmodern mess. It's about hierarchy. There are certain things that I find in good architecture, such as Craftsman houses, but this high/low culture thing—I try to work against that. I photograph in a certain way so that there's an importance placed on every subject.

RA: They may share their status as "low culture," but the people seem to display an agency that the buildings don't. Haven't they put the details on their bodily surfaces intentionally?

CO: Well, no. They have done it on purpose, but a lot of what goes on the body in terms of tattoos isn't completely planned out architecturally either. Some people do a full sleeve where it's all totally planned out, but some people choose to have a lot of different styles on their arms.

RA: Some people plan their bodies architecturally?

CO: I think they do. I plan my body architecturally. I figure out what design does. For most of my friends when they're completing their bodies and their tattoos, design and placement and everything is symbolic. I'll eventually have this arm sleeved, so that my cuttings and tattoos will end up all relating to one another. Even though there are all these different styles of tattoos, it will all have some kind of reason for being there.

RA: This may be too literal, but are you saying that your body is like a mini-mall, in that it happens over time and is partly planned but partly not?

CO: Yes. It's accumulative, whereas some people I know don't do accumulative. Some people go in, and they'll plan from here to here [shoulder to wrist] an entire sleeve, and it has to all go together. I'm more interested in history. I like that whole sleeve, and I like the way it looks, but I'm more interested in what happens if this tattoo is eight years old, and then what happens down the line. It's like building a building really slowly, I guess. Because all of sudden something that might have happened in my life, or some kind of connection, will end up being part of the architecture of my body.

RA: Architectural theory has argued many times that the best way to make a good building is to make it like a body. The values are usually different from the ones you're using, terms like solidity, permanence, and proportion, rather than accumulative and history.

CO: But I think that's fascistic. You know that gets into fascist architecture in a certain way. That's something I'm interested in getting away from, this idea that the perfect body would be the perfect building. I'm not interested in that notion of perfection. I don't believe in it.

Taco Trucks

Emergent Urbanism in Los Angeles

Ted Kane

LA Forum Pamphlet #3
Polar Inertia: Migrating Urban Systems
2007

> The evolution of a species is inseparable from the evolution of
> the environment. The two processes are tightly coupled as a single
> indivisible process.
> — James Lovelock

Everyday in Los Angeles fleets of over 4,000 mobile restaurants migrate through the streets in search of business.[1] The trucks respond to the daily changes of the city and its customers, piggybacking on the larger infrastructure of freeways, power, telephone, and water systems to find a market for their services. The taco truck, or what the health department terms a Mobile Food Preparation Unit (MFPU)[2], follows its own path among an infinite number of potential routes through the city, yet the trucks' patterns of collective behavior reveal active responses to elements in the city. The truck is a fluid and mobile infrastructure overlaid onto existing roadways; as a mobile and adaptable system, the taco truck network provides a useful tool for exploring the underlying dynamics of a city—revealing spaces that would be impossible to discover using static models and conventional mapping tools.

Mobile Patterns

The typical day for a taco truck business begins before 5:00 a.m. in one of over 30 commissaries regulated by Los Angeles County.[3] At the commissaries, the taco truck owner pays an average of $25 a day for a parking space, hot and cold water

LA Forum Reader

hookups, drains for cleaning the trucks, as well as access to a wholesale market for food, drinks, ice, and propane. These commissaries are spread across the region, creating a dispersed network of centers from which a steady flow of restaurants span outward along independent routes. After preparing the truck and supplies a truck will typically head out by 6:00 a.m. Each taco truck starts on equal footing, serving a potential market of 10 million residents.[4]

The extraordinary competition among the trucks guarantees that they are drawn to areas of demand. Because of their adaptive nature, their appearance is an indication of a certain type of condition in the city that might not otherwise be visible. From the infinite potential paths, patterns of clustering unexpectedly emerge, resulting from the unique overlay of particular geographic, social, and economical conditions that together create an ideal breeding ground for a taco truck. For example, the appearance of a taco truck in the wealthy neighborhoods of Beverly Hills or Malibu might seem unexpected, and yet they are tapping into a market of gardeners, nannies, and day laborers who are isolated from affordable food. Following a taco truck for a day, such spaces of transient density suddenly become apparent, including the late night streets of Hollywood Boulevard, where prostitutes congregate; the city parks during soccer matches; day-labor pick-up and construction sites; downtown factories, warehouses, film, and TV location shoots; and the beachfront streets where surfers and sunbathers gather. Mobile restaurants are naturally drawn to these spaces of temporary density located on the periphery of established commercial districts, in areas that benefit from the cheap food and convenience of a curbside restaurant. Taco trucks reconfigure these transient spaces into ad hoc restaurant zones whenever and wherever the situation warrants.

Urban Connections

Communication is critical to the success of a taco truck, as a route is compiled from connections developed with factory foreman, construction contractors, and business owners, culled over many years. In this effort, the cell phone has become a driver's indispensable tool, allowing for feedback from customers and adaption to different client schedules. The most lucrative routes for a mobile restaurant are at the factories around Downtown L.A. where each 20-minute stop can serve several dozen clients. The taco truck owner will work closely with the site supervisors to time his stops with breakfast, lunch, and coffee breaks, and through such service the drivers are able to inspire loyalty from clients and establish referrals to other similar sites.

The success of a taco truck business is closely related to an owner's ability to establish social and geographic connections to the city. Knowledge of the city and the areas of density is one of the things that distinguish an experienced driver from a beginner. A new driver must start by establishing a route through the city that will bring steady business, but this process is made more difficult by the unwritten code among drivers, which impedes them from encroaching on another truck's territory unless specifically invited by a customer. This seniority system requires a new driver to span out farther beyond the established routes to find business. To accomplish this he will need to work the periphery of established sites in hope of finding underserved areas, or he may chose to work off hours when most of the trucks have finished their routes. It is common in the business for a beginning driver to start by taking on the route of an experienced driver with an established client base. The established driver will then expand his business by purchasing a second truck, thus becoming both a driver and manager of two routes and through this process eventually accumulating a fleet of several food vans.[5] Innovation comes with the introduction of new drivers; their constant searching uncovers previously undiscovered pockets of demand, creating complex niche markets and co-operatives that evolve through the constantly changing local conditions.

Cultural Symbols

The popularity of the taco truck is symbolic of a cultural shift visible in the growth of Latino residents in Los Angeles, where Latinos now make up 47% of the population.[6] The immigrant population has created a fertile market of customers seeking the familiar foods from their homes at affordable prices; the common use of Spanish at the mobile restaurant also removes the language barrier that might otherwise make eating out less likely for new immigrants.[7] The connection of the taco truck or the *lonchera* to the immigrant community has triggered cultural battles among communities insecure about an influx of unfamiliar food and culture. In New Orleans, where a large population of immigrant construction labor relocated following Hurricane Katrina was soon followed by a boom in taco trucks. New Orleans recently passed laws to outlaw taco trucks exposing an anti-immigrant sentiment that manifested itself as a fear that taco trucks are unhealthy or would result in a loss of indigenous culture.[8] Such cultural food wars have popped up in other California cities including Salinas and San Bernardino, where taco trucks have also been banned from city streets. The health issue is often the reason cited for a city to ban taco trucks, even when the trucks are in compliance with health codes, as occurred in New Orleans—evidence of the power this cultural symbol has in exposing underlying tensions.[9]

    The taco truck is predominantly a small business enterprise with the owner also acting as driver. Taco trucks work from the bottom up in forming a client base, and this personal connection to their clients may explain the passion many Angelenos feel toward particular trucks.[10] Through the development of a loyal clientele over time, an experienced taco truck will often graduate into a semi-permanent facility located in one or two locations for extended periods of the day. This change happens when the truck finds a location niche that can be exploited without the need for constant roaming, or when it develops a cooperative agreement with a business to use its parking lot as a basis of operations. The truck owner's goal is to find a location that has a density of clientele to sustain it for an extended period of the day, as this setup saves gas and establishes a repeat customer base who knows where to find the truck. While the transient taco truck moves quickly among lower-density locations to serve a diverse mix of needs, the semi-permanent truck takes on the location memory of a fixed restaurant. Many of these semi-permanent restaurants also take on the look of fixed restaurants with outdoor seating and the capacity for customers to call in orders, for pick up. A notable example of this type of food van is the La Isla Bonita seafood van that has been parking in the same spot on a Venice street from 6:00 a.m. to 5:00 p.m. for over a decade, tapping into the needs of a regular crowd of construction workers, gardeners, beach goers, gym rats, and film industry workers. On Alameda Blvd in Downtown L.A. another semi-permanent taco truck regularly occupies the corner of an industrial parking lot where it caters to a steady flow of truck drivers, garment workers, and security personnel.

Sedentary Trucks

In 2006, lobbying efforts by fixed-site businesses with grievances about lost parking due to taco trucks persuaded the Los Angeles City Council to pass a law limiting the time that a taco truck can park in a commercial area to one hour, after which the truck must be moved more than a half-mile away for at least an hour before it can return to its original location.[11] Although irregularly enforced, this law has increased the occurrence of taco trucks leasing a parking spot in commercial business lots during off-business hours, which allows them to park for extended periods without moving. This arrangement benefits both the truck, providing a fixed presence and saving money on gas, as well as the commercial business, providing extra income during off-business hours. Such an arrangement is most common on busy arterial roads like Venice Boulevard or Western Avenue, where there is enough drive-by traffic to bring a steady flow of customers, compensating for the extra expense of a leased space.

    The popularity of taco trucks and the advantage their flexibility brings has influenced several permanent restaurants to abandon their fixed location in favor of mobile restaurants, as their neighborhoods change or business wanes.[12] It is also common for fixed taco stands to simultaneously operate taco trucks in their parking lots. One such taco restaurant on Hoover Avenue has a taco truck parked in its lot near the street to act as advertising; ironically, the truck often has a line, while the fixed restaurant is empty. Some explanations for this might be the value associated with mobility, including the cheap price structure and speed of service implied by a truck, which makes the mobile restaurant more attractive to a potential customer.

Mobile Urban Models

In biological terms, the taco truck could be considered an adaptive system where adaptation is the process by which an organism fits itself to its environment.[13] Only a few rules govern the behavior of taco trucks including the financial pressures of fuel prices, the social pressures of territoriality, and the governmental pressures of traffic/parking and health laws. It is out of these frictions and customer demands that patterns develop in the physical reality of the city. The taco truck's adaptation to its physical environment exposes a pattern we can interpret and document through observation, providing a useful tool for seeing the transformation of urban space through time. However, we cannot map this system as a fixed entity, because it's just one part of an infinite number of pathways and interrelated networks that make up the city. Los Angeles is a system co-evolving with its population, and can't be understood as a fixed entity, each moment the city reinventing itself, as are its inhabitants. Through the exploration of the impermanence inherent to the taco truck and other temporary forces, spaces of the city can be read and understood through their situational relationship rather than their fixed form. In this way, the city can be better understood as a collection of interactions, which combine to create spaces of community, and it is through the exploration of these interactions that governments and planners can hope to provide a qualitative influence by fostering the emergence of positive relationships in the city. We can gain valuable insight about our culture by picking up the wheel behind a taco truck and discovering another way of mapping the city through the forces of economy, regulation, and politics, that a driver of a taco truck discovers inherently.[14]

References

Baudrillard, Jean. *America*. Verso Press, 1988.
Bustillo, Miguel. "Hold the tacos, New Orleans says." *Los Angeles Times*, July 14, 2007.
Castells, Manuel. *The Rise of Network Society*. Blackwell Publishers, 1996.
Holland, John H. *Hidden Order: How adaptation builds complexity*. Perseus Books Group, 1995.
Katz, Jesse. "Wheels of Fortune." *Los Angeles Magazine*, October 2006.
Kelly, Kevin. *Out of Control: The new biology of Machines, Social Systems, and the Economic World*. Perseus Books Group, 1994.
Soja, Edward. *Postmetropolis: Critical Studies of Cities and Regions*. Blackwell Publishers, 2000.

Notes

1   According to the Los Angeles County Department of Public Health Services there are around 2,400 registered and around 1,500 lapsed registered mobile restaurants (MFPU). It is estimated that there are several hundred unregistered vans operating illegally.
2   MFPU is the term given to taco trucks by the State of California in their California Uniform Retail Food Facilities Law (CURFFL) Article 12, which is enforced in Los Angeles by the Los Angeles County Department of Health Services.
3   All MFPUs must operate out of a commissary by state law. The commissaries are private business and are regulated by the Los Angeles County Department of Health Services.
4   Based on the current U.S. Census for L.A. County.
5   Los Angeles is the epicenter of taco truck fabrication with several factories. A fabricator on Slauson has been in business for over 25 years and brings in buyers from around the state and country. A new truck costs around $100,000 with financing available.
6   See the Los Angeles County data sets published by the U.S. Census Bureau: http://quickfacts.census.gov/qfd/states/06/06037.html
7   From an interview with Luis Castro, the manager of Slauson foods commissary, he estimated that 80% of the workers have Spanish as their only language, but that most owners are bilingual. Personal interview with drivers also confirmed this ratio.
8   See *L.A. Times* article "Hold the tacos, New Orleans says" by Miguel Bustillo where in examines the growing Latino population in New Orleans that has quadrupled in the last four years while the overall population has decreased by half, causing tensions and fear among locals that New Orleans will lose its food history.
9   The Los Angeles County Health Department by California Law requires a yearly inspection, along with random inspections if there is a reason to suspect non-compliance. Since the trucks must be washed out nightly and leftover food disposed of, a regulated taco truck is most likely cleaner than fixed restaurants, this despite their reputation as roach coaches.
10   When asked, nearly every Angeleno seems to have a favorite taco truck restaurant to discuss. For some particularly passionate reviews of dozens of L.A. taco trucks see http://tacohunt.blogspot.com

11   See L.A. City Ordinance 177620, available at: http://cityclerk.lacity.org/CFI/
DisplayOnlineDocument.cfm?SRT=D1&cfnum=05-2220
The amendment to the municipal code limits food vender parking in commercial areas
for up to an hour, after which they must move their trucks more than a half-mile away for
at least an hour before they can return. In residential neighborhoods this ordinance limits
parking to 30 minutes.
12   This occurred on several restaurants in Culver City where a taco stand was also
operating a taco truck, eventually the stand closed leaving only the truck.
13   See John Holland's book *Hidden Order: How adaptation builds complexity* for
a thorough examination of complex adaptive systems (cas).
14   As Jean Baudrillard once wrote: "The point is not to write the sociology or
psychology of the car, the point is to drive. That way you learn more about this society
than all academia could ever tell you." Perhaps the point is also to drive a taco truck,
and discover a city that might otherwise remain invisible to urban studies.

Inter-
lude:
Some
News-
letters.

L.A. Forum
for Architecture and Urban Design

Newsletter 5

3454 West First Street
Los Angeles, California
9 0 0 0 4

(213) 389 - 6730

Officers:
Christian Hubert, *President*
Aaron Betsky, *Vice President*
Ann Zollinger, *Secretary/Treasurer*

Newsletter Editors:
Aaron Betsky
Natalie Shivers

Board of Directors:
Shelly A Berger
Aaron Betsky
Benjamin Caffey
Craig Hodgetts
Christian Hubert
John Kaliski
Doug Suisman

November, 1988

Futurist Flaneurs & Fashion

Ray Ryan

Ran into Ettore Sottsass at the new Giorgio Armani shop on Tuesday. At first one didn't recognise him but noticed his bespoke tailoring and elegant manners. Nothing about his person mimicked or amplified the general vulgarity of where he stood - which recalled Beau Brummel's dictum: "the severest mortification a gentleman could incur was to attract observation in the street by his outward appearance".

Sottsass, debonair creator of Olivetti gadgetry and Memphis "banal design", is in town to realise the Mayer/Schwarz Gallery across the street. He is following a path from the via Montenapoleone constructed by the engineer Ferre, the enigmatic Gigli and the fabulous Fendi sisters. Together with the Armani and Vitadini stores, his presence may be seen as part of the Milanisation of Rodeo Drive.

Entering the Armani store with aviator precision, into Benjamin's "interieures", one remembers Rossi's description of Schiele "entering...a more private area, not of abstraction but of obsession...the repeated self-portrait with all its narcissistic and almost obscene variations". Indeed, with its layers of International Style steel and glass, it does look like one of those "Obsession" advertisements. Highly cleansed and monochromatic assistants float and glance in little ethereal groups, the chill removed by gold screens which emit the anonymous luxury of another Klein, (Yves).
Advanced dandiacal espionage confirms that the Adriana Vitadini boutique is indeed by Gae Aulenti. Signora Aulenti, the grey granny of Milanese minimalism, came to town with the understated control of a soothing detective and implanted her barely perceptible oeuvre, shipped en masse from Italy, on the promenade. One could wonder here if the expert viewing of paddocks by

Degas could not be shifted to the thoroughbred automobiles of Beverly Hills. Suffice to say that Aulenti continues her line of generic distillation of things which, like Loos who liked his beef rare and his columns Doric, produces a funereal corporeality.

Of course, "Less is More" is quintessential Dandy: Dandy and Modernity being so interwoven, the former without the latter being mere foppishness and vice versa kitsch.

Baudelaire understood the need for shopping and the relationship between materiality and materialism. Bijan, indulgently nostalgic for pre-Ayatollah Tehran, is full of things and never one of them beautiful. The autonomous objects of Sottsass are taking up positions. Between Dessau and Sesame Street, they wink and flirt and challenge the refined sensibilities of Johannes van Tilburg. Exuding wit and tone and the slyly sexual materiality of Loos, black marble temple fronts pose with flesh pink chevrons to combat the ordinary. Like the dumb cacophany of Harpo Marx, they jest at our hautiness.

Up above, Carlo Mollino, impeccibly scarved, rolled across the sky.

workshops in Van Nuys, Los Feliz, Watts, City North and Boyle Heights. The workshop process is based on a similar, and very successful, program developed by the National A.I.A. called Regional Urban Design Assistance Team (R/UDAT).

The process begins with a steering committee made up of community members and staff from the various city, county and state agencies that represent the area. Organized by the Planning Department, the committee begins its work by gathering important background information on the demographics and history of the district including an investigation of existing and proposed projects and programs. This material is used to develop a mission statement and issues brief.

To conduct the workshop a team of pro-bono architects, planners, landscape architects, urban designers, housing specialists, developers, economists, transportation experts, and other consultants is assembled from the Los Angeles area. During four days of intensive work, the team interviews 50 to 100 interested community members and agency representatives; tours the area guided by local experts; and develops design, planning and economic strategies that address the issues and opportunities identified by the community. By the end of this period the team has produced a 60 to 80 page camera-ready document that is printed on the fifth day and presented to the community and the City Planning Commission on the Seventh Day.

The unique aspect of this process is that it is proactive rather than reactive (which is the usual role for a planning department). The workshop gives the community, the city staff and the team a chance to look at the community as a whole, not as a series of separate autonomous projects. This approach not only creates a vision for the community, it also develops a sense of neighborhood both architecturally, through linkages, gateways, landmarks and other significant places, and politically, through the establishment of committed resident and merchant organizations.

One key element of these programs is the continuing involvement of the community from the very beginning of the process. Such involvement is essential if the community is to feel committed to the ideas generated by the workshop and, more importantly, to the implementation of those ideas.

Four of the five workshops have already been held: Van Nuys in October 1988, Los Feliz in March 1989, Watts in June 1989, and City North in December 1989. Each of the charettes has generated a unique set of solutions particular to the areas in which they were held.

The Van Nuys workshop focused on the government center along Van Nuys Blvd., between Oxnard St. and Victory Blvd. Here the team recommended the creation of new office buildings, cultural attractions and retail shops to create a Valley Civic Center. They further proposed the reinforcement of the historic "Crossroads of the Valley" at Van Nuys and Victory boulevards by intensifying development of retail activity there. Mixed use, parking management, and landscape and streetscape improvements were all recommended to unite the community and create a sense of place in the vast wasteland of the valley. Since the workshop, the design standards proposed by the team for a new city office building and the zoning and land use recommendations they developed have been used by

plan for community develo
and renovated housing, the
the Watts Towers, and a c
station. Increased citizen
ingredient in the success of
and the team recommende
issues. The team called atte
potential as a location for ligh
due to its light rail lines alo
from Long Beach to Downt
corridor. The team's ideas
included in the program tha
Agency is producing on for

The most recen
north of the Civic Center
cultural center of Los Ange
Chinatown, El Pueblo, Un
L.A. River, Elysian Park an
shop was the most public
workshops. City North offe
to connect the vital and we
landform elements of the a
in the heart of a major city.

and in sync
with the times

for every purpose

and pocket book

LINOLEUM

REPRESENTS
material,

sensory memory triggering
device, commenting on painting,

(DE KOONING/ABSTRACT EXPRESSIONISM AND POLLACK/SPLOP AND BLOP,
PALATIAL SURROUNDINGS, PERSIAN RUGS, MARBLE ENTRIES,
planks,
mosaic,
flagstone, masonry, textiles, quake
rag rugs, straw tile, tailored floors,
raybelle/a pattern de

repres

luxe car design or borrowe
being produced by John
dimensional graphic patt
decorative scoring of stu
stucco, boomerang kidne
effectively altered their p
and the use of individua
lamps.

Occasionally period
as iconographic referen
stucco box was often flat
where builders wanted to
ity. Butterfly roofs were s

The lighting and lan
istic as the ornament. Pla
such as dracena and sag
objects or graphic accent
was equally as important.
took personal pride in the
boat, "Melody Ann", for
vehicles for theming. The
hotels (the Algiers, the F
Palms, the Dunes, etc.).

Ultimately, the mos
their disregard of conve
ornament and the boldne
readily discernible in rec

John Chase   Note:
Box"
Home

sal for that office building
lan for the area.

ed on the opportunity to
into a dynamic neighbor-
he team recommended
Blvd. and Vermont Ave.
k, the retail districts along
orth, the many hospitals
Metro-Rail stop at Sunset
d urban design improve-
avenues, including the
shops that front on the
the adjacent residential
strian activity. The crea-
ncouraged to implement
arette. The Los Feliz
esidents group, has con-
n community meetings
roject of the urban design
ues.

m developed a strategic
cupational training, new
a cultural center around
center at the light rail
on was seen as a vital
jects in the community
p workshops on specific
area's often overlooked
and regional commercial
ntury Freeway, another
third along the Alameda
ltural center have been
munity Redevelopment
Tower Art Center.

for City North, the area
that is the historic and
at ways to link together
, Terminal Annex, the
ilroad yards. This work-
est attended of all the
n a unique opportunity
ed historic, cultural and
eatly underutilized land
e major linkages in the

community, and to the areas outside of it, is the Los Angeles
River. This workshop called for the development of a mixed-
use park district as the first step in the greening of the river. The
other important connection is the proposed Pasadena Light
Rail Line. Here the team recommended that stops be created
in Chinatown and the mixed-use river park as well as the
planned terminus at Union Station. North Broadway and
Alameda St. were proposed to be linked to create a principal
arterial north-south street. A network of public open spaces and
pedestrian connections between Union Station and Olivera
Street would further encourage the sense of community for
these presently separated places.

Recently, the Planning Commission asked the
Planning Department to reconvene the steering committee to
determine the best next step for the ideas developed by the
team. The possibilities for this work range from a policy
statement about the greening of the river to the funding of a
specific plan for the area.

The impact of the City North workshop empha-
sizes the importance of this program. The combined involvement of the community, the city government and the design
and planning professions provides a unique forum for the
investigation and discussion of urban issues that affect Los
Angeles. This participatory approach is an effective means of
generating solutions that reflect the needs and aspirations of
everyone concerned.

Deborah Murphy

porch rugs,

not to
IMITATE ANY OTHER MATERIAL
but a 'DISTINCTIVE'
of materiality

FORUM NEWS

The Forum now has a permanent home, its own telephone line an
Substation for Architecture, 2798 Sunset Blvd., L.A., CA 90026 (2
series of presentations of theories about Los Angeles. The next discussion series will also
Another planned series will include an exam
Playa Vista. The series
develop

Forum

for Architecture and Urban Design

3454 West First Street
Los Angeles, California
90004

Watch out for "Out there Doing it–the sequil":
outdoors at the Schindler House
on Monday evenings in July and August.
Speakers will include Janek Beilski,
Buresh/Guthree, Charles and Elizabeth Lee,
Paul Lubowiki, Josh Schweitzer,
Hulbert/Zebria, O'Herlihy/Warner and
others T.B.A.

To:

Place
Stamp
Here
×

News Letter

#7

los angeles forum for architecture and urban design

"Home price figures
are like noses:
everybody has one.
And like noses,
everybody's figures
are different than
everybody else's."

LA Times, April 23, 1989

The Playa Vista Alternative

Last month Maguire Thomas Partners and their design team unveiled their scheme for the new town of Playa Vista which will be sited on the old Hughes Aircraft estate. The design team is made up of five firms: Duany and Plater-Zyberk, Moore Ruble Yudell, de Bretteville and Polyzoides, Hanrah/Olin, and Ricardo Legorretta.

The renderings and plan suggest a town whose formal structure is made by overlaying several urban scales: large sectors, smaller neighborhoods, and their centers. Using both early American traditional towns, such as Savannah and Charleston, and Los Angeles urban fragments as models, Playa Vista will be a dense, gridded town designed in modules based on a 5 minute walking distance. While there are to be two dominant centers, a commercial center at the base of the bluffs to the south and a marina center to the north, the town's most distinctive character will thus be its small neighborhoods. The residential areas will be modelled after Los Angeles courtyard housing, but will also feature other attached unit types such as the quadplex, duplex, large villa, row house, and terrace house. Corner retail (designated for pubs, small markets, etc.) will be placed in each small neighborhood. These clusters will also feature a small park, often containing an institutional building such as a library, a small theater, or a post office.

While this gridded morpho of the town, Playa Vista will take advantage and with the renovation of Ballona Creek. T with row houses and continuous public walk The Corps of Engineers' concrete basin (iro be planted heavily to create public esplanad

Like Duany and Plater-Zy entire town will be governed by both an Urb The necessity of coding comes not only from control, but also from the difficult political c preservation of the wetlands as a habitat for protection of the views from the bluffs (as w the area were some of the major concerns of Maguire Thomas was told by local politician issues, no project would survive the approva mandate to make the design process accom ensure the recognition of these concerns.

So far, the Playa Vista proj of the nearby residents. Moreover, it could b problems of the rest of the basin. One of the Vista design is to create a pedestrian commu but also for those who work there. Commut reduced by encouraging car-pooling and by and shop within walking distance at lunch h amount of affordable housing will be built in both live and work there.

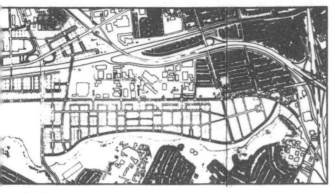

Playa Vista
proposed site plan

My own interest in the Beverly Center began when I saw it begin to rise up over the ghosts of former swampland and a kiddie park along Beverly and Third. It was the clearest possible expression of squeezing money out of a site. It was so big, so brown, and so bare of any real articulation or any relationship to the street (day-glo Beauborg Center escalators notwithstanding) that I thought of it as building rather than architecture. It is this absence that is so shocking - the Beverly Center reminds one of all the virtues a building can have in an urban setting because it is so bereft of them. One of the purposes of the Forum's 33D6E6 Project is to discover how a lumpen mass like this could conceivably be reconnected to the larger city.

Shopping
for
ARCHITECTURE:

The Sequel

ccount for the look of most
de location with a marina
s two islands will be covered
e Naples in Long Beach.
called Ballona Creek) will
vo banks.
n of Seaside in Florida, the
nd an Architectural Code.
ners' desire for aesthetic
such a project. The
f endangered birds, the
em), and control of traffic in
nts of adjacent communities.
ss they responded to these
. In fact, it was their
mmunity participation to

s to be a success in the eyes
of a solution for some of the
ortant goals of the Playa
nly for those who live there,
to the town would be
ommuters with places to eat
er work. In addition, a large
ouse many of those who do

This is the competition that asks: what does it mean to shop and to die in Los Angeles? Here we have all these big heaps of single-use stuff hunkered down next to each other. Is there a meaningful way in which the Beverly Center can say to Cedars Sinai: "Give me your sick and your dying and I will heal them with a one-time designer's close-out sale, this weekend only"? Is it possible for the Beverly Connection and Ma Maison Sofitel to be integrated into a larger urban whole?

The Beverly Center neighborhood is a reflection of the American Way of suburban development, big single-use complexes. America is the land of the college campus, the industrial park, and the shopping center. We break experience into categories, we isolate our needs and satisfy them one at a time. It is like a la carte. You eat all of the steak before going on to the mashed potatoes. It creates a peculiarly American sort of culture. Our daily missions are accomplished one by one, but never integrated. Americans compose their individual character piece by piece from a kind of de facto catalog. One doesn't absorb culture in the U.S., one

119

vance copies of the soon-to-be available, Rizzoli-published, rum book, <u>Experimental Architecture in Los Angeles</u>, have n sighted but not yet in bookstores. Substantial discounts members are being negotiated. Plans to work with)CA to mount an exhibit in the TC showcasing the work hose in the book hit the skids with MOCA's announcement t the TC would close for 18 months after "Helter elter." Alternative venues are sought. • **Activities** • er Lipson, answering the call of the open road, left vn and his position of Activities Committee chair. Our t series, "The Spring Collection," will be chaired jointly Marc Tedesco and Aaron Betsky. • **Pamphlet** • The rum's next pamphlet <u>The LA School Reader</u>, rumored to approaching book-size, is in the works. • **Help Needed** he Activities, Publications and Exhibitions Committees need new participants. If you'd like to get involved¬ ve a message on our machine 213-852-7145.

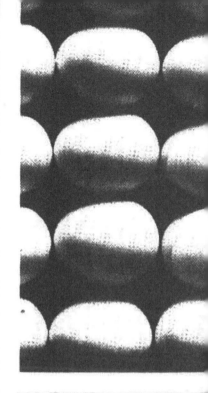

19

92

lovely e

los angeles

sprin

I accepted the job I knew it was going to be precar
But I didn't want to be holier-than-thou about what
coined "entertainment architecture," which is not

continued on p

THE Los An
FORUM

835 NORTH KINGS ROAD WEST HOLLYWOOD C

ARCHITECTU
NEWSLETTER February 1993
IN THIS ISSUE:
The Mediated Environment **URBAN**

Essays on EuroDisney and other urban landscapes by Fran
B. Lesser, Jonathan Massey, Dana L. Webber, Nicholas Lo
Larsen, and more *Nomadic Thoughts.*

ANDRE

*SEPTEM
c'est pa
a broad
Disneyla
engage*

PHOTO ESSAY BY
KRISTINE LARSEN

with the corporate side—hotels, offices, convention centers—of the company famous for theme parks and cinematic fantasy.

continued on page 3

geles

FOR

9

E AND

ESIGN

Gehry, Andrea Kahn, Nina
oto essay by Kristine

ON THE OUTSIDE LOOKING IN (OR, SOME UNTHEMED THOUGHTS
HN ON EURODISNEY)

0, 1992; A FRIEND'S APARTMENT, PARIS: "Agriculture,
yland" states a farmer in the studio of France Telé 2, during
the ECC referendum returns. (Agriculture, c'est pas
ell, maybe, or maybe not. Both are big business, both
gn trade. Both seem to incur major losses, both beg the
trols. Of course, agri-business always depends on the

Los Angeles looking east, 1960.
UCLA Department of Geography aerial photo
archives, Spence Collection

ltiple centers in the same metropolitan area,
reasing fragmentation of social and economic life,
d a simultaneous consolidation of wealth and power
all patterns that have been reproduced across the
be.

In Los Angeles, the middle and upper
sses of this city continue to retreat behind electronic
es and lines of security patrols, demonstrating the
d of radical social polarization that was previously
ributed to third world countries. Meanwhile waves of
migrants, with an uncanny astuteness for the way the
ce of this city has successively been occupied, have
ated elusive and nearly imperceptible focal points for
ir communities in the midst of previously undifferen-
ed suburban sprawl. And while few people are brave
ough to predict the outcome of the massive building
jects taking place downtown, the new and lingering

dismantling of the military industrial complex can
longer be lobbied away. The city seems, somehov
have grown to the extent of its tolerable limits. Ar
with even fewer identifiable urban markers, such
Inland Empire or Orange County have become me
lises in their own right, not simply a part of Greate
Angeles. The collapse of the real estate market de
blow, both financial and symbolic, to the eternal
optimists of Southern California, while the riots
articulated the frustration caused by decades of
economic and racial inequity with an urgency that
it difficult for even the most intransigent and entre
power players to ignore. Our focus has contracted
with our hopes and our economy at a time when
theory is finally speaking to us: as it is in fact lived
in relation to an imported model to which we coul
aspire. It is impossible for anyone who lived here

Los Angeles Forum
for Architecture and Urban Design

Fall 2013
Newsletter

The
ver Truck

- Li Wen
SPACE SPEED FORM

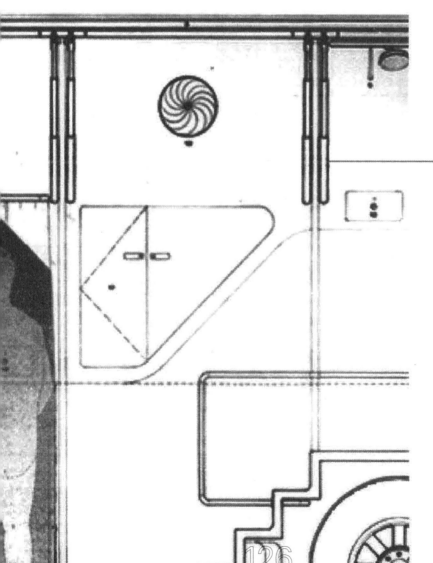

t uses the desire to provide showers
less as a generator for creating architecture
ries of urban moments.

SPECIFICATION

14 shower stalls pe
solar panels moun
18-wheeler trailer.

Each stall is equipp
penser, washboarc

All materials are o
of maintenance.

Energy is stored in
to generators exte
trailer.

Water is supplied I
public system of fi

Water is heated ar
and expansion tan

Each Shower/Truc
dant who will trave
parking lots.

Delivery, pick up a
trailer will be by lo
contributing their

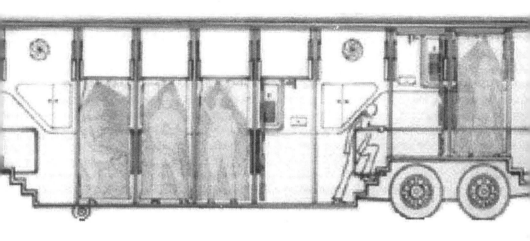

or they have no home. Cleansing facilities need to be brought to the
s for in Los Angeles at least, they are not mobile on the scale of the city.

lots for the most part seem to be such a lot of wasted space because
form only one function. No other space in the city is afforded this
The single-minded nature of parking is what makes most lots such dead
lust as at the beach, where people play roller-hockey and sail-skate in
ow of the Cirque de Soleil's tent, the parking lots of Los Angeles are
I urban stages for various human activities.

N THE LIFE

It's lunchtime downtown. Pershing Square is teeming with visitors,
and passers-by. Traffic is thick, the sky clear, and the noise dense.
ishes from the Square's fountain and splashes on the surrounding cob-
s.
Out from the corner of your view, you see a large 18-wheeler pull up to
er of 5th and Olive, enter into the parking lot and stop with a hiss. A
umps out from the cab, checks several dials on the trailer and flips a
The long walls of the trailer, which are implanted with solar panels rise
truts, like gull-wing doors, to reveal stainless steel innards. Curtains
hin stir in the breeze. The truck attendant pulls out a large hose and
one end to a nearby fire hydrant, the other end to the rear of the trailer
-release levers. He turns the hydrant on. The hose swells with the
of water; the needles on the dials jump as purring emanates from deep
e stainless torso - evidence that the solar panels have kicked the on-
enerators into gear. The nearby clock tower chimes 12:00.
The Shower/Truck is now open for service.

It's almost 4:0
attention to such things
Johnson struggles to fir
depression the enemy.
avoid Johnson. He kno
nowhere to go but mov
those who seem suscer
because he knows that
He still remem
pulling up and unfoldin
man handed him a tow
available. Soon there w
bering out of their afte
was about to take his fi
and wearing a cleaner s
memory of water peltin
locks that stuck with hir
back to the Palisades to
Johnson looks
starts setting up. He m
the beach. This will be

sia. It is the goal of the school to enable all of our students to spend a semester working in a foreign country.

SC is dedicated to more than just excellent professional training. The University has developed a new, strong general education program paralleling the architecture curriculum. This

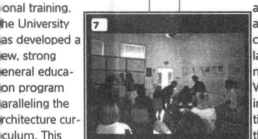

program will insure that all of our graduates have the opportunity to develop knowledge in a wide range of areas, to become renaissance men and women.

ROBERT DEAN H. TIMME

collaborative and to take risks; to look beyond the boundaries of a problem. For our part, the university is opening an extension of our architecture school in collaboration with Mesa Community College in San Diego, and will bring affordable, accredited architectural education to a population of several million people. Woodbury has initiated formal ties with ELEA, the association of Latin American schools of architecture.

The university intends that its willingness to take risks, seize opportunities and embrace constructive change is a clear example to our students. For them and for the practice of Architecture the bar is continually being raised.

LOUIS M. DEAN NAIDORF

confronted by sponsoring a diverse range of activities, electives, and internships; by bringing nationally and internationally recognized architects, designers, critics, and historians to the University community; and by making available a dynamic faculty and group of visiting critics. The Department actively recruits (and has been fortunate to retain) faculty representing both established and emerging voices in design education and practice, each of whom is expected to be highly motivated and propositional, serving as an inspiration to students who will realize the importance of developing an articulate position with regard to design in varied imaginative and material contexts.

LINDA CHAIR POLLARI

VITO ACCONCI	SERTRO SCULPTURE PROGRAM, VIENNA		
	Howard Adams	USC, Harris Hall	11-5-97 @
	Stan Allen	Woodbury U.	10-23-97 @ 7PM
Kevin Appel & Tom Baldwin	FORUM *Fake Estate* '97 Lecture Series	MAK Center	
Art by Architects Exhibit	Armory Center for the Arts, Pasadena		
	Dave Bailey & Sam Durant	FORUM *Fake Estate* '97 Lecture Series	MA
	Ann Bergren	UCLA, Perloff	10-2-97 @ 6:30PM
	William Bruder	USC, Harris Hall	10-1-97 @ 6PM
	William Bruder Cal Poly Pomona	11-3-97 @ 12AM	909
	Bernard Cache	UCLA, Perloff	11-13-97 @
	Todo Cambia (by Kcho)	MoCA Focus Series Exhibit	
Joe Carmen	Woodbury U.	1-29-98 @ 7PM	
	Peter Cook	SCI-Arc 11-5-97 @ 7:30	
Steven Erlich Architects	World Beat Architecture Exhibit	Hollyhock Hou	
Fire in the Library Fires in the Mind	Physicist/mathematician Dr. Zhen Su S Astronomer Richard Terrile & performa Writer /autodidact Bettyanne Holtzman		
Ann Friedberg	UCLA, Perloff	12-4-97 @ 6:30PM	
	Carlos Fuentes	Mandeville Auditorium, UCSD	10
Garden A Garden of Eden on Wheels Exhibit	Museum of Jurassic T		
	Frank Gehry	USC, Harris Hall	10-29-97
THE Getty Center	Opens December 16, 1997	Parking reserva	
	Diane Ghirardo	SCI-Arc 10-15-97 @ 7:30	3
Irving Gill Tour & Lecture Event w/ Marvin Rand Society of Archite Ted Wells at 714.495.6009 or SofAH @ W			
JOE Goode	*The Maverick Strain* Performance	Sushi Performanc Organized by InSite 97	
Bob Gysin & Partners Exhibit Form Zero Bookstore, SM	February 1998		
HELLO *Again! A new Wave of Recylced Art and Design* Exhibit	Municipal Art Ga		
Craig Hodgetts & Ming Fung	SCI-Arc	11-19-97 @ 7:30	
	Coy Howard Cal Poly Pomona	11-10-97 @ 12AM	
	Robert Irwin	SCI-Arc 10-31	
Masterworks: Italian Design, 1960-1994 Art Center College of Design	10-18		
Thomas Jeffries *Recycled Materials in Architecture* Municipal Art Gallery Theater			
	Wes Jones	UCLA, Perloff	10-30-97 @ 6:30PM
	Ray Kappe	SCI-Arc 9-10-97 @ 7:30	
Jeff Kipnis/Greg Ulmer	Woodbury U.	2-26-98 @ 7PM	
	Lars Lerup	SCI-Arc 10-22-97 @ 7:30	
C.J. Lim / Studio 8 Exhibit	Form Zero Bookstore, SM	TBA 1	
	Mark Linder	Woodbury U.	11-6-97 @ 7PM
	Sharlene Silverman Lyon	USC, Harris Hall	11-12-97 @
	Mark Mack	USC, Harris Hall	
Randell Makinson	USC, Harris Hall	11-19-97 @ 6PM	213.74
Winy Maas	Woodbury U. @ PDC	4-23-98 @ 7PM	
	Gordon Matta-Clark, films	UCLA, Dickson SCI-Arc MoCA, Ahmanson Aud.	
Gordon Matta-Clark	*Anarchitecture* Exhibit MAK Center @ Schindler Exhibit on view thru 1-18-98		
Riyuji Miyamoto Exhibit	Form Zero Bookstore, SM	APRI	
	Eric Owen Moss	SCI-Arc	11-12-97
Eric Owen Moss & Aaron Betsky Icons in the Sprawl Symposium @ Sa			

129

AND B

(FROM PAGE 12)

1 EDITORIAL STATEMENT:
FROM ANALOG
TO DIGITAL
AND BACK AGAIN

After a long hiatus, the *LA Forum Newsletter* is back in print. But the return to pulp and ink is not as perverse as it sounds. Throughout the 1990s, the publication of a physical newsletter was a defining endeavor of the LA Forum's efforts to disseminate ideas about architecture and urbanism into the community. A decade ago the newsletter transitioned to a low-overhead online version, where obscurity led with seeming inevitability to total dor-

b
c
u
d
F
L
tl
s
r
T
A
n
b
tc
tl
tl
o
a
a
e
a

130

ACK

ons with tall tales of ran-
and modernisms, lost
isms, and had-to-be-there
tes. Last summer, the LA
n's retrospective exhibition
ished Business shuffled
gh our archives. This
g, the Getty Foundation
es its Pacific Standard
initiative with *Modern
tecture in L.A.*, a citywide,
institutional look at the
environment from 1940
90. But as the legacy of
esigners and critics of
Oth century hangs heavy
ead, our appreciation
onsciousness of that leg-
ajole and threaten us at
turn. Frank Lloyd Wright
ay and Charles Eames

SPRING 2013

131

III.
Hunches

Re: Hunches
Michael Sweeney

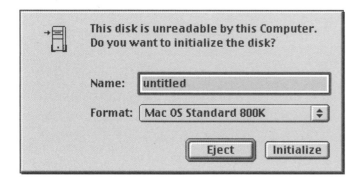

The LA Forum's publication history is allergic to consistency; our messy shelves of pamphlets, booklets, unpaginated photos, newsletters, and loosely thematic books telegraph the consistent ideological heterodoxy contained within. This abject refusal of "format" is not accidental; rather it was and is in and of itself an experimental, experiential critique of those pesky publication standards in which all articles fit within self-similar layouts and presentations.

This intentional uniformity of physical, graphic treatment in then-contemporary journals like *Assemblage* was as much of an ideological statement of editorial intent as was the Forum's refusal of the same. In a city that still largely lacks the type of publishing infrastructure and its commensal professionalized support for narrow, specialized discourse commensurate to the East Coast, the Forum's publications instead heavily borrowed from zine culture. Instead of crafting an institutional façade in the vein of *Oppositions*, the early Forum pamphlets traffic in curated anarchy. By themselves, the first seven pamphlets published by the Forum between 1988 and 1995 in the immediate pre-World Wide Web era include four almost-traditional "pamphlets,"[1] two photo collections[2], and one HyperCard stack on a 3.5-inch Macintosh floppy disk.[3] Of these seven, *Recombinant Images* and *ArchInfo* stand as hunches—as templates not necessarily of future physical publications, but of the types of hybrid, projective polemics that would soon become bread and butter for online discourse.

Physically, *Recombinant Images* is an envelope of 12 black-and-white 5 x 7s accompanied by four similarly sized, light double-sided pages of text and endnotes. There is little inherent ordering to the images, but they are all composed of nighttime multiple exposures of the quotidian Los Angeles—billboard frames, loading docks, opaque industrial tools, and Metropolitan Detention Center. The text rightly locates the project within the lineage of Moholy-Nagy, Duchamp, and Stockhausen as an exploration of the recontextualization of the as-found, but these images have a more immediate specific and local resonance. Both the formal characteristics of their framing and fragmentary subject matter, as well as the specific mechanics of their creation (focused shots instead of photograms or Stan Brakhage's direct manipulation of the film stock) owe even more of a debt to film noir. Aside from their cover text, the recombinant images present themselves as a collection of scene fades from unknown films, trading on our collective store of filmic images we all have of Los Angeles.

This ambiguous dialogue between the "types" of writing that participate in the larger streams of institutional architectural discourse, and more personal, idiosyncratic pieces that limn the edges of fiction and popular culture is present to a degree in almost all of the pieces anthologized in this book, starting from the very beginning with *Swimming to Suburbia*. Largely that complexity is still self evident on the pace, though in this regard *ArchInfo* is the most fundamentally altered here in both its presentation as well as the subjective reception(s). It is still a critical examination of the technological impact on perceptions of space and time and on the development of L.A. (thought inherently colored by the intervening twenty two years), but critically its entire inherent structure and the format by which it was intended to be consumed is now virtually inaccessible.

Conceived as a structural experiment in how writing and discourse about architecture could be/would be fundamentally re-ordered by emerging network technologies, its discursive text is fragmented and interspersed with low-res images, multiple authors (including Aaron Betsky and Sanford Kwinter), and editorial notes. Instead of a singular narrative or voice, the organization willfully disorders and jumbles the textual continuity with intent to provoke intertextual connections. Originally, it was published not as a book, but as a small black cardboard box filled with index cards and a 3.5-inch floppy disk. The cards and the database saved on the disk contended substantially the same information and the intent was for the user to experience this publication on-screen—by clicking forward and backward through the HyperCard stack. The stack of randomly ordered cards was originally intended as a backup to deal with the immediate issues of software incompatibility (the disc format and required software was Macintosh-only, which made it inaccessible to large swaths of the public even at its release). Today however, it is only because of those index cards that we can access this publication at all. Both the 3.5-inch floppy hardware and the Apple's HyperCard software long ago disappeared from the market, so it is essentially impossible to experience *ArchInfo* as originally intended.

Even in 1995, the very object of the 3.5-inch floppy telegraphed the impermanence of the *ArchInfo* project—discs never were intended to last nor (to a degree) was the critique. Rereading the Forum publications of the era that bracket *ArchInfo*, its exploration of space, time, and L.A. tracks apace the critical (re-)evaluation of the existing city and its planning alongside Marco Cenzatti's *Los Angeles and the L.A. School* and Flusty's *Building Paranoia*. The key difference is that it makes the uneasy reality of post-Uprising Los Angeles' transitory existence into a feature instead of a bug. Here, the idea of Los Angeles' urban form is mapped onto a theoretical neo-Gibsonian image of cyberspace. As Betsky writes:

> "Cyberspace is mythic; it is a space that may have existed, but may now be gone; may still be in existence; may have started; may happen in the future, or maybe never nowhere. It is an analogous space, the space of the mirror, commenting on our own predicament. It could be the very essence of architecture."

If in fact L.A. has always been the first-draft of a metropolis, then it is the relationships in the database that matter— not the indexical patterning.

Notes

1   *Ecology of Fantasy, The Los Angeles Boulevard: Eight X-Rays of the Body Public, Los Angeles and the L.A. School: Post Modernism and Urban Studies and Building Paranoia*

2   *35mm Works and Recombinant Images*

3   *ArchInfo*

ARCHINFO: Architecture and Information
Douglas MacLeod
1995

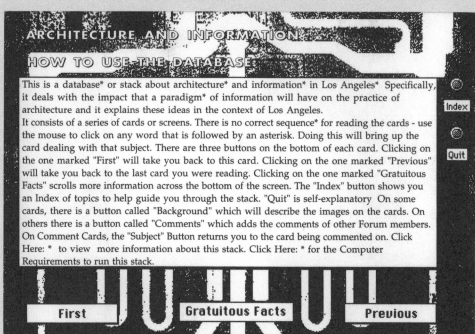

HOW TO USE THE DATABASE

This is a database* or stack about architecture* and information* in Los Angeles* Specifically, it deals with the impact that a paradigm* of information will have on the practice of architecture and it explains these ideas in the context of Los Angeles.

It consists of a series of cards or screens. There is no correct sequence* for reading the cards - use the mouse to click on any word that is followed by an asterisk. Doing this will bring up the card dealing with that subject. There are three buttons on the bottom of each card. Clicking on the one marked "First" will take you back to this card. Clicking on the one marked "Previous" will take you back to the last card you were reading. Clicking on the one marked "Gratuitous Facts" scrolls more information across the bottom of the screen. The "Index" button shows you an Index of topics to help guide you through the stack. "Quit" is self-explanatory On some cards, there is a button called "Background" which will describe the images on the cards. On others there is a button called "Comments" which adds the comments of other Forum members. On Comment Cards, the "Subject" Button returns you to the card being commented on. Click Here: * to view more information about this stack. Click Here: * for the Computer Requirements to run this stack.

Index

Quit

First **Gratuitous Facts** **Previous**

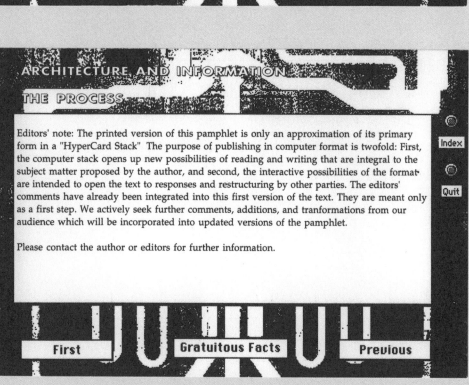

THE PROCESS

Editors' note: The printed version of this pamphlet is only an approximation of its primary form in a "HyperCard Stack" The purpose of publishing in computer format is twofold: First, the computer stack opens up new possibilities of reading and writing that are integral to the subject matter proposed by the author, and second, the interactive possibilities of the format are intended to open the text to responses and restructuring by other parties. The editors' comments have already been integrated into this first version of the text. They are meant only as a first step. We actively seek further comments, additions, and tranformations from our audience which will be incorporated into updated versions of the pamphlet.

Please contact the author or editors for further information.

Index

Quit

First **Gratuitous Facts** **Previous**

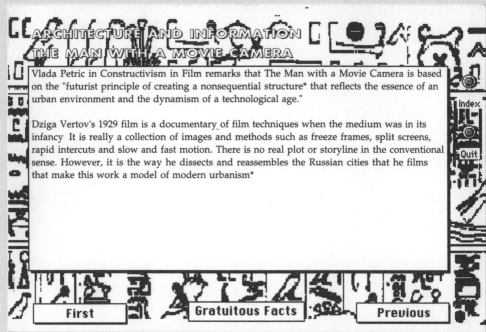

Vlada Petric in Constructivism in Film remarks that The Man with a Movie Camera is based on the "futurist principle of creating a nonsequential structure* that reflects the essence of an urban environment and the dynamism of a technological age."

Dziga Vertov's 1929 film is a documentary of film techniques when the medium was in its infancy It is really a collection of images and methods such as freeze frames, split screens, rapid intercuts and slow and fast motion. There is no real plot or storyline in the conventional sense. However, it is the way he dissects and reassembles the Russian cities that he films that make this work a model of modern urbanism*

Index

Quit

First | Gratuitous Facts | Previous

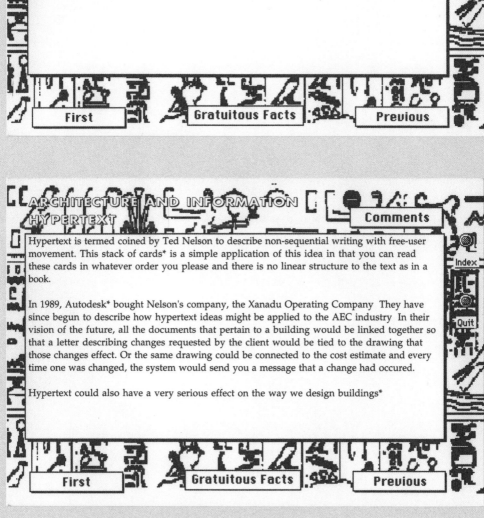

Comments

Hypertext is termed coined by Ted Nelson to describe non-sequential writing with free-user movement. This stack of cards* is a simple application of this idea in that you can read these cards in whatever order you please and there is no linear structure to the text as in a book.

In 1989, Autodesk* bought Nelson's company, the Xanadu Operating Company They have since begun to describe how hypertext ideas might be applied to the AEC industry In their vision of the future, all the documents that pertain to a building would be linked together so that a letter describing changes requested by the client would be tied to the drawing that those changes effect. Or the same drawing could be connected to the cost estimate and every time one was changed, the system would send you a message that a change had occured.

Hypertext could also have a very serious effect on the way we design buildings*

Index

Quit

First | Gratuitous Facts | Previous

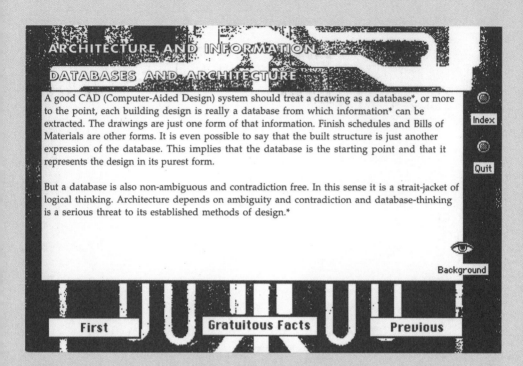

DATABASES AND ARCHITECTURE

A good CAD (Computer-Aided Design) system should treat a drawing as a database*, or more to the point, each building design is really a database from which information* can be extracted. The drawings are just one form of that information. Finish schedules and Bills of Materials are other forms. It is even possible to say that the built structure is just another expression of the database. This implies that the database is the starting point and that it represents the design in its purest form.

But a database is also non-ambiguous and contradiction free. In this sense it is a strait-jacket of logical thinking. Architecture depends on ambiguity and contradiction and database-thinking is a serious threat to its established methods of design.*

Index

Quit

Background

First   Gratuitous Facts   Previous

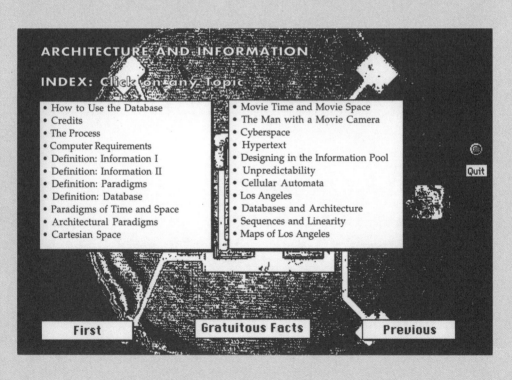

INDEX: Click on any Topic

- How to Use the Database
- Credits
- The Process
- Computer Requirements
- Definition: Information I
- Definition: Information II
- Definition: Paradigms
- Definition: Database
- Paradigms of Time and Space
- Architectural Paradigms
- Cartesian Space

- Movie Time and Movie Space
- The Man with a Movie Camera
- Cyberspace
- Hypertext
- Designing in the Information Pool
- Unpredictability
- Cellular Automata
- Los Angeles
- Databases and Architecture
- Sequences and Linearity
- Maps of Los Angeles

Quit

First   Gratuitous Facts   Previous

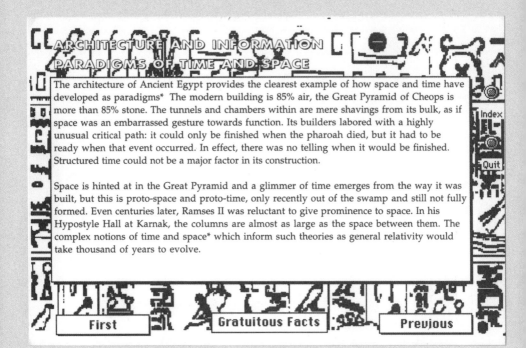

The architecture of Ancient Egypt provides the clearest example of how space and time have developed as paradigms* The modern building is 85% air, the Great Pyramid of Cheops is more than 85% stone. The tunnels and chambers within are mere shavings from its bulk, as if space was an embarrassed gesture towards function. Its builders labored with a highly unusual critical path: it could only be finished when the pharoah died, but it had to be ready when that event occurred. In effect, there was no telling when it would be finished. Structured time could not be a major factor in its construction.

Space is hinted at in the Great Pyramid and a glimmer of time emerges from the way it was built, but this is proto-space and proto-time, only recently out of the swamp and still not fully formed. Even centuries later, Ramses II was reluctant to give prominence to space. In his Hypostyle Hall at Karnak, the columns are almost as large as the space between them. The complex notions of time and space* which inform such theories as general relativity would take thousand of years to evolve.

Index

Quit

First   Gratuitous Facts   Previous

ARCHITECTURE AND INFORMATION

ARCHITECTURAL PARADIGMS

If Kuhn's objections are ignored, it is possible to interpret architecture in terms of paradigms. It becomes clear, however, that these paradigms work on a number of different levels or dimensions. There are perceptual paradigms*, such as those of time and space, which are fundamental to our understanding of the world around but which are still constantly evolving. There are stylistic* paradigms*, such as Modernism, which flash in and out of existence.

Index

Quit

First   Gratuitous Facts   Previous

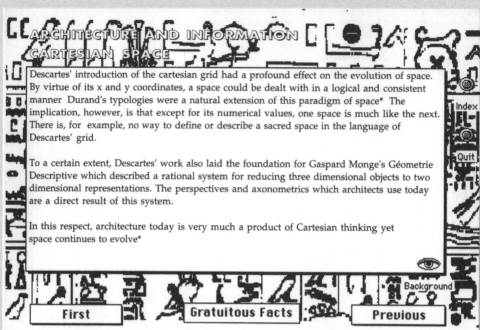

Descartes' introduction of the cartesian grid had a profound effect on the evolution of space. By virtue of its x and y coordinates, a space could be dealt with in a logical and consistent manner Durand's typologies were a natural extension of this paradigm of space* The implication, however, is that except for its numerical values, one space is much like the next. There is, for example, no way to define or describe a sacred space in the language of Descartes' grid.

To a certain extent, Descartes' work also laid the foundation for Gaspard Monge's Géometrie Descriptive which described a rational system for reducing three dimensional objects to two dimensional representations. The perspectives and axonometrics which architects use today are a direct result of this system.

In this respect, architecture today is very much a product of Cartesian thinking yet space continues to evolve*

Index

Quit

Background

First | Gratuitous Facts | Previous

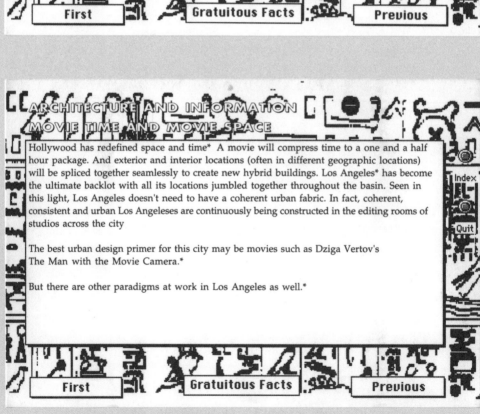

Hollywood has redefined space and time* A movie will compress time to a one and a half hour package. And exterior and interior locations (often in different geographic locations) will be spliced together seamlessly to create new hybrid buildings. Los Angeles* has become the ultimate backlot with all its locations jumbled together throughout the basin. Seen in this light, Los Angeles doesn't need to have a coherent urban fabric. In fact, coherent, consistent and urban Los Angeleses are continuously being constructed in the editing rooms of studios across the city

The best urban design primer for this city may be movies such as Dziga Vertov's The Man with the Movie Camera.*

But there are other paradigms at work in Los Angeles as well.*

Index

Quit

First | Gratuitous Facts | Previous

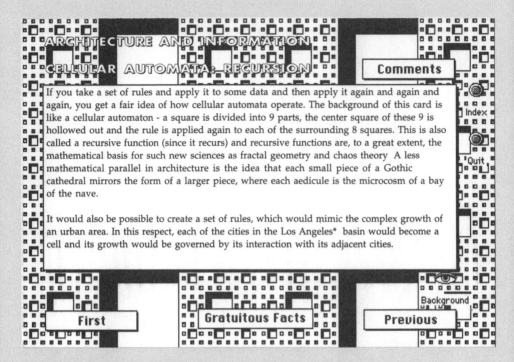

Comments

Index

Quit

If you take a set of rules and apply it to some data and then apply it again and again and again, you get a fair idea of how cellular automata operate. The background of this card is like a cellular automaton - a square is divided into 9 parts, the center square of these 9 is hollowed out and the rule is applied again to each of the surrounding 8 squares. This is also called a recursive function (since it recurs) and recursive functions are, to a great extent, the mathematical basis for such new sciences as fractal geometry and chaos theory A less mathematical parallel in architecture is the idea that each small piece of a Gothic cathedral mirrors the form of a larger piece, where each aedicule is the microcosm of a bay of the nave.

It would also be possible to create a set of rules, which would mimic the complex growth of an urban area. In this respect, each of the cities in the Los Angeles* basin would become a cell and its growth would be governed by its interaction with its adjacent cities.

Background

First   **Gratuitous Facts**   **Previous**

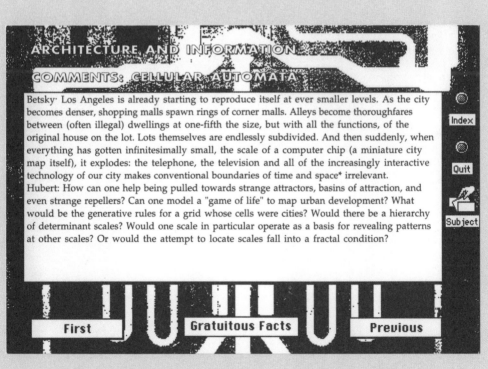

Index

Quit

Subject

Betsky· Los Angeles is already starting to reproduce itself at ever smaller levels. As the city becomes denser, shopping malls spawn rings of corner malls. Alleys become thoroughfares between (often illegal) dwellings at one-fifth the size, but with all the functions, of the original house on the lot. Lots themselves are endlessly subdivided. And then suddenly, when everything has gotten infinitesimally small, the scale of a computer chip (a miniature city map itself), it explodes: the telephone, the television and all of the increasingly interactive technology of our city makes conventional boundaries of time and space* irrelevant.

Hubert: How can one help being pulled towards strange attractors, basins of attraction, and even strange repellers? Can one model a "game of life" to map urban development? What would be the generative rules for a grid whose cells were cities? Would there be a hierarchy of determinant scales? Would one scale in particular operate as a basis for revealing patterns at other scales? Or would the attempt to locate scales fall into a fractal condition?

First   **Gratuitous Facts**   **Previous**

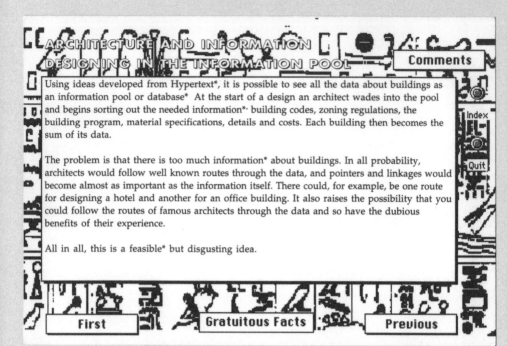

Comments

Index

Quit

Using ideas developed from Hypertext*, it is possible to see all the data about buildings as an information pool or database* At the start of a design an architect wades into the pool and begins sorting out the needed information*· building codes, zoning regulations, the building program, material specifications, details and costs. Each building then becomes the sum of its data.

The problem is that there is too much information* about buildings. In all probability, architects would follow well known routes through the data, and pointers and linkages would become almost as important as the information itself. There could, for example, be one route for designing a hotel and another for an office building. It also raises the possibility that you could follow the routes of famous architects through the data and so have the dubious benefits of their experience.

All in all, this is a feasible* but disgusting idea.

First | Gratuitous Facts | Previous

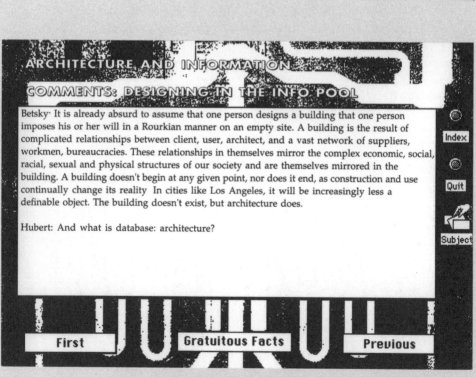

Index

Quit

Subject

Betsky· It is already absurd to assume that one person designs a building that one person imposes his or her will in a Rourkian manner on an empty site. A building is the result of complicated relationships between client, user, architect, and a vast network of suppliers, workmen, bureaucracies. These relationships in themselves mirror the complex economic, social, racial, sexual and physical structures of our society and are themselves mirrored in the building. A building doesn't begin at any given point, nor does it end, as construction and use continually change its reality In cities like Los Angeles, it will be increasingly less a definable object. The building doesn't exist, but architecture does.

Hubert: And what is database: architecture?

First | Gratuitous Facts | Previous

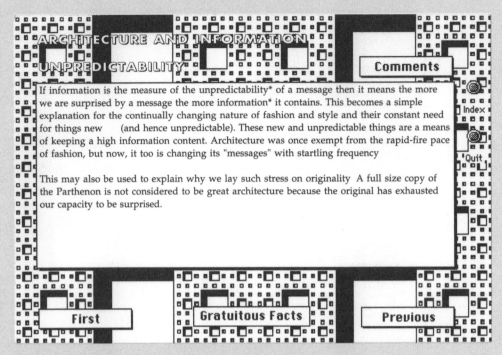

Comments

Index

Quit

If information is the measure of the unpredictability* of a message then it means the more we are surprised by a message the more information* it contains. This becomes a simple explanation for the continually changing nature of fashion and style and their constant need for things new   (and hence unpredictable). These new and unpredictable things are a means of keeping a high information content. Architecture was once exempt from the rapid-fire pace of fashion, but now, it too is changing its "messages" with startling frequency

This may also be used to explain why we lay such stress on originality A full size copy of the Parthenon is not considered to be great architecture because the original has exhausted our capacity to be surprised.

First   **Gratuitous Facts**   **Previous**

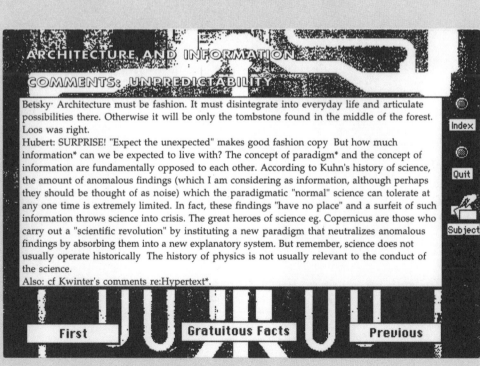

Index

Quit

Subject

Betsky· Architecture must be fashion. It must disintegrate into everyday life and articulate possibilities there. Otherwise it will be only the tombstone found in the middle of the forest. Loos was right.

Hubert: SURPRISE! "Expect the unexpected" makes good fashion copy But how much information* can we be expected to live with? The concept of paradigm* and the concept of information are fundamentally opposed to each other. According to Kuhn's history of science, the amount of anomalous findings (which I am considering as information, although perhaps they should be thought of as noise) which the paradigmatic "normal" science can tolerate at any one time is extremely limited. In fact, these findings "have no place" and a surfeit of such information throws science into crisis. The great heroes of science eg. Copernicus are those who carry out a "scientific revolution" by instituting a new paradigm that neutralizes anomalous findings by absorbing them into a new explanatory system. But remember, science does not usually operate historically The history of physics is not usually relevant to the conduct of the science.

Also: cf Kwinter's comments re:Hypertext*.

First   **Gratuitous Facts**   **Previous**

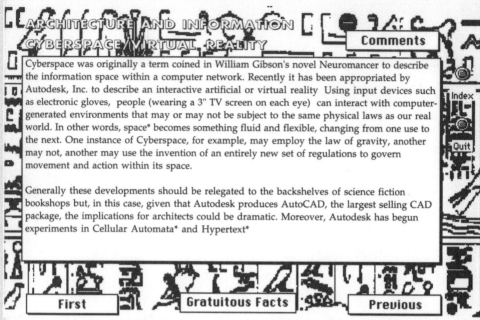

Comments

Index

Quit

Cyberspace was originally a term coined in William Gibson's novel Neuromancer to describe the information space within a computer network. Recently it has been appropriated by Autodesk, Inc. to describe an interactive artificial or virtual reality Using input devices such as electronic gloves, people (wearing a 3" TV screen on each eye) can interact with computer-generated environments that may or may not be subject to the same physical laws as our real world. In other words, space* becomes something fluid and flexible, changing from one use to the next. One instance of Cyberspace, for example, may employ the law of gravity, another may not, another may use the invention of an entirely new set of regulations to govern movement and action within its space.

Generally these developments should be relegated to the backshelves of science fiction bookshops but, in this case, given that Autodesk produces AutoCAD, the largest selling CAD package, the implications for architects could be dramatic. Moreover, Autodesk has begun experiments in Cellular Automata* and Hypertext*

First   **Gratuitous Facts**   **Previous**

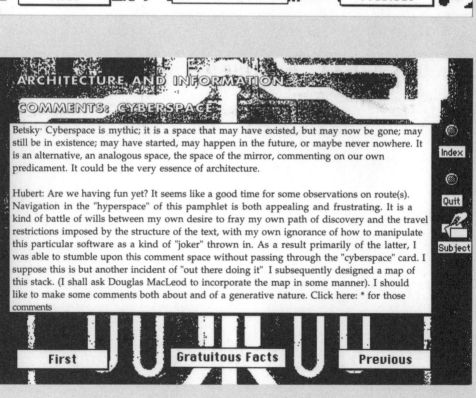

Index

Quit

Subject

Betsky· Cyberspace is mythic; it is a space that may have existed, but may now be gone; may still be in existence; may have started, may happen in the future, or maybe never nowhere. It is an alternative, an analogous space, the space of the mirror, commenting on our own predicament. It could be the very essence of architecture.

Hubert: Are we having fun yet? It seems like a good time for some observations on route(s). Navigation in the "hyperspace" of this pamphlet is both appealing and frustrating. It is a kind of battle of wills between my own desire to fray my own path of discovery and the travel restrictions imposed by the structure of the text, with my own ignorance of how to manipulate this particular software as a kind of "joker" thrown in. As a result primarily of the latter, I was able to stumble upon this comment space without passing through the "cyberspace" card. I suppose this is but another incident of "out there doing it" I subsequently designed a map of this stack. (I shall ask Douglas MacLeod to incorporate the map in some manner). I should like to make some comments both about and of a generative nature. Click here: * for those comments

First   **Gratuitous Facts**   **Previous**

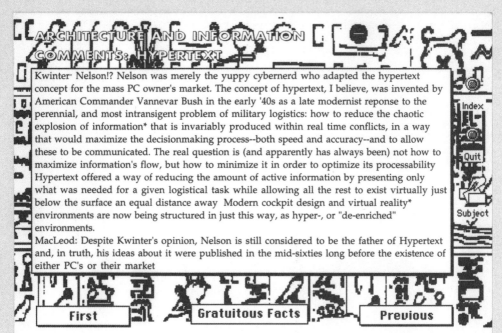

Kwinter· Nelson!? Nelson was merely the yuppy cybernerd who adapted the hypertext concept for the mass PC owner's market. The concept of hypertext, I believe, was invented by American Commander Vannevar Bush in the early '40s as a late modernist reponse to the perennial, and most intransigent problem of military logistics: how to reduce the chaotic explosion of information* that is invariably produced within real time conflicts, in a way that would maximize the decisionmaking process--both speed and accuracy--and to allow these to be communicated. The real question is (and apparently has always been) not how to maximize information's flow, but how to minimize it in order to optimize its processability Hypertext offered a way of reducing the amount of active information by presenting only what was needed for a given logistical task while allowing all the rest to exist virtually just below the surface an equal distance away Modern cockpit design and virtual reality* environments are now being structured in just this way, as hyper-, or "de-enriched" environments.

MacLeod: Despite Kwinter's opinion, Nelson is still considered to be the father of Hypertext and, in truth, his ideas about it were published in the mid-sixties long before the existence of either PC's or their market

Index

Quit

Subject

First   Gratuitous Facts   Previous

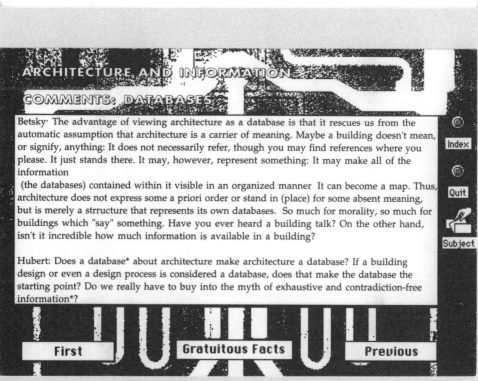

Betsky· The advantage of viewing architecture as a database is that it rescues us from the automatic assumption that architecture is a carrier of meaning. Maybe a building doesn't mean, or signify, anything: It does not necessarily refer, though you may find references where you please. It just stands there. It may, however, represent something: It may make all of the information
 (the databases) contained within it visible in an organized manner It can become a map. Thus, architecture does not express some a priori order or stand in (place) for some absent meaning, but is merely a strructure that represents its own databases. So much for morality, so much for buildings which "say" something. Have you ever heard a building talk? On the other hand, isn't it incredible how much information is available in a building?

Hubert: Does a database* about architecture make architecture a database? If a building design or even a design process is considered a database, does that make the database the starting point? Do we really have to buy into the myth of exhaustive and contradiction-free information*?

Index

Quit

Subject

First   Gratuitous Facts   Previous

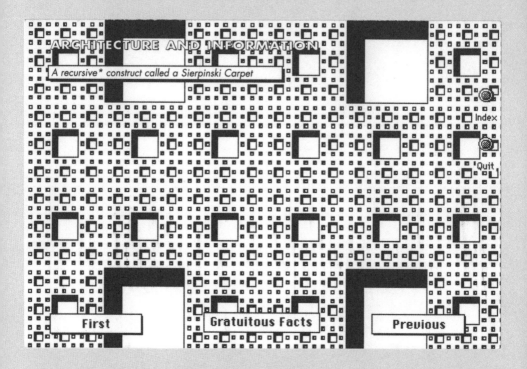

ARCHITECTURE AND INFORMATION

A recursive* construct called a Sierpinski Carpet

Index

Quit

First   Gratuitous Facts   Previous

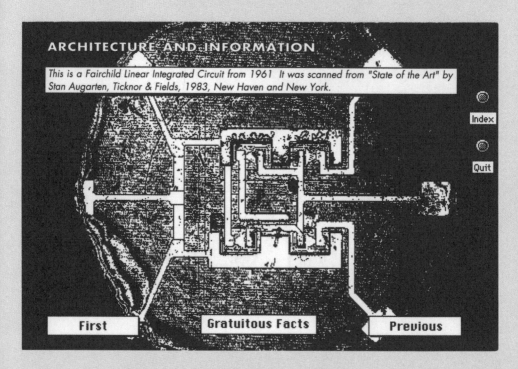

ARCHITECTURE AND INFORMATION

This is a Fairchild Linear Integrated Circuit from 1961 It was scanned from "State of the Art" by Stan Augarten, Ticknor & Fields, 1983, New Haven and New York.

Index

Quit

First   Gratuitous Facts   Previous

Recombinant Images in Los Angeles
Central Office of Architecture
1989

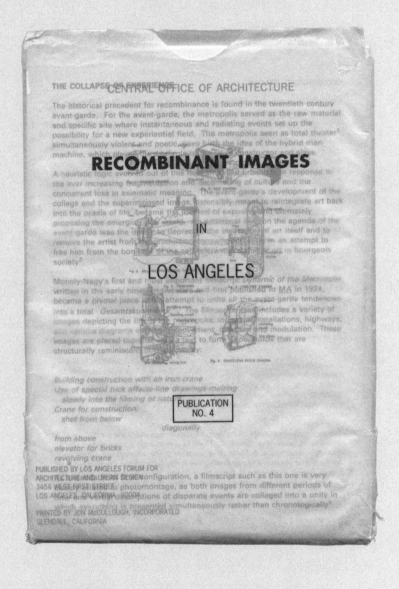

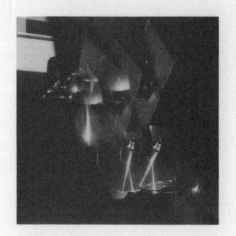

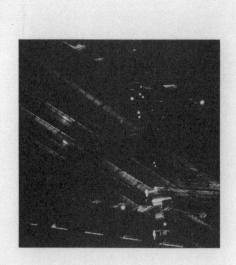

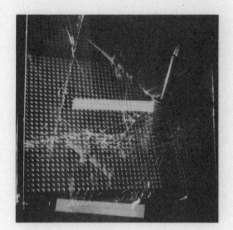

RECOMBINANT IMAGES

The camera as a machine-eye registers a series of images. The scrambled syntax implied by these images radically breaks the normative praxis of linear single image cognition. The screen space of the recombinant image acts as a collector and homogenizer of all events, allowing for the coexistence of the possible with the impossible. These images embrace chance and the found object for their absolute aesthetic absenteeism[5] but more importantly their purpose is to unveil the metropolis in a complex and simultaneous manner proper to its character. From the production- aesthetic point of view they depend on the superimposition of found urban artifacts pulled from their functional context and treated as 'fragment' and empty sign. As analogical constructs they posit a virtually collapsed space-time synonym, becoming both appearance and apparition. Paradoxically, the effect is that of a real scene, a synopsis of actions, produced by originally unrelated space and time elements which demand reconciliation. Ultimately they are quite unstable images.

Duchamp's coinage of the term *inframince*, the combination of two french words, the prefix "infra" (under) and an adjective "mince" (thin), in English becomes *infrathin*[6] For Duchamp the meaning of the word "thin" is stretched to accomodate a multitude of spatial, erotic and metaphysical phenomena. In his own words describing "The Large Glass: "Painting on glass seen from the unpainted side gives an infrathin." We can assume that *infrathin* means not only physical thinness, but signifies a plane of interference and or simultaneity in communication(s) where phenomena are subjected to various recombinant forces.

Kind of Sub-Title
Delay in Glass instead of "picture" or
"painting"- "picture on glass" becomes
"delay in glass"-but "delay in
glass"-does not mean "picture
on Glass"[7]

The superimposed layers of the recombinant image share the similar 'thinness' of Duchamp's *infrathin*. These layers exist in a collapsed (discontinuous) space and time, that unstable plane where disparate elements are forced to coexist. Phenomenally, this collapse results in the compression of experience; experience that has been erased in the final image except for its traced memory, understood as that which is the in between the between.

Karlheinz Stockhausen's *musique concrète* opus, *Hymnen* composed in 1966 at the WDR Studio for Electronic Music, incorporates the phonic "ready-made" As with Duchamp, Stockhausen depends on the latent meaning of the found object and its reuse in a new context to posit new meaning. Stockhausen divides *Hymnen* into four separate pieces. Each of the the the four center around a specific set of national anthems and each is dedicated to a specific musician (Boulez, Pousseur Cage,and Berio)[8] In addition to national anthems, further found sounds, such as recordings of public events, recorded conversations, sounds from short- wave radios, demonstrations, the christening of a ship, a chinese store and a diplomatic reception have been used. Restructured and modulated by electronics, sound or 'noise' in the most basic sense (now standard fare in techno-scratch music), and fragments of the spoken word become the basic raw material for the piece itself.

When one integrates known music with unknown new music in a composition, one can hear especially well how it was integrated: untransformed, more or less transformed, transposed, modulated etc. The more self-evident the WHAT the more attentive the listener becomes to the HOW.

Hide what you compose in what you hear
Cover what you hear
Place something next to what you hear
Place something far away from what you hear
Support what you hear.
Continue for a long time an event you hear
Transform an event until it becomes unrecognizable.
Transform an event that you hear into the one you composed last.
Compose what you expect to come next.
Compose often, but also listen for long periods to what is already composed, without composing.
Mix all these instructions[9]

C O A 1989

Ron Golan
Eric A. Kahn
Russell N. Thomsen

THE COLLAPSE OF EXPERIENCE

The historical precedent for recombinance is found in the twentieth century avant-garde. For the avant-garde, the metropolis served as the raw material and specific site where instantaneous and radiating events set up the possibility for a new experiential field. The metropolis seen as total theater[1] simultaneously violent and poetic, gave birth the idea of the hybrid man-machine, which played the dual role of the city's constructor and slave.

A heuristic logic evolved out of this new amplified-urbanism in response to the ever increasing fragmentation and decentering of culture and the concurrent loss in axiomatic meaning. The avant-garde's development of the collage and the superimposed image, ostensibly meant to reintegrate art back into the praxis of life, became the method of exposing and ultimately proposing the emerging new world. An additional item on the agenda of the avant-garde was the desire to deprecate the institution of art itself and to remove the artist from the production-consumption cycle in an attempt to free him from the bondage of the self referential status of art in bourgeois society[2]

Moholy-Nagy's first and most important filmscript *Dynamic of the Metropolis*, written in the early nineteen-twenties and first published in *MA* in 1924, became a pivotal piece in his attempt to unite all the avant-garde tendencies into a total *Gesamtskunstwerk*.[9] The filmscript itself includes a variety of images depicting the life of the metropolis: industrial installations, highways, and various diagrams exhibiting movement, direction and modulation. These images are placed together with a text to form *Typophotos* that are structurally reminiscent of Dada poetry:

Building construction with an iron crane
Use of special trick effects-line drawings-melting
   slowly into the filming of nature.
Crane for construction:
   shot from below   *diagonally*

from above
elevator for bricks
revolving crane

As it stands in its final configuration, a filmscript such as this one is very closely related to photomontage, as both images from different periods of time and verbal descriptions of disparate events are collaged into a unity in which everything is presented simultaneously rather than chronologically[4]

NOTES

(1) Kristina Passuth, Moholy Nagy, (Thames and Hudson, New York 1985), p. 45

(2) Ibid.

(3) Peter Burger, Theory of the Avant Garde, (University of Minnesota Press, Minneapolis 1984), p.53

(4) Joseph Caton, The Utopian Vision of Moholy-Nagy, (UMI Research Press,Michigan 1984) p.79

(5 Duchamp, Madrid 1984 exhibition catalogue to Marcel Duchamp Retrospective, (Fundacio Joan Miro, Bacelona). p. 176

(6) Ibid. Yoshiaki Tono, "Duchamp and "Inframince"" pg. 54

(7) Richard Hamilton. A Typographic Version of Marcel Duchamp's Green Box, The Bride Stripped Bare By Her Bachelors, Even (Jaap Rietman Inc., New York 1976). p. O

(8)Robin Maconie, The Works of Karlheinz Stockhausen (London, Marion Boyars and Oxford University Press 1976), p.21

(9) Karlheinz Stockhausen,Liner Notes to "Hymnen" (Electronic and concrete music), (Deutsche Grammofon), 1966.

PUBLISHED BY LOS ANGELES FORUM FOR
ARCHITECTURE AND URBAN DESIGN
3454 WEST FIRST STREET
LOS ANGELES, CALIFORNIA 90004

PRINTED BY JON McCULLOUGH, INCORPORATED
GLENDALE, CALIFORNIA

Cathedrals of the Culture Industry

Kazys Varnelis

Forum Annual
2004

Arriving in Los Angeles in 1996, I was struck by its lack of significant civic monuments. Only the diminutive Isozaki Museum of Contemporary Art, huddled beneath the improbably tall skyscrapers of downtown and compromised by being forced largely underground, hinted that compelling monumental architecture might be a proper aspiration for a city. Indeed, it has always seemed ironic that historically, the home base of what Theodor Adorno and Max Horkheimer called "the culture industry," has been unconcerned with its own appearance. While New York and Chicago invented skyscrapers to represent their aspirations, Los Angeles remained content without significant monuments. Perhaps no physical embodiment could represent the ethereality of Hollywood. Perhaps to try, and thereby risk failing, was something the Industry could not allow itself. Complicating matters was the conflicted position of real estate developers and civic boosters. Promoting the city as the locus of an idealized suburban lifestyle was always at odds with the idea of the city as an urban center with public amenities.[1] Whatever the reason, the city's inability to develop a civic expression lends it an air of transience, as if to underscore the ephemeral nature and fleeting importance of show business.

Today, however, Los Angeles promises a dramatic reversal, transforming itself into a cultural destination of the first order, adorned with architectural monuments to house its cultural institutions and announce its presence on the world stage. The reshaping of the city began with the 1997 opening of Richard Meier's $1 billion+ Getty Center and reached a crescendo in 2002–2003 with the consecration of Rafael Moneo's Cathedral of our Lady of the Angels and the inauguration of Frank Gehry's Disney Concert Hall. Together with the Renzo Piano proposal for the Los Angeles County Museum of Art, an expansion of the Museum of Natural History by Steven Holl, an intervention into the UCLA/Hammer

Museum of Art by Michael Maltzan, and the renovation of the Getty Museum in Malibu by Machado and Silvetti, Los Angeles is rapidly becoming a destination worthy of even the most sophisticated connoisseur of the global architectural neo-avant-garde. What a contrast to the pages of the *Dialectic of Enlightenment*, in which Adorno and Horkheimer, exiled to the city in the 1940s damned the entertainment business for caring about nothing more than the bottom-line, producing easily digestible and vapid pieces for consumption by the docile masses.[2] How, then, might a city defined by this watering-down of culture into a transient froth come to reconceive itself as a showcase of architecture, the most permanent of art forms?

Rather than remaining an event of merely local importance, Los Angeles's abandonment of its bottom-line mentality to metamorphose from a featureless field of sprawl into a horizontal museum of international architecture reflects the newfound alliance between neo-avant-garde architecture, museums, and cities. In this, perhaps, Los Angeles is merely a laggard. Regardless how late, the "Bilbao-effect" has finally hit Los Angeles.

The museum is the crux in this transition. For not only is the contemporary city conceived of as a dispersed museum of neo-avant-garde monuments, these are dominated by the typology of the museum. This is a surprising about-face, for until recently the museum defined itself in opposition to the present. When Jean Cocteau stated "The Louvre is a morgue; you go there to identify your friends," he succinctly summed up the museum of old. Presenting in columned halls the accomplishments of cultures past, museums served as monuments, embodying collective achievements of nations while demonstrating the reach of empires through a display of their plundered loot. But beyond that representational role, the early museum sought to transform the citizen-subject. Appearing at the birth of modernity, museums served to align the newly invented nation-state with higher, universal values by teaching these eternal truths to the public. Contemplation of the aesthetic object removed from its physical and functional context would allow bourgeois subjects to develop the refined taste and understanding of the ideal previously possessed only by the aristocracy. With the process of nation-building complete by the early twentieth century, however, the museum's role became largely obsolete. Apart from a handful of polemically-oriented museums of modern art, museums became storehouses of history, Cocteau's morgues. Cultural production became dominated by the culture industry and its products for mass consumption or by a vanishingly small avant-garde, possessing a polemical critique that by its nature could only be understood by a select few. So, too, when advocates of the avant-garde created museums of their own, they retained the museum's élite stance, verifying their cultural superiority through their ability to appreciate works the uncouth public saw as too difficult or too dissonant.[3]

Today the art museum no longer speaks with the condescending voice of a benevolent élite but rather joins the culture industry to address the public as a market, enticing audiences with popular exhibits and an architecturally stunning environment in which the museum's stores and restaurants are as important a draw as the works of art. No longer is it enough merely to house the past in dignified quarters: the contemporary museum must be not so much distinguished as distinctive. Today, virtually every museum commission, regardless of size, seeks a work by a cutting-edge architect to ensure the a barrage of media coverage that can draw maximum attendance.[4] As if to assert their global significance, museums in smaller cities aggressively court an international pantheon of architects as well. The list of architects for commissions in second-tier American cities alone tells a narrative of cultural aspirations: the Toledo Museum of Art's Center for Glass will be by Kazuyo Sejima and Ryue Nishizawa, the Milwaukee Museum of Art will be expanded by Santiago Calatrava, the Walker Arts Center in Minneapolis by Jacques Herzog and Pierre de Meuron, Akron's Museum of Art by Coop Himmelblau, Cincinnati's Contemporary Art Center by Zaha Hadid and so on. The LACMA competition itself invited solely signature firms: Koolhaas, Morphosis, Steven Holl, Daniel Libeskind, and Jean Nouvel. Corporate architects no longer need apply for major museum commissions.

The result is attractive not only to museum administrators and donors, but also to local governments and tourist bureaus. After all, the Guggenheim Museum's branch in Bilbao has succeeded wildly, drawing in huge crowds and promoting tourism in the formerly depressed backwater town. Nearly 500,000 foreign tourists visited the complex in 2001 and even following September 11 it suffered only a minor dip in attendance.

As radical as the new focus on the museum's appearance is the revolution in curatorship. No longer do museums act as caretakers of their collections, cultivating a devoted local following; they must exhibit growth in attendance and revenues or be considered failures. The need to fill halls, necessary to both justify and pay for the new structures, has accompanied a curatorial populism meant to draw big crowds. Not only do museums turn to blockbuster exhibits of Van Gogh, Picasso, Rembrandt and the other familiar names, more and more they mount shows on themes previously considered "low" or outside the purview of the art museum. The "Art of the Motorcycle" at the Guggenheim Bilbao proved the success of such a strategy, drawing in the fifteenth biggest daily audience worldwide in 2000. The danger is obvious: does luring in crowds come at the expense of attention to permanent collections or the teaching mission of the institution?

Even more controversial is the policy of "deaccessioning" or selling works, often to help pay for new construction. Pioneered by Guggenheim director Thomas Krens, deaccessioning gave museums a new source of revenue, but it also compromised the museum's autonomy, tying it more closely to a postmodern economy in which culture was thoroughly permeated by capital.

A recent *New York Times* article by Deborah Solomon raises questions about the sustainability of the Guggenheim. While the Guggenheim Bilbao continues its success with a show on Frank Gehry that was the most well-attended in the museum's history, taken as a whole the Guggenheim has run into difficulties. The Guggenheim Las Vegas, designed by the superteam of Koolhaas and Gehry failed to draw the anticipated crowds. Coupled with declining revenues from the Manhattan location after the terrorist attacks this caused a financial crisis at the museum forcing Krens to slash its annual operating budget from $49 million in 2001 to $25.9 million in 2002, lay off 79 of its employees, about a fifth of the staff, close a branch in SoHo and postpone a number of major shows. More seriously, from 1998 to 2001, Krens has dipped into the museum's endowment to cover operating expenses, precipitating a decline from $55.6 million in 1998 to $38.9 million at the end of 2001. Even so, the museum continues to plan for a $680 million branch on the East River in lower Manhattan, yet another Gehry designed project. Krens doesn't see this as a contradiction: "It's easier to raise money for a building than a show. A building is permanent."[5] Should the lower Manhattan Guggenheim be built, the long-term feasibility of the Bilbao branch may be in question. With a much larger version in a city obviously far richer in other tourist amenities, will vacationers still flock to Bilbao?

With the economic sustainability of contemporary museum expansion strategies an open question, what of the architecture? What does this spectacular proliferation of neo-avant-garde objects mean? Although it is almost fifty years old, André Malraux's "Museum Without Walls" gives us a prescient model for not only today's curatorial practices but also for the consequences of the global proliferation of the neo-avant-garde museum. With the invention of the color photolithographic plate Malraux believed a supermuseum of art had been created, its collection encompassing any work of art that could be photographed:

> In our Museum Without Walls, picture, fresco, miniature, and stained-glass window seem of one and the same family. For all alike-miniatures, frescoes, stained glass, tapestries, Scynthian plagues, pictures, Greek vase paintings, 'details' and even statuary—have become 'color-plates.' In the process they have lost their properties as *objects;* but, by the same token, they have gained something: the utmost significance as to *style* that they can possibly acquire. ... Thus it is that, thanks to the rather specious unit imposed by photographic reproduction on a multiplicity of objects, ranging from the statue to the bas-relief, from bas-reliefs to seal-impressions, and from these to the plaques of the nomads, a 'Babylonian style' seems to emerge as a real entity, not a mere classification – as something resembling, rather, the life-story of a great creator. Nothing conveys more vividly and compellingly the notion of a destiny shaping human ends than do the great styles, whose evolutions and transformations seem like long scars that Fate has left, in passing, on the face of the earth.[6]

Where the 19th-century museum removed objects from their contexts to subject them to a coherent narrative imposed by the state's experts, unleashing the image from any physicality made it possible for us to classify and reclassify works of art according to our desires, a process that anticipates the search function of the Internet image bank. For here, in the steady glow of the computer monitor, a pornographic fascination with the image can be played out: masterpiece after masterpiece march in an endless parade across the screen. This too is the model for the art museum of the 21st century: concern with establishing enduring narratives of historical periods gives way to short-term blockbuster shows drawing together art from sources around the globe, temporary thematic exhibits that aim to recontextualize works, and new media such as video art, computer-based art, and Internet art allowing shows to be mounted simply through the loading of appropriate data. The art museum's model is no longer that of the tomb, it is that of the data bank. Once again, Thomas Krens proves to be the most ambitious museum director, hiring Studio Asymptote to undertake a much-trumpeted but never-opened project for a Virtual Guggenheim that would exist on the Internet. Given that they are unwilling to act as storehouses of collective memory, today's museums cannot act as traditional monuments. The volatile memory stored within the museum-databank is subject to disappearance if the power—of leveraged multinational capital—is switched off. Like databanks, today's museums can be anywhere: they occupy a placeless continuum and engage in dialogue with each other across continents more easily than across town. The self-contained nature of the contemporary museum leads it to disengage from the city fabric—here the Getty Center's perch atop a hill approachable only by freeway is exemplary. And if the Guggenheim Bilbao initially appears to have a greater connection to the city, its most remarkable aspect is that this is a ruse: the museum has virtually no architectural influence on Bilbao beyond the park on the banks of the Nervion.

Reading an urban environment as a museum-city inevitably means ignoring the urban context, which exists only as a place to buy dinner and shop for clothes. The only continuity discernable between its isolated structures is through reproduction, either in a series in a monograph or in comparison drawn by some critic. But here again, the emphasis is more on a relationship between products scattered across the globe or at best across a city. Traditional typological boundaries break down in our attempt to understand the products of the museum-city: their function as contemporary architectural masterworks overcomes traditional divisions between concert hall, airport, and museum. Only thus can Disney Concert Hall be compared to the Guggenheim Bilbao. What is important now is only that the object be recognizable and distinct.

The reconfiguration of the contemporary city as a field of isolated master-works is anticipated by the interest in autonomous form that emerged during the 1970s, not incidentally the decade of professional adolescence for today's superstar architects. With the defeat of modernism, the neo-avant-garde of that day turned to the only strategy that could give relevance to architecture: affirming its right to exist through formal games to display in the gallery. Manfredo Tafuri described the scene: "It is no wonder then, that the most strongly felt condition today belongs to those who realize that, in order to salvage specific values for architecture, the only course is to make use of 'battle remnants,' that is, to redeploy what has been discarded on the battlefield that has witnessed the defeat of the avant-garde."[7] Thirty years later, today's knights have no battle to fight. Buoyed by the museum industry's belief that neo-avant-garde architecture is necessary for maintaining the bottom-line, architecture seems to have a function in society again. Thus today's neo-avant-garde abandons the melancholic irony of the "exasperated objects," as Tafuri called them, of the 1970s or the "violated perfection" of the 1980s. Aldo Rossi's idea of the building as emptied sign is gone: there is no meaning to evacuate. Architecture is now utterly self-referential, proclaiming its success, the victory of pure form.

What has been lost in all this is the possibility of architecture as an agent of social change. The ancient role of architecture to represent the sacred has been resurrected, only now rather than God, we worship the alliance of culture and industry that creates a new global order and gives architecture relevance.

The result is not so much a field of monuments but a field of tombs. Adolf Loos suggested that architecture as art could only be found in that which evades the everyday: the *monument*, the creation of an artificial memory, and *the tomb*, the illusion of a universe beyond death.[8] The museum buildings of today certainly do little to represent the contents of the volatile databank within and, given the rapid obsolescence of architectural fashion—one of the buildings that OMA proposes to tear down at LACMA is a 15-year-old structure by Hardy, Holzmann, Pfeiffer—these structures may not be around for long in any event. Rather, a virtual world is created in which architecture is the most significant of arts and its products lord over the city as cathedrals did. Where Loos's tomb presented an order beyond death, the museum-city presents a utopian dream of architecture, profoundly relevant to society through the heroism of its forms alone.

To comprehend the neo-avant-garde's role in society, Tafuri turned to Walter Benjamin's essay "The Author as Producer."[9] As Benjamin explained, what ultimately matters is not the *attitude* of a work to the conditions of its day but rather its *function* in them. Thus, Tafuri found the debates of his day to be merely peripheral and pointless: with the task of planning taken from it by economists, architecture's relevancy was gone, it had become a thing of the past. Adopting Benjamin's method today, we read the contemporary monument as demonstrating the global economic order of late capitalism in which the construction of museums and large-scale real-estate investment are compatible. No longer does Los Angeles need to rely on Disneyworld or Jon Jerde's Universal Citywalk: these are the monuments of a less sophisticated time. The culture industry is now strong enough and hungry enough to absorb the neo-avant-garde. But the impact of all this great architecture on the city fabric is fleeting. The exasperated objects of Piranesi's Campo Marzio plan, which Tafuri read as an anticipation of the 1970s neo-avant-garde, have been replaced by self-contained jewels punctuating Koolhaas's junkspace.

Turning back to LACMA, we should follow Benjamin to ask not what this project means but rather how it will be funded and why. For if the LACMA competition signifies anything, it is the ascendancy of the city's elite to global status. The museum expects that a large part of the construction will be financed by billionaire Eli Broad and, in turn, the structure is seen as a prerequisite for the display of his collection. But the source of Broad's riches reveals the ruse of contemporary architecture's success. Known as "the King of Sprawl," Broad made his riches by building more cut-rate homes in suburban America between the late 1950s and 1980s than anyone else. As a founder of Kaufman Broad (now KB) Homes, Broad did more to create the contemporary condition of suburban sprawl, than anyone else. Now over the last 20 years, Broad has increasingly dissociated himself from home-building, managing a large insurance firm instead. But Broad's shift is the product of the home market becoming too risky for investment, not because of a moral transformation. Today, however, Broad proclaims sprawl too expensive and hopes to underwrite a transformation within

Los Angeles. Not only has he promised funds for LACMA, he served as founding chairman of MOCA and also raised tens of millions to ensure that the Disney Concert Hall would be built. Although it would be easy to see this public beneficence on Broad's part as penance, akin to the building of cathedrals by barons to justify the pillaging of the surrounding countryside, he insists that this is not the case.[10]

What then is the rationale behind Broad's decision to fund Los Angeles's transformation into a museum-city? More broadly, what is the ultimate consequence of the museum-city for architecture and urbanism? In its emphasis on the singular object, the museum-city acts to reinforce the persona of the hero-patron, such as Broad. The museum-city also domesticates any transformative force claimed by architecture, reducing it to a producer of affect for a greatly expanded culture industry. Disconnected from the field of sprawl they punctuate, the monuments of the museum-city serve as an *alibi*, paying lip-service to the idea of the urban environment even as they take attention away from everyday life in the city and its increasing unaffordability. When it is economically feasible to revive city centers, they are taxidermized, turned into historic districts functioning primarily as tourist attractions or playgrounds for the global elite. But if the city becomes nothing more than isolated historic districts and monuments in the sprawl, even if the cathedrals of the culture industry have funded the neo-avant-garde with lucrative jobs for the moment, what will become of the profession if the fashion for architecture passes?[11]

Notes

1   See William B. Fulton, *The Reluctant Metropolis: The Politics of Urban Growth in Los Angeles*, (Point Arena, CA: Solano Press Books, 1997), particular chapter 9, "The Taking of Parcel K," which surveys the history of the Disney Concert Hall.
2   Theodor Adorno and Max Horkheimer, *Dialectic of Enlightenment* (New York: Continuum, 1969).
3   Ortega y Gasset's attack on modernism is a response to this, as is the sociological analysis of Pierre Bourdieu. No matter how brilliant the latter, it is of limited use for us today given the changed condition of the museum described below.
4   A personal anecdote illustrates the situation: I was consulted by representatives of a new museum in a small American city recently to aid them in their choice of an architect. Above all, I was instructed, they wanted guaranteed front page coverage in the Arts Section of *the New York Times*.
5   Deborah Solomon, "Is the Go-Go Guggenheim Going, Going ..." *The New York Times* (June 30, 2002).
6   André Malraux, *The Voices of Silence*, trans. Stuart Gilbert, Bollingen Series, no 24 (Princeton: Princeton University Press, 1978), 44, 46.
7   Manfredo Tafuri, *The Sphere and the Labyrinth*, (Cambridge, Mass.: The MIT Press, 1987), 267
8   Adolf Loos "Architecture," 1910. Roberto Schezen, ed. *Adolf Loos: Architecture 1903-1932*, (New York: Monacelli, 1996), 15. Mine is very much a Tafurian reading of Loos, see Tafuri, 375.
9   Walter Benjamin, "The Author as Producer", *Reflections* (New York: Harcourt Brace: 1978), 220-38.
10   Mark Arax, "Convention is Just an Introduction to Eli Broad's vision of Downtown; Once the King of Sprawl, Billionaire Turns his Sights to Reviving the City's Heart," *The Los Angeles Times*, August 6, 2000.
11   See also the questions raised in Joe Day's essay for the Los Angeles Forum for Architecture and Urban Design website, "MEIERED, MoCA's recent exhibition What's Shakin: New Architecture in LA," http://www.laforum.org/shakin/index.html

Returning to L.A.

Chava Danielson

LA Forum Newsletter
February 1994

> Ignored for so long as aberrant, idiosyncratic, or bizarrely exceptional,
> Los Angeles, in another paradoxical twist, has more than any other place,
> become the paradigmatic window through which to see the last half
> of the twentieth century.
> — Edward Soja, *Postmodern Geographies*

For a century and a half, exiles escaping the burdens of climate or of politics, or simply hoping for some impossible stroke of good luck, have been drawn to Los Angeles. Overlooking the immediate beauty of what lay before them, they planted elm trees.

Urbanists, who traveled here to study the place, too saw only the metaphoric desert. They turned their attentions elsewhere, promising to return once a city finally emerged.

A great many projects were proposed that attempted to give the sprawl of Los Angeles the clarity or legibility it was said to lack, but they have been continually thwarted by the reality that to live here meant to live without self-consciousness, without the burden of an urban identity. Angelenos, as a whole, continually refused either nostalgia or a higher sense of civic duty in choosing where to live, to work, how to travel between them, or which parts of the city would be central to their lives. Other forces have formed this place, with honesty and cruelty that has left most students breathless.

In this light it is both highly ironic and absolutely predictable that Los Angeles would become the focal point for intense inquiry by a new generation of theorists and critics. It is a reflection of the maturation of both the metropolis and of urban theory, social criticism, and their practitioners.

What has changed in the discussion of urbanity is the acceptance of simultaneity. That a multitude of forces coincide at any given moment in history to produce colliding and contradictory trends is now accepted as part of the post-modern experience. Multiple centers in the same metropolitan area, increasing framentation of social and economic life, and a simultaneous consolidation of wealth and power are all patterns that have been reproduced across the globe.

In Los Angeles, the middle and upper classes of this city continue to retreat behind electronic gates and lines of security patrols, demonstrating the kind of radical social polarization that was previously attributed to third world countries. Meanwhile, waves of immigrants, with an uncanny astuteness for the way the space of this city has successively been occupied, have created elusive and nearly imperceptible focal points for their communities in the midst of previously undifferentiated suburban sprawl. And while few people are brave enough to predict the outcome of the massive building projects taking place downtown, the new and lingering residents of the neighborhoods immediately adjacent have just been presented with the cleanest and most expensive public transportation, the best library services, and the slickest architectural monuments in the short history of this enormous basin. Suddenly, Los Angeles, once thought underdeveloped and ill defined, is understood as a highly charged urban landscape.

This focus of intellectual attention on the nature of urban life in Los Angeles has coincided with a moment that finds Angelenos uncommonly interested in civic self-reflection. The smoke screen of decades of boosterism is beginning to clear—to reveal a crisis-ridden but strangely compelling place. It seems that, as this city developed, the intense individualization in the daily life of its people found spatial expression in an almost continuous suburbanization and expansion across the Southern California landscape. The incessant expansion found an economic analog in an almost continuous rise in the value of real estate that somehow, it was assumed, would continue unabated. Our optimism had been given material form. Meanwhile, 30 years of sporadic deindustrialization have finally taken their toll, now that the dismantling of the military industrial complex can no longer be lobbied away. The city seems, somehow, to have grown to the extent of its tolerable limits. Areas with even fewer identifiable urban markers, such as the Inland Empire or Orange County, have become metropolises in their own right, not simply a part of Greater Los Angeles. The collapse of the real estate market dealt a blow, both financial and symbolic, to the eternal optimists of Southern California, while the riots articulated the frustration caused by decades of economic and racial inequity with an urgency that made it difficult for even the most intransigent and entrenched power players to ignore. Our focus has contracted along with our hopes and our economy at a time when urban theory is finally speaking to us: as it is in fact lived, not in relation to an imported model to which we could only aspire. It is impossible for anyone who lived here during the 1960s and 1970s to imagine that a book such as Mike Davis' *City of Quartz* would become a regional best seller, but it describes events and phenomena that suddenly the citizens of Los Angeles are struggling to understand.

The urgency of the discussion of urbanism and urban issues has not left architects unaffected. As for anyone else, it has become important to understand in a new sense, beyond the time-worn metaphors of liberation and sunshine, what it means to be a part of this place. Could there be an architecture that admits, or that is in fact genuinely susceptible to, the urban pressures of Los Angeles without either reducing this urgency to simplistic contextualism or indulging in images of instability that become little more than iconography? The answer is unclear, or perhaps untested, but is certainly part of a larger question: what impact can, and should, architecture ever have on people's lives?

Inter-
lude:
Down-
town

On Broadway
Downtown Los Angeles

Robert Adams

LA Forum Newsletter 5, 1994

North, past the Arcade Building by several blocks, is the Victor Clothing Store owned by Ramiro Salcedo. Aside from selling clothes and appliances, Victor Clothing, thanks to the efforts of jn Salcedo, is full of artifacts that reveal important qualities of Broadway's history not found in the files of the CRA or Building Department, or the archives at the Grand Central Library. Referring to the photographs under the plate glass of his desktop, Mr. Salcedo traced the rich history of then unpaved *Forte Calle* before it was named Broadway, the social and shopping center of Los Angeles 30 years ago where the street cars would pass by old City Hall. Fifty autographed portraits of movie stars, many of them Hispanic, hang along the south wall above the changing rooms, now used for storage. The large room is surrounded by a series of painted murals. Commissioned by Mr. Salcedo, the 14-year-old artist represented daily life on Broadway and in L.A., including himself kneeling, just above Mr. Salcedo's shoulder in the photo above. Ramiro Salcedo tells the story of the restaurant down the block where he would eat lunch when he used to go out on the street. Beyond providing good food, twice a day the restaurant owner would sweep the sidewalk the length of one block as a service to the other shop owners, and due to his success certain "others" looted and burned his restaurant, driving him off Broadway. It was then that things were not quite as they appeared, that there among the action of Broadway was a hidden and compelling array of people working, peculiar spaces, austere large walls, signs leaking into the city, and other associations specific to Broadway.

Above Victor Clothing is another Salcedo business called Top Hat Bridal, run by Ramiro Salcedo's sister and mother. A pale green garment production studio in the back is operated by Carolina Lugunas, sister-in-law of the Salcedo family. Unlike the mass production garment industry managed by ANJAC, Carolina Lugunas measures each client, marks and cuts every piece of textile, and assembles exquisitely detailed wedding gowns.

Off Broadway, from the Biltmore Hotel heliport overlooking Pershing Square, one can see the two KRKD Radio towers atop the Arcade Building. A building in the foreground was removed creating a gap, framing a small portion of Broadway. From Bunker Hill, Broadway leaks through several of these openings, and specifically from the heliport, one can see the Cameo Theater with rooftop billboard displaying an outdated Cherry 7UP advertisement.

The Cameo, formerly Clune's Broadway, was the first theater on Broadway made specifically for the new technology of cinema. Designed by Alfred Rosenheim in 1913, this long narrow theater had a sky window above the audience and an electronic billboard at the entrance composed of hundreds of light bulbs and a digital clock. Later, a billboard proportioned for 24 30-inch by 40-inch poster boards advertising the feature film replaced this sign. From the street this billboard was repetitive advertising, much like the posters that advertise Snoop Doggy Dogg, Industria del Amor and others wrapping the scaffolding arcade surrounding the vacant Broadway Department Store. As seen from the Biltmore heliport and other Bunker Hill buildings, this sign appeared as a quilted pattern of blurry image and text. The Cameo closed a couple years ago and was converted into retail shops occupying the lobby and light storage in the auditorium.

Other building cuts along Broadway produce large exterior rooms that are surfaced for parking. Each lot has a small food shack that is out-scaled against an eight-story blank wall. The demolished building exposes a new wall, leaving behind an outline of its section. These large austere walls are windowless. Some have painted signs that hint at the interior, telling what is being produced or who controls the building. One is painted a rich, deep red. Most, like the metal industrial shed, indicate nothing of their contents. The Sun Drug Co. Bldg. is surfaced with a lace-like pattern of ceramic tiles much like the lace on a dress in the display case of Sussy's Brides. This particular building is occupied and active with garment production. Instead of a Miller Beer advertisement, such as the one on the Hotel Figueroa, a six-story sewing machine is painted on the south facade of this garment building, telling of the work going on inside and identifying the location of the garment district.

A survey was made of Broadway between Fourth and Seventh streets, to determine building use, occupancy, and square footage utilized. The long plan represents not the familiar building footprint, but rather the compression of Broadway buildings against the street. The most obvious example of this is between Fourth and Fifth street on the west side of Broadway where the empty Broadway Department Store and the recently closed Newberry's bracket a few buildings in the center of the block. A perpetual clearance sale forced all products down to the ground level, escalators were boarded up sealing off the upper floors, and finally the metal gate closed, leaving only the inlaid terrazzo sign "Newberry's" in the sidewalk floor. Instantly these buildings become voids in the city, the modern ruins of Broadway. A long, narrow shop (30 feet by 120 feet) uses only the first 20 feet of available space to sell clothes; the long back room remains empty. Another flat shop selling an eclectic variety of goods is less than six feet in depth, while Babak Saghian's clothing store finds itself in the five-foot gap between the Cameo Theater and the Pantages Theater.

On Sunday driving east on Sixth Street, Bunker Hill is quiet with few people on the street. Past Grand Central Library, past Pershing Square approaching the intersection at Broadway, and then slowing for the hundreds of people packed onto the sidewalks. On Sunday, Broadway triples its daily population of security guards acting as jewelry store bouncers, street vendors selling mangos, cucumbers, and ice cream, leaflet distributors handing out coupons for haircuts or religious propaganda, street people collecting cans from restaurants, street preachers raising books and voices to the passersby, shop owners yelling "three for one" for socks and earrings, an accordion player in front of Clifton's Cafeteria, a man selling chewing gum, a Salvadorian woman selling pornographic magazines from one of the many green news-booths, LAPD passing out parking tickets as fast as they can, layers of signage on the walls and strewn across the sidewalk. Focused on the street, one seldom looks up into the buildings or to the sky. Driving east on the 10 towards downtown, beyond the aqua-green artificial horizon of the Convention Center, the two KRKD radio transmission towers on top of the Arcade Building again are visible in the city. The Arcade Building had a complex program that included a post office, pharmacy, offices, restaurants, a basement assembly hall, and KRKD Radio. The Arcade is one of the few Broadway buildings to accept the daily activity of the street within its long blackened glass-covered arcade connecting to Spring Street. As a short cut to the bus stops on Spring Street, this heavily traveled corridor contains electronic stores, swap meets selling many types of gadgets, a *botica*, restaurant, and hair salon; the former basement assembly hall is now a parking garage.

At night, the vacancy along Broadway is more apparent as security lights come on only in the active buildings. The street activity of the day is reduced to a few waiting buses below the windows of the Yorkshire Apartments, a group of street cleaners in orange suits working at 4:00 a.m., and the occasional lone person walking down the street. Closed to the street, the dormant Arcade Building projects nothing but an ominous facade of dark windows.

Broadway is a place that is constantly under speculation by investors, business people, developers, and architects. Broadway is a social center for 2.5 million Hispanic Angelenos. Broadway is supported by the garment and jewelry trades industries. Broadway, like other major retail/production streets in America, is a familiar street typology in downtown landscapes. Broadway is open for, and deserves, further consideration as a place to learn from and act upon.

Downtown

Todd Gannon

laforum.org, 2007

Like many Angelinos, I come from the Midwest. And in Midwestern cities like the Cleveland of my birth, when somebody says Downtown, everybody knows what is being talked about. Downtown is where the tall buildings are.

Los Angeles, of course, could never suffer such a simple definition. After decades of sub-, ex-, post-, hyper-, and even new urban legends, Downtown L.A. is less a specific geographical entity than a mythical conceptual specter. These ghost stories continue to provoke abject fear and perverse infatuation in roughly equal measure, enough to sustain a cottage industry of academic ghostbusters bent on capturing downtown's elusive spirit or disproving its very existence.[1]

No doubt you've ventured your own bold predictions for Downtown or participated in incessant comparisons to the West Side and the East Coast. But what exactly is it we love and loathe, promote and dispel? Nobody seems quite sure, and definitions, if ventured at all, are uniformly tentative. As one colleague recently opined, "I don't know what it is, but I don't think it's just where the tall buildings are."

Most sources will tell you that the term "downtown" was coined in New York City, a function of Manhattan's river-bound geography and upstream development. Through the 19th century, as American cities mushroomed across the continent, the term quickly dissipated to signify the urban core of any major metropolis. Sure, there are variations—in Chicago you're in the Loop, in Philadelphia it's Center City. But local inflection notwithstanding, Downtown, in pragmatic, unequivocal, American vernacular, signifies our version of the European *centro storico*.

Yet the term's original usage, still prevalent in its place of birth, does not connote a place so much as a direction. As the original settlement of Manhattan Island expanded northward, Downtown proved an expedient geographical shorthand, distinguishing the old town from more valuable developments on higher, more northerly ground. As delivered to us, the term signifies the area of tall buildings at the tip of Manhattan only by implication. In New York, as every subway sign makes clear, downtown simply means "south of here."

In each case, we begin to see the deep roots of the term's phantasmal connotations. One variant implies an allegiance to an established, often imagined, typological model of urban density, aesthetics, and inhabitation. This is Petula Clark's "Downtown," that catchy jingle of promise and possibility that, when applied as urban strategy, tends to devolve into saccharine nostalgias for a past that never existed. The other notion pushes us further into the realm of the impossible. Downtown as direction denotes a place where, by definition, one cannot be. Always a bit further south, this Downtown remains an elusive concept, one step ahead of even the most intrepid urban denizen.

To me, whether cast as sappy nostalgia or ghostly inaccessibility, impossibility seems unlikely to provide a viable foundation for an urban agenda. But a third, more positive inflection may prove more effective.

In 1979, the National Basketball Association adopted the three-point rule. By juridical decree, the professional court was divided into two distinct zones, with an extra point awarded for baskets scored from beyond the top of the key. The three-point rule forever altered the game, requiring new strategies for coaches and players and new terminology for sportscasters and fans. The slam-dunk, muscled in at close range by brute force, gained a long-distance counterpart as players developed alternative techniques to provide high-value scoring "from downtown."

This to me seems an apt metaphor for L.A. architecture as well as our slippery notion of Downtown. In basketball parlance, downtown is not that place in closest proximity to the goal (that's "the paint") but rather a much larger peripheral zone whose boundaries oscillate according to who has the ball. It's the place difficult shots come from, a place that prizes technique over tenacity, marksmanship over muscle. To score from the inside, you need only be a bully; to shoot from downtown, you have to innovate with the game and master its techniques.

This is what L.A. architecture is all about. The East Coast may remain the seat of architectural power in the United States, but L.A. routinely draws the most daring innovators. From Neutra and Schindler to the current crop of cutting-edge digital fabricators, generations of architects have abandoned traditional city centers to hone unorthodox techniques in our unorthodox urban context. This innovative bent is what gives L.A. architecture its distinctive character and what makes us so easy to tell apart from our more traditional East Coast counterparts. While New Yorkers scrap it out in the paint, we fire three-pointers.

Take Frank Gehry's Bilbao, still architecture's most dramatic three-pointer to date. Though its effects emanate from Northern Spain, Gehry launched this potent attack on traditional European urbanism from Los Angeles, half a world away. And as its cool swish resonated around the globe, one could almost hear critics shouting in breathless disbelief, "Gehry delivers FROM DOWNTOWN!!"

Long before Gehry's one-in-a-million shot, L.A. architects routinely delivered high impact, unconventional architecture, always finding dispersal and distance a crucial asset. Leaving behind time-honored and tightly bound East Coast rules, L.A. architects relentlessly innovate and strike from the outside. So I prefer to leave the impossible downtown of ghost stories and urban legends to others. My Downtown is not a forgotten core to return to, but rather an unruly zone at the periphery—the best place to score from.

Notes

1   Even Reyner Banham, always a dependable apologist for architectural misfits, would only begrudgingly acknowledge Downtown. Withholding a fifth ecology, Banham instead tossed off a dismissive "Note on Downtown" toward the end of his book "because that is all Downtown Los Angeles deserves."

Downtown ... Again

Peter Zellner

Forum Annual, 2004

Spectacle

The future of Downtown Los Angeles is in play again. The Grand Avenue
Project is the biggest public redevelopment spectacle to come to town in a long
while. Under the banner "Re-Imagining Grand Avenue, Creating a Center for
Los Angeles," the newly invigorated push to revitalize L.A.'s center is once again
focused on Bunker Hill, the area around the recently completed Walt Disney
Concert Hall.

The Grand Avenue Project is being promoted and organized by the Grand
Avenue Committee, a public/private partnership that aims to "transform the
civic and cultural districts of downtown Los Angeles into a vibrant new
regional center which will showcase entertainment venues, restaurants, retail
mixed with office buildings, a hotel, and over 1,000 new housing units." Directed
by the Los Angeles Grand Avenue Authority, a joint power entity formed by
the union of the Community Redevelopment Agency of the City of Los Angeles
(CRA/LA) and the County of Los Angeles, the Grand Avenue Committee has the
singular agenda of creating a more than 3.2-million-square-foot regional center.
Also planned for redevelopment is the existing County Mall, a little-used public
space that stretches from the Music Center at the top of Bunker Hill to City
Hall at the bottom of the hill. Ingenuously, the enhanced park is being promoted
as "L.A.'s own Central Park." The fact that the County Mall is neither central to
Downtown Los Angeles—or greater Los Angeles or for that matter—nor, at 16
acres, anywhere close to Olmstead and Vaux's 843-acre urban oasis seems beside
the point. What matters most is that the entire project is hinged on the premise
that Downtown L.A.'s dead-after-5:00 p.m. curse can be finally vanquished.
Eli Broad, billionaire tract house developer, patron of the arts and architecture,
and vice chairman of the Grand Avenue Committee said recently, "We're hopeful
we'll be able to create a street where people will stay after work and one that
will be a draw for the entire region." Bringing foot traffic to Downtown L.A. after
dark could cost $1.2 billion. Of this, approximately $300 million will be required

for public infrastructure, and approximately $900 million will be needed for real estate development. If successful, the project will generate 16,000 long-term jobs and raise $85 million annually in local, county, and state taxes.

Circus

Eight teams of developers and architects, comprised of some 60 individual firms, responded to the RFQ issued for the project. The Grand Avenue Committee's County Supervisor Gloria Molina, Councilwoman Jan Perry, the CRA's Bud Ovrom, and L.A. County CAO David Janssen reviewed the submissions and announced in late January 2004 that five teams had been shortlisted to compete for the job:

Grand Avenue Development Alliance, a consortium led by Australian property giant Bovis Lend Lease with Arquitectonica of Miami, Manhattan-based Gary Edward Handel + Associates, MVE & Partners, and RTKL;

Forest City Development of Cleveland, owners of the 42nd St Retail and Entertainment Complex in Times Square and developers of the recently unveiled Downtown Brooklyn Basketball Arena designed by Gehry Partners;

J. H. Snyder Company, the L.A.-based developers of the local Water Garden business park, with private equity real estate investment group Lubert-Adler Partners and the Jerde Partnership, Johnson Fain, and the recently re-formulated Rios Clementi Hale Studios; and

The Related Companies, backers of the $1.7 billion Time Warner Center at Columbus Circle in Manhattan, with architects Skidmore, Owings & Merrill under partner David Childs, and Elkus Manfredi.

Operating as Bunker Hill Ltd., only one other team is primarily Los Angeles-based—Weintraub Financial Services with the Bronson Companies, Apollo Real Estate Advisors, and the Vornado Realty Trust. The local consortium counts Gehry Partners, LLP as their architect with landscape architects the Olin Partnership and the promising L.A. firm Daly Genik Architects.

Curiously, Gehry, who would seem to be Bunker Hill Ltd's trump card, has downplayed his role, publicly announcing that he is not so much interested in the design of the project as its potential for urbanism. "For me, it's not important if I do a building—I've got Disney Hall. I'm more interested in the urban planning," Gehry recently stated. Nevertheless rumors of all-star designer involvement have spread with Jean Nouvel and Zaha Hadid pegged to join the Gehry-led team. Earlier yet, Sir Norman Foster was temporarily aligned with Donald Trump's team, which has since fallen out of the bidding process.

Notably absent from the redevelopment frenzy is the local dream team of Ming Fung, Craig Hodgetts, Thom Mayne, and Eric Owen Moss who have joined together in discussions with a number of potential developers, but for the moment remain (strangely) on the sidelines. Should that team ultimately join the Grand Avenue fray it could also include Wolf Prix/Coop Himmelblau, designer of the new Central Los Angeles High School #9 and Steven Holl, architect for the new Los Angeles County Natural History Museum. Also conspicuously out of the running in this redevelopment frenzy is Dutch urbanist and iconoclast Rem Koolhaas, whose last two ventures in Los Angeles, a scheme for the Los Angeles County Museum of Art's new facilities on Wilshire and headquarters for Universal Studios over the hill in the San Fernando Valley both fizzled after losing funding.

Amnesia & Erasure

Despite, or perhaps because of the optimism surrounding the project, there seems to be a state of amnesia about the number of "ground-breaking" and largely unsuccessful fresh starts Bunker Hill has been given over the last five decades.

The view that many Los Angelenos hold of Downtown as one of the city's final redevelopment frontiers seems endemic, and its power wards off any bad flashbacks associated with the numerous failed efforts to redevelop Bunker Hill. Granted, L.A. is coming off a blissful decade of major civic achievements— Richard Meier's Getty Center, Rafael Moneo's Cathedral, and of course Walt Disney Concert Hall. Additionally, Angelenos have witnessed an overhaul of the city's infrastructure, including a $2 billion Alameda Corridor transport conduit, a new subway system, a linked light rail network, and an "intelligent" metro bus line. So perhaps accordingly, the city's dismal record Downtown has yet to spark any questions about the viability or the reasoning behind the latest attempt to revive Bunker Hill. Indeed, the redesign, promotion, and marketing of Bunker Hill's future are something of a local tradition in line with L.A.'s infamous skill for manufacturing the future while destroying its history.

As early as 1950/51 the newly established CRA tagged the then-down-at-its-heels Bunker Hill as "Redevelopment Area Number One." Overlooking the downtown of the 1930s and 1940s—the L.A. that Raymond Chandler called "that old whore"—Bunker Hill was a community of reportedly 10,000 low income, largely immigrant and minority residents living 10 to a room in squalid, disintegrating structures. The initial master plan developed by the City Planning Authority called for the complete clearing of the area. In its place the study proposed a series of 20-story-high public apartment blocks arranged around octagonal shaped courtyards. The scheme, widely pilloried, was scrapped and by 1959 the firm of Charles Luckman and Associates was retained to develop a new master plan. Luckman, former CEO of the Lever Company and later partner with William Pereira, planner of Irvine, one of this nation's largest master planned communities, put forward a new scheme that envisioned for some 11-million-square-feet of office and retail space, 2,000 hotel rooms and 3,000 residential units. Not coincidentally, Luckman's plan also proposed that Bunker Hill be scraped clean, graded, and neatly divided into a series of gridded zones connected by overhead walkways and moving sidewalks.

It would be 15 years before the Luckman plan for Bunker Hill could begin to be fully implemented. In the intervening years, amendments were made for cultural facilities and significant height variations. The master plan was refined again in 1968 by Bay area firm WBE—Wurster, Bernardi & Emmons—by which time the Bunker Hill High Rise Apartments, the first new structures on the Hill, were completed. By 1970, Bunker Hill was shaved clean. Save the 40-story Union Bank tower there was very little new construction completed or in the ground. Aerial photographs from the period 1973–74 look less like Los Angeles than images of Rotterdam after it was bombarded in 1940. Aside from those few lone towers, Bunker Hill was effectively the largest construction site in North America.

Déjà Vu

From 1975 until the mid-1980s close to 20 housing, retail, and office structures were erected in and around Bunker Hill. These included five major buildings—the Bonaventure Hotel, the Security Pacific National Bank (now the Arco Towers), the Arco parking structure, the Los Angeles World Trade Center, and the Figueroa Courtyard. The construction boom that emerged in the early 1980s drove the development of the Angelus towers, the Citicorp Center towers, the Marriott Downtown, and the Wells Fargo Center. This active new city core would lead the CRA to conduct a nationwide competition for a mixed-use 11-acre development to be situated at the top of Bunker Hill.

In February of 1980, the CRA announced that proposals from five North American developers had been accepted for the 11.2-acre L-shaped site between the Music Center and the Central Business District. Projected for the site was a mix of office and commercial space (70%) and residential (30%) with 1.5 percent of the cost of the project earmarked for the construction of the Museum of Contemporary Art and a related park on 1.5 acres. Additionally, the CRA had stipulated the reinstatement, Disney-style, of the "restored" Angel's Flight funicular. The shortlist included:

Metropolitan Structures Inc., with Fujikawa, Conterato, Lohan and Associates, the successor firm to Mies van der Rohe;

Olympia York/Trizec Western with SOM;

Cabot, Cabot & Forbes with A.C. Martin and Davis Brody Bond;

Bunker Hill Associates with Arthur Erickson, Kamnitzer, Cotton, Vreeland and Gruen; and

Maguire Partners with Harry Perloff, Barton Myers, Edgardo Contini, Charles Moore, Lawrence Halprin, Cesar Pelli, Hardy Holzman Pfeiffer, Ricardo Legoretta, Frank Gehry, Sussman Prejza, Carlos Diniz, and Robert Kennard.

By June of 1980 the competition had come down to pair of final competitors— Arthur Erickson's team and the super group led by Harvery S. Perloff, Dean of the School of Architecture at UCLA, that would come to be known as the All Stars.

Arthur Erickson vs. the L.A. All Stars

Canadian Erickson's winning scheme, the so-called California Center, presented a composition of several towers connected by a plinth arranged around a swirling center at the site's "city-end," the California Plaza. Essentially its parti developed from an established, homogeneous modernist gesture unified by an unremittingly banal language—tower blocks and excavated courtyards.

The All Stars' scheme, by contrast, abandoned the singular modernist gesture in favor of a sort of postmodern orchestrated chaos. In the place of a unified nod to the master plan developed by Luckman, the All Stars presented an exquisite corpse—nine projects approximately connected by a variety of public spaces developed by Moore and Halprin. Emblematic of Moore and Gehry's adventurous and often outré public work of the period (Moore's Piazza D'Italia or Gehry's Loyola Law School) the entry was rejected.

Criticism of Erickson's winning project came fast and sharp. Invited to comment on the competition process, Rem Koolhaas declared that the Erickson scheme "poignantly evokes what is no longer there: conviction, seriousness, invention." He continued to add that "for lovers of Los Angeles' 'no-topia' both schemes are disappointingly alien to locale mythology. In fact the images they offer are similarly removed from the L.A. myth of the freeway, of low intensity, etc. Granting it would be another kind of nostalgia to condemn L.A. to a perpetual life without a center of gravity, it is surprising that the image of downtown is presented here as merely an East Coast one seen through rose-tinted polaroids."

Equally scathing, Michael Sorkin wrote of the winning entry, "the Erickson presentation, instead of actually supplying any evidence of good design, sought to overwhelm by a mass of visual codes signifying good design. Instead of architecture, one was exposed to a banal lexicon of renderer's icons for urbanity: flapping banners, balloons, push carts with mustachioed vendors" Sorkin added, "one would expect a cogent expression about the particular character of Los Angeles, one of the world's wonder cities. This requires an act of imagination, an act which unfortunately proved unnatural to most of the entrants."

Hope

Given the increasingly celebrated reemergence of Downtown as a bona fide residential and cultural center, and the entrenchment of L.A. more generally as a center for contemporary architectural experimentation, it seems vitally important now to re-examine the future imagined for Bunker Hill yesterday as a way to sharpen our ideas about Downtown today. One wonders if the current excitement building around the Grand Avenue Project will spark an interest in a genuinely new discussion about Downtown's prospects or will we be treated yet again to the usual, quotidian developers' exigencies that are too often passed off as urbanism.

"We want a great mixed-use project that works economically," says David Malmuth, real estate consultant with Robert Charles Lesser Co. and a board member of the Grand Avenue Committee. Malmuth, who helped conceive the recently completed Hollywood & Highland mall, brought Michael Eisner to Times Square while at Disney Development in the early 1990s. He claims that the need now at Bunker Hill is "to move more towards a process that's about urban planning ideas and a financial approach, as opposed to a pro forma that's not going to be accurate—and that everyone knows is not going to be accurate." What remains to be seen is what the current definition of "urban planning ideas" means. If the notion of bringing a miniature version of 42nd Street or a Central Park to L.A. seems to define the outermost limit of what the Grand Avenue Committee is willing to picture as urbanism, then one is forced to wonder how far we have come since the CRA announced its first set of plans for Bunker Hill some 50 years ago.

The 1980 All Star Team

The journey Bunker Hill has made from tabula rasa to Walt Disney Concert Hall hardly seems like a coherent trajectory. However, somewhere in its history Bunker Hill presents a case for the return to something akin to urbanism or at least the will to experiment with our accepted ideas about Los Angeles. "It's difficult within the public environment not to ask for something that is so specific," Malmuth remarks. "But then you're locked into disappointment, and you'll build gradually toward failure. I want to get a great project built here." While Malmuth may be correct in terms of any assessment that could be made about Bunker Hill's lost opportunities and erased history, Walt Disney Concert Hall creates a powerful argument for innovative urban form and it must be said here that its success has been entirely dependent on its specificity and the clarity of its vision for L.A.'s future.

In the 24 years that have passed since the last major competition held to determine the future of Bunker Hill, it seems as if Los Angeles has devolved from being the subject of wonder—think of Banham's paean to this city—to being a center increasingly concerned with simulating the picturesque urbanisms of the East Coast or 19th-century Europe. The intricacy and complexity of the development process not withstanding, one hopes that what remains of L.A.'s distinctiveness as a contemporary city—its history of architectural experimentation, idiosyncratic forms, and cultural diversity—will provide the Grand Avenue Committee with enough impetus to back a motivated team with a courageous scheme for Grand Avenue. This city deserves a proposal for Grand Avenue that is unapologetic about exceeding our present demands of urbanism or the litany of disappointing plans that have been foisted on Downtown Los Angeles.

Special thanks to Mauricio Munoz for research assistance and archival image sourcing.

IV.
Santa Anas

Regarding Santa Anas
Mimi Zeiger

No reading of Los Angeles is complete without a mention of the city's legendary desert winds. Hot, dusty, and mythic in their force to undo everyday urbanisms and architectural experiments with an evening gust, the Santa Anas mark a necessary counterpoint to more temperate understandings of the built environment.

Joan Didion compares the weather pattern to catastrophe, writing, "[T]he violence and the unpredictability of the Santa Ana affect the entire quality of life in Los Angeles, accentuate its impermanence, its unreliability. The wind shows us how close to the edge we are."

Craig Hodgetts' text *Swimming to Suburbia: Some Thoughts on the New City and How It Came to Be That Way* blows through L.A. grids like a hot wind, destabilizing assumptions of the city. Released in January 1987, the text, manifesto and monologue—one akin to Spalding Gray's *Swimming to Cambodia*, from which the title riffs. The film directed by Jonnathan Demme came out the same year. In his piece, Hodgetts' asks designers take on the city as a cybernetic, holographic project, urging us to "disassociate ourselves from the fixation on buildings and to instead look in the rearview mirror." In short, he's arguing for an expanded and self-reflexive role for architecture and architects.

Swimming to Suburbia is the LA Forum's first newsletter and initial foray into publishing (a practice that actively continues within the organization). Although not much more than a few sheets of colored paper folded and stapled together, the little pamphlet represented a rebuff to more staid publications coming out of the East Coast. Yet, the zine-like form is right for its place. Los Angeles is a land of ephemerality—of mini-marts and fallen palm fronds.

Aaron Betsky and Gary Paige edited *Swimming to Suburbia*, and when asked about its genesis, Betsky confessed an ongoing affection for sprawl. But suburbia also presented an intellectual and political stance within architecture. According to Betsky, East Coast postmodernism as promoted and practiced by Michael Graves and Peter Eisenman was a love affair with Italy: Tuscany's hill towns or reclaimed Fascist architecture in Como. But the Forum was in love with L.A.; Hodgetts would be Cyrano—or even Reyner Banham— for a new wave of practitioners. "We dedicated the Forum to seeing and knowing L.A., and this was our first manifesto towards that goal," Betsky explained, noting a desire to understand the urban landscape on its own terms.

"Many of us who came together to form the Forum had arrived a few years before that from the East Coast or Europe and were part of one of those periodic waves of immigrants whose eyes opened wide upon finding the endless grid, the collage of cultures, and the closeness of nature that seemed to be both abstract and balmy—a vernacular landscape that seemed to be fundamentally modernist," he recalled.

The extent to which the LA Forum is still obsessed with the city and with exploring deep into the sprawl is seen in later works, such as Tom Marble's *After the city, this (is how we live)*. Marble's publication is suburban screenplay that tells the story of fictional architect Nat Flemming, 42, disillusioned with his own complicity in making landscapes of beige, Spanish Colonial spec homes. In contrast to Hodgetts scorching pace, Marble's text is California cool, almost banal, but no less searing.

Los Angeles–born writer Eve Babitz is a fan of the Santa Anas. Where her colleague Didion is wary, Babitz embraces the disagreeable sirocco winds, writing "Raymond Chandler and Joan Didion both regard the Santa Anas as some powerful evil, and I know what they mean because I've seen people drop from migraines and go crazy. Every time I feel one coming, I put on my dancing spirits."

As if stirred up by the Santa Anas, Steven Flusty's "Paranoid Typologies," taken from Forum Publication #11, *Building Paranoia: The Proliferation of Interdictory Space and the Erosion of Spatial Justice* from 1994, presents a text that is agitated and suspicious. He presents a series of dystopic typologies that could only have been recognized in the years after the rise of the L.A. School and Mike Davis's *City of Quartz.* Joe Day's 1999 interview with Davis, just after the publication of the now-classic *Ecology of Fear,* veers and detours from the famous book and instead the pair embark on a prescient conversation about the future of downtown and, of course, politics.

The LA Forum has a historic tendency to publish contrarian viewpoints. In 2010, the *Late-Moderns* publication celebrated the overlooked period and included historian Alan Hess's tribute to a period he calls "Imperial Modern" and architect Welton Becket. Five years later, an issue of the newsletter was dedicated to Brutalism in Los Angeles. In it, Russell Fortmeyer interviewed Richard Bradshaw, the structural engineer behind the Theme Building at LAX.

By examining and relishing these architectural eras, the Forum is less about acts of official scholarship and more about acts of blatant enthusiasm—a perverse attitude in opposition to the rigors of the discipline. As Babitz writes of the Santa Anas, "I walked for an entire afternoon along the empty cement in 110 degrees of hot winds just to get the feel of them, alone. Everyone else was hiding inside." At times this passion for Los Angeles' landscape, sprawl, and collage of architecture might seem passé or over indulgent. That's okay. We're just walking in the wind.

Santa Anas

PARANOID
TYPOLOGIES

Steven Flusty

From *Building Paranoia:*
The Proliferation of Interdictory Space and the Erosion of Spatial Justice
Forum Publication #11
1994

Combinations of these various flavors of interdictory space[1] are gradually being incorporated into every facet of the urban environment, generating distinctly unfriendly mutant typologies.

The BLOCKHOME is a residence with a crusty core of thick blank walls, often embedded in an extended jittery perimeter of alarms, video observation cameras, and motion sensitive security lighting.

> Blockhouse: a small timber fort used as a refuge from attack throughout North America during the westward expansion over Native American land. Such structures were commonly built by settler communities for use by individual families in the event armed disputes arose between settlers and their Native American neighbors. The blockhouse was generally two stories tall. The lower floor had sheer walls with tiny loopholes facilitating gunfire. The upper floor overhung the first, thus creating a projecting ledge from which assailants with torches could be prevented from getting close enough to ignite the walls.[2]

> Blockhomes have long been prominent fixtures in high-crime, often low-income neighborhoods throughout the city. In these neighborhoods, homes gradually accrete barred windows and sturdy, well-maintained fences with locked gates to provide relative safety against trespassers and the intrusion of street violence.[3] At the opposite extreme, the blockhome has a long-standing presence in such opulent urban neighborhoods as Beverly Hills, where large mansions containing great wealth are secured against outsides by means of high walls and impenetrable hedges.
> More recently, blockhomes have been adopted in gentrifying areas, where new wealthier residents feel threatened by the established poorer community. Venice is dotted with blockhomes forced into compact bunker and tower forms by the high cost of beach-adjacent property. Isozaki's blank-sided beach studio on Speedway is set in a forecourt surrounded by plaster and frosted glass walls.

Laddie Dill's studio on Innes Place has featureless concrete facades and a courtyard held behind towering blackened steel gates. Many of these buildings clothe themselves in the trappings of the preexistent community, as with a miniature white picket fence set before the windowless corrugated metal front of Brian Murphy's Hopper House near the corner of Indiana and Electric avenues, or the exterior of the Dillon House on 5th Avenue, fitted with handleless steel doors in the unrehabilitated shell of an existing dilapidated house, and complete with an address number spray painted across the front in emulation of graffiti.

Blockhomes have also appeared in areas perceived to be subject to creeping blight, like southern Hollywood where the yards of sprawling two- and three-story Spanish Revival style homes from the 1920s and 1930s are being retrofitted with spike-topped perimeter walls.

This trend, however, is not confined to locations in flux, being visible in stable, affluent areas as well. On Royal Oak Road, in the northern foothills of the Sepulveda Pass, homes sprout such features as crenellated walls and fences made of unscalable vertical piping. Some homes include exterior video cameras to communicate the identities of visitors prior to admission through remote-controlled driveway gates. Others employ prickly plantings like bougainvillea and firethorn to establish security-oriented gardens beneath windows and surrounding the property. In areas such as this, blockhomes are embedded in a jittery ground of privately patrolled streets (the entire Royal Oak neighborhood has contracted with Westec for security services) rendered slippery with parking restrictions and/or the absence of sidewalks.[4]

An experienced thief is capable of entering and leaving alarmed properties in less than the fifteen minute maximum permitted by Underwriters Laboratories for dispatch and arrival of security patrols.[5] Nonetheless, studies suggest that such interdictory measures as home alarms do discourage more casual break-ins, reducing the likelihood of a burglary by 15 times. Anecdotal evidence suggests that this reduction is achieved by displacing break-in attempts to properties less well-defended. Home security providers cater to this conventional wisdom with advertising copy implying, "They'll take one look, and move on to easier pickings."[6] The apparent success of such sales pitches indicates that many homeowners are perfectly willing to protect themselves to the possible detriment of their neighbors.

The LUXURY LAAGER is a relatively affluent residential community sealed behind a crusty perimeter, fenced off or built within walls sometimes reinforced by a stealthy periphery of densely landscaped berms.

> laager: an autonomous encampment configured to withstand siege. Beginning in 1836, 12–14,000 disgruntled Boer farmers and ranchers undertook the Great Trek in reaction against British colonial administration of South Africa's Cape Colony and in search of fresh pasture land. These Voortrekkers penetrated into the interior in trains of ox-drawn covered wagons. These wagon trains, when circled and lashed together either

against threat of attack from the native Bantu-speaking population or as a base of cavalry operations for the subjugation of same, were called laagers. This configuration was later echoed in the layout of settlers homesteads. (Afrikaans variation of German lager, "camp," originating with fortified camps of circled wagons employed defensively by the Goths against the Roman legions.)[7]

According to city law, there are two distinct types of street gating defined according to the process of closure: gating of existing public streets by revocable permit and gating of formerly public streets subsequent to vacation. At present, 147 requests for street closures are awaiting implementations, pending city council approval of some sort of closure policy. Notwithstanding these requests, the real growth in luxury laagers has been new blank-slate developments including privately constructed streets. Such developments obviate the need for gating approvals.

Early luxury laagers from the 1950s to the 1960s were sold more on the basis of snob appeal than survivalism. Although walled off from surrounding major boulevards and lacking internal sidewalks, gates were either largely for show, as at Bel Air in the Santa Monica Mountains, or not provided at all, as at Devonshire Highlands in the northern San Fernando Valley. Real estate advertising copy of the past decade, however, suggests a preoccupation with creating hard interdiction. Advertisements tout such features with the utilitarian brevity of "Gated with 24-hour Drive-by Security"[8] or florid prose like "As you drive through the wrought iron gates, past the uniformed guard, and over the rushing stream, you will be transfixed by [the development's] natural beauty and inherent quality of design."[9]

Sealed luxury laagers with checkpoint entries and private internal security patrols may now be found throughout the L.A. area and beyond. This proliferation has led to an explosion of typological permutations that provide owned and rented residential units in a range of premium prices. Park La Brea in the Wilshire District is a complex of rental apartments built through the 1950s as a series of high-density urban tower blocks, surrounded by two-story garden court apartments. In 1990, the complex was retrofitted with gatehouses manned by forage-capped guards. High metal fencing stretches between the garden courts to block access to internal streets.[10]

The medium-density suburban townhouses of Summit in Canoga Park, completed in 1990, are set atop a tall berm landscaped so heavily as to obscure the existence of residences behind. Access is through a gate-guarded forecourt. The low-density exurban mansions at Calabasas Park are similarly reached by passage through sentry stations augmented by video cameras to record visitors' license plates. Behind the gates lay single-family houses indistinguishable from homes immediately outside the walls.

The residential development of Desert Island in the region's far eastern exurb of Palm Desert is a novel moated community. It is surrounded by "a deep 25-acre lake [that] provides total security for the owners of the spacious high-rise condominium homes."[11]

Contrary to the commonly held assumption that luxury laagers deter crime by displacing it elsewhere, evidence suggests that luxury laagers actually have little effect on crime either inside or outside the walls. Recent crime incident maps and quarterly crime reports for the period of 1988–93 were examined in six police reporting districts. The districts studied were composed largely or entirely of gated developments and adjacent reporting districts of similar, ungated properties. The study indicates that fluctuations of rates for all categories of crime within luxury laagers are similar to those outside.

This holds true even in the case of tightly secured laagers comprised of single-family homes in the Porter Ranch area of the far northern San Fernando Valley, where crime rates rose with the construction of new laagers to mirror crime rates throughout the surrounding ungated area.[12] In some cases, gating of existing developments has occurred, permitting comparison of crime rates prior to and following gating. Initial props in crime rates as a result of gating, relative to adjacent ungated areas, either fail to occur or return to re-gating levels or slightly higher within one to three quarters after gating, suggesting criminal adaptation to the newly "controlled" environment. Further, high-density urban laagers sometimes show significant rises in residential burglaries, residential robberies, and street robberies.[13]

Explanations of these findings are complex, varied, and based largely on the anecdotes and street sense of law enforcement specialists and the perpetrators themselves. First, security in any luxury laager is invariably compromised. Luxury laagers must permit the constant passage of domestic servants, maintenance workers, and visitors. Any of these individuals may engage in criminal activity or provide access to criminals, either intentionally or inadvertently. Access may also be obtained through automated gates in the process of closing, and with codes, remote controls or gate check passes disseminated by residents or stolen from residential units, rental offices, or vehicles. And, of course, perimeter walls may be scaled. Finally, departures are rarely monitored as closely as arrivals, facilitating vehicular escape even past a manned gatehouse. While gating may discourage casual amateur property crime, luxury laagers are perceived as indicative of greater wealth and thus may attract a more professional class of criminals undeterred by such permeable defenses. Further, the laager's interdictory spaces obstruct the passage of emergency vehicles as well as unauthorized visitors. The resultant absence of police patrol visibility inside the laager provides criminals a more relaxed environment in which to work. Finally, in addition to criminal intruders, luxury laagers generate their own internal crime much as any other community. In 1991, crimes committed in one cluster of laagers just outside Las Vegas included five robberies, three rapes, three murders, and a series of alleged child molestations attributed to residents.[14]

The POCKET GHETTO is a public housing project or low-income area retrofitted with street barricades and patrolled by police garrisoned on-site. Residents themselves are considered an "artificial community"[15] constituted according to perceived criminal potential by virtue of residing in areas with high numbers of reported crime incidences. Thus, the configuration of interdictory spaces in the pocket ghetto differs from that of the luxury laager in that the former is intended as much to interdict actions by the poor and allegedly dangerous residents within as those of potential intruders from without. While both types are residential communities with crusty perimeters, the interior of the pocket ghetto is made extremely jittery.

> GHETTO: originally sections of European cities where Jews settled, beginning with the Diaspora following the Roman conquest of Palestine. At first a product of voluntary segregation to retain ritual purity. Jews were later forced into ghettos as an element of increased persecution during the Crusades of the 12th century, resulting in overcrowded, walled-in ghettos locked behind gates after dark. The Nazis revived the practice in 1939. Many Nazi-era ghettos were sealed behind high walls, sometimes surmounted by bridges to permit Jews to pass from one ghetto sector to another without setting foot on "Aryan" ground. The most famous of these, the 840-acre Warsaw Ghetto, was created in October, 1940 and forcibly populated with approximately 500,000 residents. They were held behind barbed wire, later replaced with a wall ten feet tall and eleven miles long. Two years later, diminished food rations and the deportation or extermination of up to 3–4,000 people a day had reduced the population to 40,000. In the post-First World War United States, the term ghetto has referred to urban areas densely populated by minority groups, especially African Americans, generally as a product of financial or social restrictions. (Possibly Italian from borghetto, diminutive of borgo, settlement outside city walls, or getto, an iron foundry on a Venetian islet where the city's Jewish population was confined by canals with bridges raised and guarded nightly from 1516–1797, or Hebrew get, indicating divorce or separation.)[16]

One such micro-township, a mile-square area of Newton Division centering on Jefferson High called Operation Cul De Sac, has been put forward by the LAPD as "an ideal test bed […] to create a model for Citywide application."[17] Beginning in 1990, the thirty-one-block area was saturated with police officers and entirely blocked off by manned sawhorse barricades. By 1992, the sawhorse barricade perimeter had been replaced by steel fences and concrete planters blocking eight street entrances into the original Cul De Sac area and an additional nine street entrances extending three-quarters of a mile to the west. Simultaneously, however, the costs of maintaining police omnipresence proved unsustainable, necessitating manpower cutbacks.

A less labor-intensive strategy has been employed in Pico-Union, known as La Centroamericana to its residents. A roughly 20-block area has been sealed off with unmanned lines of concrete "K Rail" freeway dividers. Residents allege that undocumented Central American immigrants have, at times, been herded behind the Pico-Union barricades as a means of containment preparatory to deportation.

Much like luxury laagers, pocket ghettos appear to have little clearly attributable effect on crime. An examination of portions of the Operation Cul De Sac area shows declines of approximately 15 percent in some forms of crime during the first year of barricading. Similar declines, however, occurred in most nearby, unbarricaded reporting districts. Further, crime rates within the Cul De Sac area remained constant, with fluctuations comparable to those of crime rates in adjacent areas, following barricade and staffing reduction. Not surprisingly, total street closure was most effective in eliminating drive-by shootings.

While some police officers credit barricades with at least inconveniencing crime, others claim they merely distribute criminal incidences more widely throughout the area. Observers note that, in a further similarity to luxury laagers, any initial drops in robbery, narcotics trafficking and other street crimes that do occur within newly created pocket ghettos eventually disappear. This is due in part to the fact that barricaded streets are readily negotiated on foot but impassable to officers in patrol vehicles. Barricades thus create a comfort zone, which perpetrators learn to exploit as a safe space of operation and route of escape.

Equally significant are the effects of pocket ghettos upon community. Barricaded edges of Operation Cul De Sac and Pico-Union largely correspond to the boundaries of specific high-crime police reporting districts. These districts are derived from census tracts, as a means of rendering census data readily applicable for law enforcement purposes.[18] Census tract boundaries reflect nothing more than a unit of roughly 4,000 demographically homogeneous persons. Thus, residents of pocket ghettos are forcibly contained within physical boundaries determined not by any real neighborhood social geography, but by abstract statistical expediency. In instances, this is exacerbated by police-run checkpoints permitting entrance only to residents with identification, although manpower shortages have left these checkpoints unstaffed. As a result, actual communities are dismembered and isolated. Residents complain of severed social connections and disintegrating neighborhoods. This community disintegration, coupled with the apparent lack of long-term efficacy against crime, has led residents of one pocket ghetto in the San Fernando Valley's North Hills to call for removal of the barricades.[19]

Santa Anas

Commercial facilities have undergone similar transformations. Spaces of consumption cannot seal themselves off completely, being dependent upon customer access for sustenance. Even so, they have imposed tight controls over use to become STRONGPOINTS OF SALE resembling colonial trading stations. Similarities to colonialist institutions are particularly strong for large corporate retail outlets like supermarkets, which remain profitable by extracting as much as four dollars from neighborhoods for every one dollar returned as local employees' salaries.[20]

STRONGPOINT: a heavily fortified, tactically advantageous area in a defensive position, trading station: fortified colonialist outpost selling glass beads, tools, textiles and other articles to native populations in exchange for valuable resources brought from the interior. These resources were then handed on for export to the home country. In time, native populations were replaced or assimilated by colonists who utilized the stations for their provisioning. Diversity of merchandise selection increased and the stations became nexuses of settlement. Capt Town, known in the seventeenth century as "the tavern of the Indian Ocean" and the last provisioning opportunity en route from Netherlands to Java, was one of many trading stations that evolved into major port cities.[21]

Even the smallest strip mall has become a tightly nested series of interdictory spaces. Crusty perimeters are established by fencing off parking lots to limit points of access. The strip mall's parking lot itself has become jittery and prickly. Armed security guards are present at growing numbers of malls. Pay phones have been removed to discourage vagrants, and some of Southland Corporation's 7-Eleven convenience stores have installed exterior speakers blaring Muzak to drive away adolescent loiterers.[22] Many secured strip malls include smaller freestanding commercial spaces such as fast food outlets, surrounded by their own fenced-off outdoor eating areas and equipped with observation cameras at pay points both at indoor counters and high concrete walls accessed through steel doors. In addition to these strategies, the interior promenades of some larger malls are remotely monitored by both private security and police in on-site substations replete with holding cells.

Many structures damaged in the 1992 insurrection have been rebuilt with interdictory features. In addition to the usual fences and security stations, these strongpoints of sale are designed to thwart looting and arson. Wood frame structures, flammable and easily breached, have been replaced by single or double-thick walls of concrete masonry. Parapets have been extended to deflect firebombs thrown from street level. Display windows have been either omitted or set into concrete bulwarks two to five feet above sidewalk level to prevent automobiles ramming through to the interior. Locking glazed entries and steel lattice sliding burglar doors have been replaced with solid metal plate roll-down gates, many pre-graffitied to discourage taggers.[23]

Commercial spaces targeted toward predominantly African- and Latin-American clientele in middle- to lower-income "inner-city" neighborhoods have been most frequently converted to strongpoints of sale. This has occurred in large part because insurance companies require such features as a precondition to providing merchants in these neighborhoods with coverage. Baldwin Hills Crenshaw Plaza, reopened at Crenshaw and Martin Luther King boulevards in 1988, employs such control strategies as fenced parking lots, total video coverage, and contained loading docks. It even goes so far as to include a storefront police station serving as a base for 200 police officers, and another bay immediately across the promenade houses a municipal courthouse.

Tightened security in shopping environments has also become the norm in more affluent suburban malls, where the role of shopping as community social focus has provided a site for police contact with the general public. Police substations in mall administration offices have become standard fixtures, and often serve as the public hub for community policing and neighborhood watch operations.

Strongpoints of sale both deter and apprehend criminals in their activities against retail establishments and shoppers on the premises. Crime incident maps, however, suggest they have been less successful in preventing high rates of thefts from vehicles occurring across the expanses of large parking lots.[24] They have also been less effective in controlling patron robbery. Customers are generally identified as people with money and thus targeted for victimization while in commercial environments, but not robbed until after they have left the premises for less peopled locations. Further, while strongpoints of sale are intended to provide a sense of safety for the reassurance of customers, the secondary effects of interdictory spaces in retail environments may have the opposite effect. Conservative cost estimates of store security currently run to 16 cents for every dollar in sales.[25] It may be assumed that prices rise and sales drop as these costs are passed on to customers. Additionally, while visible security engenders a sense of comfort up to a point, there may exist a level at which visibly pervasive security discourages patronage by communication a sense of distrust while creating the impression of shopping in a war zone.

High-rise offices are outfitted as self-contained WORLD CITADELS, a crusty core set within a tery field held behind stealthy and/or slippery perimeters. The slippery perimeters are further reinforced by the tendency of world citadels to cluster together as a means of facilitating face-to-face contact between business interests. These clusters are commonly sited in locations that are either difficult to casually reach or devoid of affordable parking and pedestrian amenities. World citadels serve as the headquarters of large business concerns, most notably the supranational corporations engendering CITISTAT.

> CITADEL: a walled fortress intended to surround and protect a ruler's residences, usually built high on a hill overlooking a city. Throughout history, citadels have kept the inhabitants of surrounding towns in subjugation and/or formed a final point of defense during a siege. Well-known examples include the ancient Greeks' Acropolis and Acrocorinth and the Carcassone of the Middle Ages. The essential citadel is the Motte and Bailey castle of the 13th century Norman subjugation of Wales, consisting of an open forecourt surrounded by a palisade, behind which stood the tower of the keep. A garrison of soldiers was stationed in the keep's ground floor and charged with watching over the grounds and preventing entrance into the keep. On-site facilities might include larders, mills, bakeries, and smithies to permit normal life while under siege.[26] (Middle French, derived from Old Italian citadel(a), "little city.")

Early forms of the world citadel were inspired by New York's 1956 Seagram Building, with its glass-walled high-rise set back from adjacent properties within an empty plaza. Such open spaces were encouraged by New York City's zoning code of 1961, which provided density bonuses for the provision of pedestrian amenities. As a result, freestanding towers in empty plazas became the norm until 1975. In that year, guidelines and requirements for plaza design were implemented in response to studies indication that wide featureless stone plinths were of greater value to developers for associated density benefits than to users for implicit recreational agility.[27] These developments in both design and legislation were reflected in Los Angeles and other major American cities.

In such early world citadels from the 1970s as Arco Plaza or the original Union Bank Building, the plaza is pure prickly space, a stone-faced expanse of hardscape exposed to thermal extremes. Winds are magnified as they flow around adjacent towers, which also block sunlight entirely or magnify its heat and glare with reflective glass surfaces. Seating is either nonexistent or improvised from ledges, railings, and steps. Amenities consist primarily of gigantic steel sculptures or fountains commonly referred to as plop art or yards-in-the-plaza.

More recent developments reflect both a shared consciousness among developers and legislators of the value of user-friendly urban designs, and a differing conception of to whom those benefits should accrue. With the fragmentation of large vertically integrated firms, world citadels are now more likely to be administered by management companies competing with one another to attract multiple corporate tenants. Attractive site amenities are seen as integral to this competition by providing spaces where "office workers will find outdoor areas for noontime relaxation."[28] Municipal agencies, meanwhile, seek both to encourage tax-generating development and to create parklike additions to the city's open space inventories without directly incurring additional fiscal burden. Thus attempts are made to extract greater site amenity from private developers in exchange for subsidies provided through below-market-rate land sales or leases, tax abatements, and density bonuses. In negotiations with developers, municipal agencies have been successful in linking public subsidies to the provision of higher quality urban deign producing more habitable open spaces. This has occurred in no small part because such spaces enhance the value of the project to the developers. Municipal agencies have not, however, been particularly successful in negotiating the right of public access to these spaces. This failure may be attributed to the fact that right of free passage provides no additional benefit for the developer and entails the loss of private control over the space's users.[29] Thus, public subsidies have often been expended to create plazas accessible only at the discretion of private owners, as is illustrated by the text embossed into the small brass plaques at the property lines of L.A.'s world citadels: "Private property, right to pass by permission, and subject to control, of owners. Sec 1008 CIVIL CODE."

Recent world citadels are lushly planted and ornamented with water features. They include on-site malls uniformly equipped with eateries, express mail posts, dry cleaners, and gift shops to relieve office workers of the need to leave the premises. Newer world citadels in Los Angeles were constructed with the financial assistance of public agencies, on the assumption that the plazas would serve as a surrogate for public open space. So as not to blatantly contradict this presumption, world citadel developers tend to rely upon strategies more prone to discourage access than prevent it.

The as-yet-incomplete plaza at California Plaza, on the southeast edge of Bunker Hill, is an exemplary labyrinth of interdictory spaces. On the west side, the plaza is separated from the sidewalk by a property line expressed as a bronzed metal strip bolted to the sidewalk. Half the plaza sinks well below street level and is concealed behind a solid screen of box topiary. The other half is tucked behind a high-rise. From the east, the plaza abuts the Watercourt central performance plaza two stories above the street, casting the sidewalks below into deep shadow. Here, the plaza is reached via a remote-monitored elevator, a narrow stairway sandwiched between a hotel porte-cochere and a service vehicle entrance, or an escalator installed at the insistence of the city's redevelopment authority. The south façade at street level is a gigantic ventilator grate giving way to a subterranean vehicular entrance.

The plaza interior is studded with video cameras monitored by private security stationed within the adjacent tower's stone-sheathed elevator lobby. Private security is responsible both for ensuring that visibly inappropriate visitors do not access the elevators and for ejecting undesirables or an overabundance of less desirables form the plaza.[30]

Security provisions of world citadels are directed at maintaining the preferred user mix by preventing non-professionals and the obviously less affluent from becoming so prevalent on site as to intimidate tenant office workers and executives. Such user mix is usually maintained, even where world citadels are sited in close proximity to impoverished populations in areas devoid of landscaping and usable open space.

Notes

1   Flusty, Steven, *Building Paranoia*, Chapter 2, "Attributes of Insecurity": "Los Angeles' emergent paranoid urban environment is engendered by spaces designed to intercept and repel or filter would-be users: INTERDICTORY SPACE.
   interdict: steady bombardment of enemy positions. Routes or supplies for the purpose of delaying and disorganizing the enemy's progress, to cut off authoritatively from certain functions and privileges. (Stein, J. *The Random House Dictionary of the English Language*. New York: Random House, 1967.)
   Interdictory space is comprised of a variety of exclusionary design strategies, flavoring it with one or more of these defensive characteristics: stealthy, slippery, crusty, prickly, and jittery.
2   Hart, H.M. *Pioneer Forts of the West*. Seattle: Superior Publishing, 1967.
3   Blazek, P.V. *The Childhood Landscape*. Unpublished thesis, U.S.C. School of Architecture, 1993.
4   This use of proprietary security in the role of police surrogates or auxiliaries in residential spaces prefigures wider application, as is demonstrated by the City of Los Angeles Community Redevelopment Agency's reinforcement of the LAPD with contracted private patrol services along a 1.5-mile length of Hollywood Boulevard in the Hollywood Redevelopment Area.
5   Private security companies are unwilling to release response time figures but industry members claim 15 minutes as average, and response times of as long as 30 minutes are not unknown.
6   Television advertisement for roll-down steel shutters.
7   Hogg, Ian. *The History of Forts and Castles*. New York: Crescent Publishing, 1985, 140.
8   Promotional sheet for Mountaingate in Brentwood.
9   *Life is an Art Form*. Promotional brochure for Summit at Warner Center.
10   Some residents of these garden apartments have expressed dissatisfaction with paying monthly surcharges for maintenance of a security perimeter comprised in part of their own rental units.
11   Advertisement in *Palm Springs Life*. Rear inside cover. July 1993.
12   For example, rising crime incidents for LAPD Reporting District #1701 concurrent with construction and inhabitation of luxury laagers from 1989–93, compared with crime incident fluctuations for adjacent reporting districts of comparable population density and ungated building stock. It should be noted that crime rates are negligible throughout such affluent suburban areas as Porter Ranch, both within and outside luxury laagers.
13   Exemplified by crime incident fluctuations and categorical increases for LAPD Reporting Districts 714 and 715, prior to and following gating in 1990, compared with crime incident fluctuations for adjacent ungated reporting districts of comparable population density and building stock.

Santa Anas

14   Guterson, D. "Home, Safe Home." *Utne Reader*. March/April 1993, 62–67.
15   Operation Cul De Sac Project Summary. Los Angeles Police Dept. and Los Angeles City Council Notes 90-1165, 90-1267.
16   *Encyclopaedia Judaica*. 1978.
17   Project Summary, ibid.
18   In the Cul De Sac area, this data has been augmented with information gathered by police in a "door-to-door community survey."
19   Williams, T. "Neighborhood Gives Up on Barricades." *Los Angeles Times*, June 27,1993.
20   This 1:4 ratio may be conservative, as it assumes 100% of payroll remains in the community. Figures courtesy of the University of California at Los Angeles Department of Afro-American Studies.
21   Marshall, B. *Real World*. London: Marshall Editions, 1991, 150.
22   Heller, M. "Stores Fight Crime with Guns and Alarms." *Los Angeles Times*, August 24, 1993.
23   Lopez, R.J. "Anxiety is Building." *Los Angeles Times*, June 20,1993
24   It may, of course, be argued that incidence of theft from vehicles would be even higher in the absence of interdictory spaces.
25   Heller, M. "Stores Fight Crime with Duns and Alarms." *Los Angeles Times*, August 24, 1993.
26   Hogg, *Forts and Castles*, 39–43.
27   Whyte, W.H. *City*. New York: Doubleday, 1988, 229–230.
28   *California Plaza*. Promotional brochure. Metropolitan Structures.
29   For downtown Los Angeles, it may be argued that municipal authorities, rather than having lost some battle for plaza accessibility, knowingly collaborated with developers in the creation of exclusionary open spaces. Downtown plazas were developed under the auspices of redevelopment programs, by which "housing and services for huge numbers of residents no longer needed in the world economy were destroyed as [...]. space was allocated to profit maximizing development that provided the physical conditions to meet the needs of a new international economy." Deutsche, R. "Art and Public Space: Questions of Democracy." *Social Text 33*, 1992, 34–53.
30   Private security has a long tradition of providing property protection for businesspeople. "Special" police, common in most cities of the 19th century, were privately hired and commanded guards sworn in by, and accorded the same powers as, municipal police. In Pennsylvania from 1865 to 1930, private corporations were permitted to mobilize proprietary police forces, considered more reliable in suppressing the railroad, coal and iron industries' labor movements than the more popularly controlled municipal police forces and state militias. Walker, S. *A Critical History of Police Reform*. Lexington, Mass.: Lexington Books, 1977, 29.

On Anything but the *Ecology of Fear*

An Interview with Mike Davis

Joe Day

LA Forum Newsletter,
Urban Infrastructure
Spring 1999

Just before departing on a promotional junket for his book *Ecology of Fear: Los Angeles and the Imagination of Disaster* (Metropolitan Books, 1998), Mike Davis took a couple of hours one morning to answer some questions from the Forum. He had just completed a two-hour phone interview with *Metropolis* magazine and really didn't want to talk about the book, so we asked...

What's Next?

Joe Day: What are you working on currently for Verso?

Mike Davis: It's called *Late Victorian Holocausts*, subtitled "El Niño Famines and the Making of the Third World." In the 1870s and 1890s there were these global El Niño events and somewhere between a minimum of 35 million people and as many as 50 million people died in [the resulting] famines—the majority of them in India and China, but also in Southern Africa and Eastern Brazil. It's a short book, essentially an environmental history of these famines, but It's also trying to adjudicate this question: to what extent were these famines caused by El Niño, and what turned these into such devastating episodes? What I focus on is the increased ecological poverty brought about when the British abandoned small irrigation and destroyed the traditional village government systems for mobilizing communal labor.

JD: So, a colonial mass-agricultural system was installed and then got hammered by natural catastrophes?

MD: Right. Building roads to move food everywhere, and exporting massive quantities of food to England while millions are dying; that's what happened in China. Although, in China it's different because the right of subsistence was always considered a human right. The Grand Canal, which is the single largest man-made object on the planet, was traditionally used in China not only to move tribute grain to Beijing, but also to move rice surpluses to Northern China to relieve famines. It was a system that worked brilliantly in the 18th century, but after the foreign interventions, the Opium Wars, and the Tai Ping Rebellion, the ruling Chings had abandoned the maintenance of the Grand Canal. They couldn't move the surplus grain anymore and 20 million people died of starvation in two terrible famines, the second of which fueled the Boxer Uprising. In other words, this is either an environmental history of late-Victorian imperialism or a social history of El Niño.

Downtown

JD: I'd like to talk about a few current and specific issues in L.A. What do you make of the fast-track development of the new downtown sports facilities?

MD: With regards to downtown, it's the same old song: yet one more costly, publicly subsidized project will make downtown work. We built this huge convention center expansion but nobody came because there aren't any stores or street life. So now we'll build a sports stadium, and it goes on and on. The question is why is it in the interest of the whole city to constantly pile up investments in downtown? It's an artificial life support system for downtown hotels and businesses.

It's a slightly complicated issue for me because these convention and sports centers are a major subsidy to the hotels and I've historically been a very strong supporter of the hotel workers' union's struggle downtown. But there's still no justification for any level of further public subsidy. And in fact, this is happening while across the country there is a grassroots rebellion going on against public subsidies for professional sports centers.

The whole history of downtown since the 1920s, since the original challenge by the Wilshire District, was the leveraging of downtown with increasingly large amounts of tax expenditure to keep it artificially central or dominant.

JD: Why do you think [Mayor] Riordan has fallen into exactly the same pattern? He came into office so closely identified with the Westside.

MD: Well, he made a fortune downtown wearing several hats as an investor and corporate lawyer. In an older piece on Chinatown I discussed a deal in which Riordan made a couple million dollars buying and selling a single parcel downtown in one week. He is actually a consummate downtown insider. What fascinates me though, is that he won office by virtue of the northwest valley and he's stacked commissions with perhaps the biggest number of valley-ites in the history of the city. When Riordan came in it really looked like there might be a serious shift in power, but in the last couple of years he's proven to be a much more traditional downtown mayor in the footsteps of Tom Bradley.

JD: A few people at the LA Forum are studying the freeway expansions in Pasadena. Can you clarify the issues surrounding the extension of the Long Beach Freeway?

MD: There are two forgotten aspects to the conflict over the extension of the Long Beach Freeway. One is that it impacts El Sereno as much as South Pasadena. It's always been perceived as an issue of the white middle class in South Pasadena, that doesn't mind if traffic is stopped in Alhambra, but doesn't want its ambiance destroyed by a freeway. But there has always been another side to it: there are hundreds of homes in [more working class] El Sereno that are similarly menaced, but the opposition from El Sereno has never really been noted.

Secondly, the big problem with this freeway is that it will siphon off all of the truck traffic to the harbor. In other words, if you're coming in from the valley, the easiest thing to do, rather than get snarled in traffic downtown, is to loop to the Long Beach freeway through the City of Commerce to the harbor. L.A. since the 1940s has kept alive the idea of a separate truck freeway through downtown— an Alameda Street freeway. It is an absolutely fundamental idea, because the largest threat to early morning commutes are early morning truck accidents on the San Bernadino freeway or on the exchanges around Downtown L.A.

JD: So this freeway would effectively divert traffic out of downtown...

MD: It would take a lot of heavy truck traffic and divert it onto the Long Beach Freeway, which at rush hour is already one of the most terrifying driving experiences in Southern California with the current volume of truck traffic. And you're going to exacerbate that. I believe that Alhambra needs to take some of the traffic off Valley Boulevard, but you could deal with that separately from completing the freeway. I don't think the freeway is just the selfish white middle-class issue that it's been presented as; lots of working-class Latinos are against the project as well.

Relocating SCI-Arc

JD: Did you see the *Los Angeles Times* piece on SCI-Arc's search for new campuses?

MD: Apparently [Nicolai Ouroussoff] has me advocating a move to the old Lincoln Heights Jail. What I actually said was that before the last move to Playa del Rey, some students had advocated that, and I supported the student position. I think that anywhere but where we are would be preferable. The Harbor would be preferable; anywhere downtown would be preferable.

JD: Why move out of that belt of the city, with Dreamworks moving in? SCI-Arc will probably be priced out of the market there, but what's your argument for moving?

MD: There's very little interaction with any neighborhood or urban context possible at that site. If we were located in the harbor, we'd be in the storm center of all kinds of interesting land use battles. I'm just excited about being in any kind of heavier industrial environment, and having some relationship with what's been going on in the interesting local politics of Long Beach, the great forgotten city of L.A. County. Or, alternatively, take any of the downtown sites that have been suggested. I heard there was a 1920s auto dealership that was a possibility. It's just that now we are not within walking distance of any neighborhood or any kind of human activity. It's a very, very inert site.

JD: What do you think of the possibility of SCI-Arc operating in tandem with another school in the area?

MD: I had proposed to [former director] Michael Rotondi that SCI-Arc do this with CalArts eight years ago when I was teaching at both schools. Steven Levine at CalArts was really interested in the potential synergies between the two schools—maybe in an arrangement along the lines of the Claremont Colleges. I think SCI-Arc would be the perfect compliment to CalArts. At the time, CalArts was a lot more aggressive about responsible community involvement and was better than any of the other design schools at putting resources into the city.

FORUM
Publication

Swimming to Suburbia

Some Thoughts on the New City and How It Came to Be That Way.

Craig Hodgetts

FORUM

For Architecture and Urban Design

Los Angeles

3454 West First Street
Los Angeles CA 90004

FORUM

Newsletter

Number One

Santa Anas

INTRODUCTION TO THE FORUM

The primary purpose of the Forum is to provide a framework in which design professionals and members of the public can explore and evaluate the architecture and urban structure of the Los Angeles area. The Forum seeks to promote and coordinate scholarly research, planning studies, artistic activities, and other endeavors which can affect and improve the built environment. We seek to disseminate the results of these activities to a larger public and to encourage informed evaluations of the physical environment of the city. Through our programs, we hope to promote the establishment of an informed community of concerned professionals and members of the general public and to provide that community with a vehicle for dissemination of information to the public at large.

In its first six months of existence, the Forum sponsored two highly successful lecture and discussion series. Material presented at these and future events will form the basis for a series of publications devoted to Architecture and Urban Design in Los Angeles to be published bi-monthly. The Forum has incorporated as a non-profit public benefit corporation devoted primarily to educational purposes. We are seeking to obtain Federal and State tax exemptions and to be recognized as a Public Charity by the IRS.

In 1988, we intend to coordinate and partially support a series of studies and proposals on public space, transportation, building types, and street patterns in Los Angeles. We hope to obtain funding for these research projects from Federal and State organizations, to develop them in conjunction with the Forum's meetings, and to present them to a wider public through symposia, exhibits, and publications.

Newsletter Editor:
Natalie Shivers

Board Members:
Shelly A. Berger
Aaron Betsky
Benjamin Caffey

Craig Hodgetts
Christian Hubert
Doug Suisman

Officers:
Christian Hubert, President
Aaron Betsky, Vice-President
Suzanne Caffey, Secretary/Treasurer

MEMBERSHIP

Membership in the Forum is open to any interested individual. The $35 annual fee entitles members to free admission to Forum events, to receive the bi-monthly newsletter, and to purchase other Forum publications at reduced rates. Members are encouraged to participate in planning Forum activities. Please check the appropriate category below if interested.

Name: _____

Address: _____
_____

Telephone: _____

I am interested in participating in the following activities:

☐ publications ☐ lectures and discussions

☐ planning and development ☐ reading groups and research

☐ fundraising ☐ social events

FORUM Number One
Publication

Swimming to Suburbia

Some Thoughts on the New City and
How It Came to Be That Way.

Craig Hodgetts

Before

Santa Anas

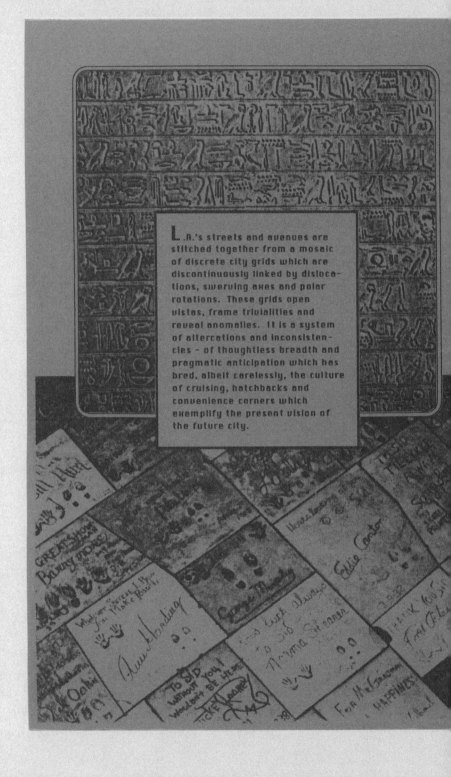

L.A.'s streets and avenues are stitched together from a mosaic of discrete city grids which are discontinuously linked by dislocations, swerving axes and polar rotations. These grids open vistas, frame trivialities and reveal anomalies. It is a system of altercations and inconsistencies – of thoughtless breadth and pragmatic anticipation which has bred, albeit carelessly, the culture of cruising, hatchbacks and convenience corners which exemplify the present vision of the future city.

In short, the city grid is the medium from which all other media emanate. People do things with it: they plan excursions and funerals, meditations and trysts, with the abandon of an action painter. The city is perhaps less an artifact than a benevolent flux in which to pursue individual destinies. Yet it seems that our ability to understand and modify urban destiny has in both theory and practice been hopelessly mired in the cramped space of our most elementary perceptions. In other words, given the universe of energy and its corollary matter, we are only able to measure and perceive the "physical" world, and consequently have developed systems of architectural "order" related to the ability of various urban objects, buildings and so on to reflect light. Because of this fixation, the planning of most cities is still at the toy block stage, while much of the rest of the world has discovered electricity.

We generally see walls and roofs as shaping our cities, but there are those of us who are frustrated by the limits of construction and its control of making and memory, and there are others who recognize the inconvenient weight and the permanence of stone as a natural way to dominate the culture as a whole. I would propose that our idea that the stone image confers status by its simple existence must be re-examined in light of the relative effort required for its realization.

Imagine, for a moment, the ponderous task of coordination in the times when even basic size and shape could only be communicated with difficulty. A world lacking FAX and stats, limited to messengers toting papyrus rolls in boats up the Nile, could hardly be blamed for the rigid geometry which came to signify civilization. That geometry was a useful tool. It got things done, enabling legions of people to work on a single product, even a simple, elemental one: there was a necessary symbiosis between the monolithic communications network and the task at hand. So it comes as no surprise to find the design for the network itself carefully incised into the rock, in effect memorializing the "chain of command" which may have been the real invention of such a culture. Thus the definition of power and rank came to reflect the rigidity of the medium in which early civilizations worked (imagine the consequences of People Magazine in stone), with the resulting geometry inferring a like status at some future time.

By the late Middle Ages, the routines and sub-routines of city building inherited from the Romans had become the structure by which urban life was evaluated. The medieval city became a familiar artifact, so much so that Giotto's toy-like depiction of formerly monumental edifices as tilted, colored, even charming objects-at-play defies their status, reducing them to the engaging companions to urban life that they had become. Buildings themselves became entertaining pleasure objects, as plentiful as Walkmen; they made you feel good, dressed up your life, and provided a defined context in which you could relate to others.

Santa Anas

The city, like a good host, was
where it was happening, and the
creative nature of man was not
only supported, but even exemplified in the complex structures
of its plazas and streets. Hence-
forth, the synthesis of man and
city was to become increasingly
reciprocal, evolving steadily away
from the paternalistic patterns of
imperialism to the point where it
became a complex communications organ capable of extending
the dynamic interchange of man
to man, man to institution, and
man to his work. It became the
"communitas:" a place which, in
my view, functioned as a kind of
media center, where the grand
and the accidental could find
appropriate accommodation,
while the exchange of goods,
information, and judgements
could multiply indefinitely.

Free interchange characterized
the city center. But by the time
Sixtus V had re-erected the
obelisk at what was to be the
Basilica of St. Peter, the Roman
in-crowd had moved on. And in
cities throughout the world, with
the rise first of wide-spread
publishing, then of railroads,
telegraph, radio and telephone,
the essential function of communication began to operate without
particular reference to its center.
Suddenly, the now-meaningless
symbolism of place and adjacency
was seen to be less compelling
than the complex symbolism
inherent in a gigantic task,
whether it be the building of
pyramids, cathedrals, spaceships,
or even cities themselves.

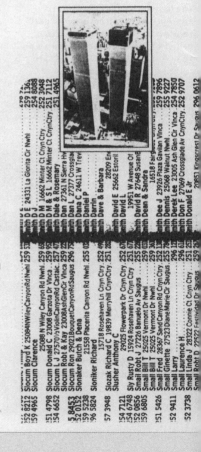

The society which discovers a
stimulant such as this task,
which, after all, requires extraordinary talents and diverse
communication, has no need for
the puffery of conventional
symbols. Thus the waning of
architectural symbolism in the
recent past makes sense. By
engaging ourselves in the
creation of a symbolically
charged and represented task,
we have finally devised a way
to make an object, a symbol
and a center which requires the
most diverse creative energies
ever assembled. This object
realizes the potentiality of our
technology to take us beyond
the realm of the city and of

Santa Anas

Los Angeles is frustrating because the ways in which we have studied cities in the past - analyzing their solids and voids, their bumps and valleys - is no more relevant today than are the fingers of phrenology which attempt to "scientifically" plumb neurological depths by describing the surfaces of the skull. This is because cities have become as quasi-electronic as the brains they house. Any analysis must address this reality. As Keith Jarrett has remarked: "There's electricity in all of us!"

Similarly, if Los Angeles is reduced to a Nolli map, it seems opaque and uninspired when compared to its European cousins. Yet we must remember that the functional shape of the new city is best described by the flux of its electronic network. The city is made up of variegated, constantly changing rhythms of bookings, orders, transactions and contacts too rich in information to be subjected to holistic analysis. The "skull" of the modern city cannot be cleverly sliced for diagnosis and cure: it is an entity requiring the sophistication of a brain-scan rather than the ministrations of a triple-0 pen. Los Angeles is a holographic city.

Let me give an example of the implications of such an analysis by comparing three musical compositions: a Gregorian chant, the Eroica Symphony, and composer Terry Riley's "In 'C'."

In the chant, we are offered a vision of unanimity: a single melodic line thick with voices of every timbre, without so much as a rhythmic defection, reflects the quality of Medieval agrarian society.

In the music of Beethoven a marked tension is apparent as themes and sub-plots vie for attention, yet the whole is clearly dominated by a single powerful idea – much, it would seem, like the Renaissance city.

Finally, in the work of Terry Riley, each of a series of three- and four-note phrases is played as often as each member of the ensemble chooses, producing a slowly evolving field of harmonic events often characterized as non-music. In fact, as is the case in a holographic image, the relationship of each unit of the piece to the whole is absolutely typical. Each moment is the whole at the same scale, even though the whole is articulated in its parts.

I believe that Los Angeles has the qualities of the Riley piece. Here, a grab-bag of style, convenience and opportunity surrounds each individual like a microcosm of the whole city, offering short-range choice from tacky to flamboyant, catering to lifestyles from monkish to raffish, creating opportunities even a champion self-stylist could never exhaust.

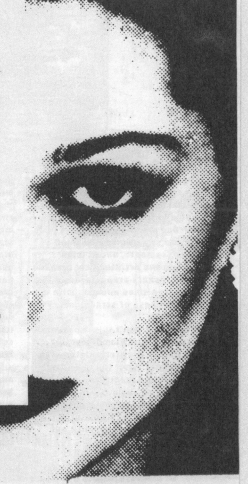

Santa Anas

Consumptive, competitive, and creative, the mythic avenues of this city, lined with trees of all species and kaleidoscopic homes, have a logic born of the individual. One man's fantasy is another's reality in a clash of advertisements, decor, wide screens and architectural bravado which flickers preposterously along tree-lined avenues with all the gaudiness of screen gems.

Or do they? Isn't this capsule re-creation of eras long gone, taken as a whole, a differentiated style unto itself? Isn't it a distinctly post-modern luxury to dwell in the midst of sham reality where the only consensus is in diversity? Are Trigger's hoof prints just another hieroglyphic? At the Chinese Theater?

Los Angeles is a city committed to images, but never to sources. An advertisement shows the bulk of the new Beverly Center as the chapeau on a dressed-to-kill model. A later ad shows it in steamboat drag, complete with stacks. A few miles away a landlocked nineteen-thirties Coca Cola bottling plant renders the steamboat in stucco. A saucer-shaped restaurant rotating atop a severely modern office slab bills itself as a crenellated antique. A serious downtown hotel takes "Things to Come" too seriously, with comic results. A gigantic Man on Horseback lights a cigarette at the focus of a long axis while multi-million dollar homes look on.

Who's kidding whom? Are the inhabitants of this place simply

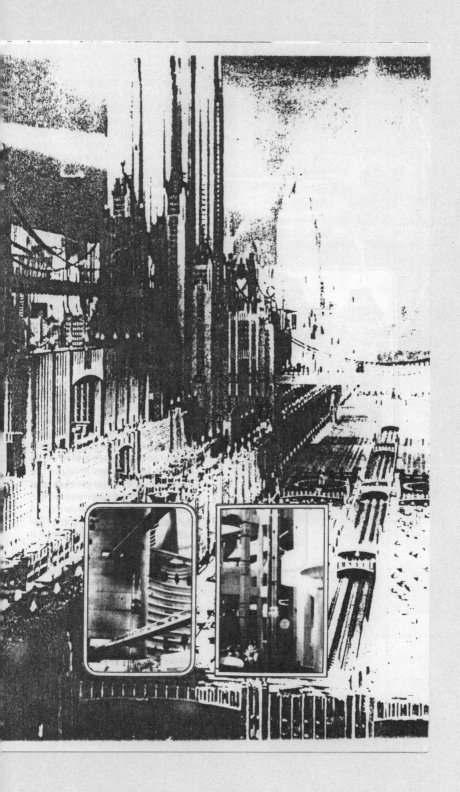

Santa Anas

gullible? Or are they able to row merrily through this shipwreck of icons as though it were a Sunday cruise? Every weekend abandoned corner lots in vacant corners of cities-within-the-city with names like Eagle Rock, Alhambra and Arcadia are blasted by the giant lights and motor generators of mobile furniture showrooms. Without the benefit of so much as a tent, with NCR's safely in the truck, and while soft sculpture surrounds them on the crumbling asphalt, the omnipresent Valley housewifes solemnly confer with their designer counterparts. They are afraid it won't go with their wall hanging. The color is wrong. The color is money. Surely the crew of the Discovery could not have felt more incongruous had they uncovered a grandfather clock rather than a black monolith in that pit on the moon.

If one avoids freeways, which promise reassurance in the form of a guaranteed destination, the surface of this planet L.A. is endlessly rewarding. It is an encyclopedia of mini-gardens and barely throttled power boats. It is like stepping off the Rue Montparnasse to explore the back alleys of Paris. No matter that Melrose Avenue is 120 feet wide, that it seems to carry more traffic than the autobahn, it is an alley nonetheless, and the pattern of freeways and street grids is topologically, emotionally, and urbanistically Beaux-Arts. No wonder Banham loved them.

Freeways focus traffic as if they were lenses, beaming the cars directly to the next interchange,

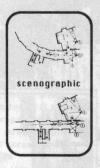

scenographic

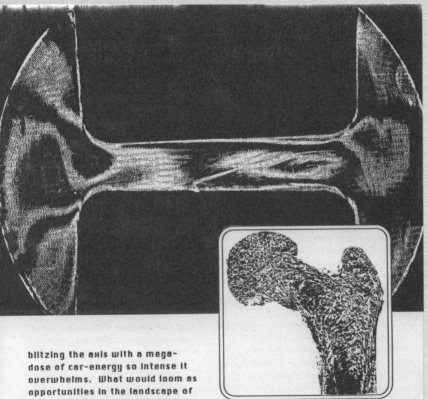

blitzing the axis with a mega-
dose of car-energy so intense it
overwhelms. What would loom as
opportunities in the landscape of
lesser cities - sites charged with a
view, perhaps a prominent bend, a
vista - here are flung at the
passing tide in a volley of words
and images which ricochet from
billboard to billboard, dazzling
with a visual racket as violent as
a Prohibition shoot-out.

I question the fact that nobody
"exploits" those locations. Why
do so few buildings address the
shifts in axis which mark sub-
divisions long since annexed? And
then I remember that there are
cars in front and behind. There is
a blonde in that one, the radio is
on, and in the distance a string of
cobra-like lamps stretches like a
veil over a parade of billboards.
And the carphone is in my ear.

Santa Anas

In fact, unless there is some particular fixed asset out there – like oil – which must be consumed on the very spot, every backyard is exactly equal to every other backyard. And it is the producer sunning by the pool, surrounded by telephones and bikini'd cuties of either sex, who makes all the deals.

The magnificent images of cities designed to emulate, and even magnify, the manifold processes of industry and culture and crime and indulgence are not unlike Gainsborough's paintings. They tranquilize, mystify, and romanticize the vitality of an as of yet uncongealed city which could be getting you off.

In this context, physical manipulation of the gross city fabric seems superfluous at best. Presumptuous and potentially damaging, cosmetic adventures like the Bunker Hill exercise seem destined to appear, like tidied-up office lobbies, wherever developers have a stake.

It might instead be more meaningful to address the way dislocations and distortions of the basic city fabric can accommodate eccentricities like the Blue Whale or the Brown Cow. Or one might consider how the message-beeper, phone banks and express mail have already created a cybernetic city. One might ask how chain stores can be given significant roles which exploit their cumulative importance. Los Angeles has already evolved a unique texture in which these elements are the principal determinants. We are already

the beneficiaries of a meta-urban state which offers proof-positive that scenography and urban function are no longer mutually exclusive. This condition suggests that uncoupling the diagram from the experience may be the catalyst which expands our definition of urban form to include explicitly scenographic intent: we can create "a good shot."

The dream each of us dreams is the locus of each individual, heating and cooling whole districts in a dynamic, sensory, always interactive experience linked to the fluid nature of the city itself. As designers, the architectural project which faces us is to disassociate ourselves from the fixation on buildings and to instead look in the rearview mirror.

Santa Anas

SUGGESTIVE SPACES

Themes no less than "Earth", "Air", "Fire", and "Water" will be the Forum's topics for investigation in a series of events entitled "Suggestive Spaces" to be held this Spring. The cosmic elements will be transposed into the local vernacular via a range of discussions and tours that will

explore the fundamental structures of Los Angeles. Each event will take place in a space evocative of the topic to be discussed, so please note the change in location from meeting to meeting. Events are free for members, $7.50 for non-members.

🏛 "Unveiling the Sky",
a discussion of the function, role, and place of tall buildings in Los Angeles with Richard Keating (Design Partner, Pereira Associates), Mike Davis (Professor of Urban Geography, UCLA), and Thom Mayne (Partner, Morphosis; Professor, SCI-ARC).
Tower Reception Room, Los Angeles City Hall, 200 N. Spring St.
Monday, January 25, 7:30 p.m.

🏛 Tour of Sylmar Aqueduct Filtration Plant
and a discussion (tentatively scheduled) with Bill Morrish, Professor of Architecture at USC, whose investigations of the L.A. water system were published in Issue #16 of Modulus.
Saturday, March 26, 1:00 p.m.

🏛 Discussion of the Los Angeles landscape
with Pamela Burton, landscape architect with Burton and Spitz
April 23, time and place t.b.a.

🏛 Tour of Union Oil Refinery, Wilmington.
Limited number of places available. Call 389-6730 for information and reservations.
Time and place t.b.a.

THEORY TOWARDS ARCHITECTURE

The SCI-ARC Reading Group will meet biweekly to discuss the application of particular theories and modes of thinking to architecture. Occasional guest speakers will be invited to discuss both their own work and interpretations of the relationship between theory and architecture.

Meetings will be held Monday evenings at 7 p.m. at SCI-ARC. The cost is $20 for Forum members and SCI-ARC faculty and staff, $30 for non-members, and $10 for students. Call Ann Bergrin (213-821-3494) or Aaron Betsky (213-938-6626) for more information.

Schedule (Tentative)
🏛 Discussion with Mark Wigley: "Derrida".
Monday, January 18.

🏛 Text: "Plato's Pharmakon", by Jacques Derrida.
Monday, February 1.

🏛 Text: "Thinking", by Hannah Arendt.
Monday, February 15.

🏛 Selected texts by Svetlana Alpers, Donald Preziozi, Norman Bryson.
Monday, February 29.

🏛 Text: The Order of Things, by Michel Foucault.
Monday, March 14.

🏛 Discussion with Cornel West: "Post-Modernism"
Monday, March 28.

🏛 Selected texts by Anthony Vidler.
Monday, April 11.

Built by Becket

Alan Hess

Forum Issue 7: Late-Moderns
2010

The mid decades of the 20th century were the heyday of Imperial California. The Golden State's population swelled, its youth revolutionized the nation's commerce and culture, its entertainment industry colonized the globe, and its aerospace industry ruled the future.

Like all ascendant empires, Imperial California required an architecture to manifest its glory. No architect exceeded Welton Becket's influence in this period of expansion. The young man from Seattle who became a confidant of Walt Disney and architect for Buffy Chandler had arrived in L.A. in the 1930s at a time when he could substantially reshape the city. The highlights of his career are impressive: Hollywood's Capitol Records building gave Hollywood an instant postwar icon; Parker Center embodied all that was progressive and modern in city governance; Bullocks Pasadena showed that the new suburbs could be elegant; Los Angeles International (with Pereira & Luckman and Paul R. Williams) was a gateway to tomorrow; Fashion Island, the UCLA Medical Center, Pauley Pavilion, the Cinerama Dome, the Beverly Hilton, the plan for Century City, and crowning them all the Music Center—a latter-day Acropolis for the arts. Each is a Becket design. Put them together and you have a comprehensive catalog of the era's confidence, innovation, and progress.

Consider the number of landmarks in this list. Becket buildings molded our image of L.A. in this era. Even vanished Becket buildings have left an indelible after-image: the Pan Pacific Auditorium remains a part of the mental landscape of L.A. long after the actual building burned and crumbled.

So it should be surprising that Becket's name is not widely recognized or revered today. Mid-century modern design is undergoing a welcome renaissance, but the architects we identify with it are mostly known for their residential design: Neutra, Eames, Lautner, Koenig, Ellwood—unlike Becket, whose work was largely civic, commercial, and corporate.

Why aren't Becket's monuments similarly celebrated? One possible reason: many Angelenos still harbor ambivalence about this era, which confirmed their city as a unique world capital. The era was the high watermark of suburbanization, constructing a city from a web of freeways, housing tracts, office buildings, and shopping malls—everything that has become fashionable to dismiss as "sprawl." The polycentric city of today, woven together from hubs in Santa Monica, Westwood, Century City, Burbank, Downtown, Costa Mesa, and elsewhere, was cemented during this era, with the considerable architectural aid of Becket. Despite the fact that suburbanization is Los Angeles' natural inheritance, we

Santa Anas

prefer to live it, not think about it.

Another reason: Becket's very success. His buildings captured the personality of mid-century L.A. so well that they served as templates for many other buildings. His pioneering planning ideas were so influential that they established a norm. Becket buildings have blended with the pattern and texture of our postwar suburban metropolis so seamlessly that we take them utterly for granted. The suburban shopping mall set in its parterre of parking was pioneered by Bullock's Pasadena; the suburban civic design of Becket, Gruen, Pereira, A.C. Martin's prototype malls adapted modern space and uses with an abstracted neoformalism of tapering columns and curving façades.

A fresh look at Welton Becket's career and influence would not only help us to understand his era, but ours. We would not be the city we are today if this era had not set us on a course with its innovations, its reach, its scale.

What was the Becket style? Modern, clean, well organized, on budget. At their best they could be as elegantly composed as a Neutra building (Parker Center) or as original as a Lautner building (the Capitol Records cylinder). With a prolific output and an enormous staff—in the 1960s Welton Becket and Associates was the largest architecture firm in the nation—not all the office's work was as fresh or innovative as these. The daunting challenge to large-scale corporate architecture in the second half of the 20th century was to supply industry and government with the shelter and symbols they needed, while avoiding blandness and oppressive size. Welton Becket and Associates did not always escape those pitfalls. But measured by the best of their buildings, Becket's record bears comparison to any other large firm in the nation.

Becket had arrived in Los Angeles from his native Seattle at the right time. The multi-centered metropolis, the commercial suburban city that he would help articulate, was already taking root in the early 1930s.

Los Angeles fancied itself, even then, as the City of Tomorrow. Becket and partner Walter Wurdeman's winning competition entry for the 1935 Pan Pacific Auditorium captured the city's optimism and progressivism. The masterful Streamline Moderne composition was instantly popular. Its fluid pylons seemed a portal to the future. It was Becket's first iconic design.

With the end of World War II, the entire architectural profession realized that the face of the American city was about to change dramatically. No one yet knew exactly how.

But Wurdeman and Becket (renamed Welton Becket and Associates after Wurdeman died unexpectedly in 1949) set out to rethink almost every genre of urban architecture: shopping centers, workplaces, recreation venues, hospitals, housing, education, culture. On the way they reorganized the traditional architecture office to handle the increasingly large and complex projects that governments and developers demanded.

Their 1947 Bullocks Pasadena was one of the first department stores in the nation to step out of the traditional downtown and into suburbia. But the old, formal downtown department stores, modeled on palazzos, had to be reconfigured for the larger, open sites in low-rise suburbia, had to be restyled for its casual lifestyles, had to be reshaped to deal with the automobile. New forms followed new functions.

Mastering the Late Moderne style as they had the Pan Pacific's Streamline Moderne, Wurdeman and Becket oriented Bullocks' main entries to the auto parking terraces (elegantly landscaped by Ruth Shellhorn) in an innovative and fully realized design. Becket followed Bullocks Pasadena with a succession of shopping centers evolving the type: Stonestown in San Francisco, Bullocks Westwood and Northridge, Seibu (now the Peterson Automotive Museum), malls such as Del Amo and Fashion Island, and literally dozens of others across the continent.

The modern workplace? The Prudential Center on Wilshire, the General Petroleum building downtown, Capitol Records in Hollywood, Parker Center in the civic center explored different solutions to the need for flexibility in dynamic industries. They lead to Welton Becket office towers from Houston to Bartlesville to Oakland, for Ford, Kaiser, Phillips Petroleum, and Equitable.

Americans began vacationing in droves in the 1950s, and Welton Becket (with Pereira & Luckman and Williams) designed the LAX jetport. Becket designed modern tourist towns at Canyon Village at Yellowstone for the National Park Service, Hawaiian Village in Honolulu for Henry J. Kaiser, and hotels at Walt Disney World in Orlando and Las Vegas.

Though he and Wurdeman began their partnership designing Tudor mansions for movie stars in the 1930s, they also helped to design the classic ranch-style tract houses of Panorama City (idealized in their 1943 House of Tomorrow on Wilshire Blvd.) in 1950 for developers Fritz Burns and Henry Kaiser. As master planner for UCLA, Welton Becket and Associates designed much of the extensive Medical Center, dormitories, the student center, many classroom buildings, and Pauley Pavilion.

In the ultimate assertion of the multicentric city, Becket planned Century City, converting the old movie factory into a new type of downtown. To fulfill the cultural and recreational needs of the new city, he built the Memorial Sports Arena (where JFK was nominated for president in 1960), the Cinerama Dome, and finally the Music Center. Magnificently modern, the Dorothy Chandler Pavilion's walls swell outward and its columns taper tautly as if responding to unseen forces within. Its self-confident, inventive ornament, and its cascading neo-baroque staircases express the assured opulence of American mid-century might.

The Music Center is a shopping center of culture. As a public space in the heart of downtown, the big boxes of the Chandler and Ahmanson linked by arcades, plazas, and fountains mirror the shopping malls of the suburban metropolis. The similarity (seen also in Pereira's L.A. County Museum of Art) is hardly coincidental. Welton Becket was, after all, an architect who knew how to design successful shopping centers—the large public spaces and de facto town plazas of Southern Californians.

Like the Agora in ancient Athens, Les Halles in Paris, Fifth Avenue in New York, the buildings of the public marketplace have always been as important to great cities as cathedrals and palaces. Los Angeles architects adapted that urban constant to the 20th-century city of housing tracts, regional malls, and freeways.

Becket played a significant role shaping the region and the era behind the scenes too. None proved more consequential than when he advised his friend and Holmby Hills neighbor Walt Disney to abandon an architect's design for his new amusement park in Anaheim. Design it yourself with your movie studio staff, architect Becket urged the moviemaker. Given the impact of Disneyland in planning, suburbanization, and culture, no advice more far-reaching was ever given in 20th-century architecture.

This brief list doesn't give full credit to Becket's entire work. Welton Becket and Associates spanned the global corporate culture (Hiltons in Havana, Cairo, and Manila, office buildings and shopping centers from Newport Beach to New Jersey) before Becket died in 1969.

Yet for all the national and international scope of his work, Becket remained a Los Angeles architect. From the beginning of his career, he was designing the City of Tomorrow. He mastered the fundamental forces that shaped the 20th-century city: technology, commerce, and popular culture. The high art modernists who made it into the history books addressed the first issue successfully, but rarely the second and third. Without aspirations to high art, Becket responded to these urban forces with pragmatism and innovation. City leaders were in philosophical agreement with him; note that the Music Center patrons did not need to and did not choose to reach to New York or Europe to tap an architect of sufficient ability to conjure up a suitable landmark.

Today, Los Angeles can begin to rediscover this complex, sometimes vexing, but undeniable part of the history that made us who we are. We can face Becket's faith in Los Angeles as we begin to see the interplay emerging between the 35-year-old Music Center and its new neighbor: Frank Gehry's Disney Hall doesn't rebuke or ignore the Music Center; its curves respond to and enhance it, creating a stronger unified cultural center atop Bunker Hill. This is a superb example of how new architecture can acknowledge our past (and our identity) as we move along new paths.

Growing from a two-man office into the largest in the world, prepared to handle any project of any size and any complexity, Becket's career rode the trajectory of 20th-century Los Angeles. Today, 35 years after his death, Welton Becket's legacy is still inescapable as one cruises the region. His contributions have not faded. They have simply become so integral to the fabric of the city that we no longer notice them.

But we should. We cannot afford to take the buildings of Imperial California for granted. We cannot afford to deface a seminal landmark of suburbia like Bullocks Pasadena. In these buildings lie the key to the balances, the forces, the character, the urban rules—whether we approve of them or not—of our suburban metropolis. Architects must understand the tradition and legacy that lies behind the organic life of the city. In understanding them lies the workable solutions to the urban challenges of today.

Adapted from remarks delivered at "Built by Becket: Centennial Celebration," March 4, 2003, organized/hosted by the L.A. Conservancy Modern Committee and previously published in the accompanying catalog/driving guide.

Buildings Demanded It

An Interview with Richard Bradshaw

Russell Fortmeyer

LA Forum Newsletter
Summer 2015

Architecture in Los Angeles never claims to be about engineering. This is not an engineer's city in the manner of New York or London, where architecture routinely calls on engineers to solve big problems of height or urban connectivity. A lack of engineering heroics may explain why Los Angeles hasn't bothered to claim much of a Brutalist legacy—at least in the terms we may associate with Reyner Banham and the Smithsons, to keep it simple. To this day, the city has no solidly enduring, locally established engineering firms outside of aerospace and infrastructure. The engineering ideas behind the city's architecture, or what the trendy may call engineering's "innovation," have mostly remained invisible, with a smattering of examples we may now reverse engineer as Brutalist exceptions. Sometimes we owe that to the subjugation of engineering within an architect's office (think Ellerbe Becket, now part of AECOM) or to the starts and stops of a local economy fueled mostly by production housing (think Eli Broad). Even architecture's literature—already threadbare when it comes to engineering—is scattershot, if not downright unreliable, on Los Angeles engineering.

The structural engineer Richard Bradshaw may be the most well-known and influential engineer the city has produced—although, out of his penchant for underplaying his hand, he would certainly disagree. His lack of heroics aligns perfectly with the Los Angeles sensibility. Bradshaw's best-known project, the Theme Building at Los Angeles International Airport (1961), owes its success largely to its structure. He's contributed to so many of the essential mid-century houses we celebrate that Bradshaw struggles to remember them all. But his key contributions to engineering he can recall in detail. The LA Forum's Russell Fortmeyer asked the long-retired engineer, who now lives in Northridge, to reconsider two of his structures in light of the Brutalist conceptions of structural expression, functional clarity, and material transparency: the University of California Los Angeles' Pauley Pavilion (1965), by architect Welton Becket; and the Tarzana Ice Rink (1960), designed with architect Carl Maston.

Russell Fortmeyer: I wanted to start talking about the Pauley Pavilion as an example of Brutalism because its structure, at least in its original incarnation, is so clearly celebrated on both the interior and exterior.

Richard Bradshaw: In that case, I have a great affinity for Brutalism, because what I've worked on my whole life is to make the structure express the form of the building. I love that, and it's what I tried to do, and did do, in many cases. In that case, I am a Brutalist.

RF: Can you tell you me about working with Welton Becket on that project?

RB: The structure, when I was called in on it, was a basketball pavilion, so therefore the general size and shape of it was set. It was to be a rectangle around 300 feet wide and 400 feet long, which in those days was a good-sized structure. What immediately jumped into my mind was that it was a natural for a space frame, which is a two-way grid of trusses. The problem with space frames up until that point was that everybody recognized the greatness of them, but they couldn't analyze them because before computers, we had to analyze it by hand. People like Lockheed had mainframes, but they were changing rapidly at the time and what they had owned became obsolete. The aerospace industry had these white elephants that cost millions of bucks and probably had the same capacity as my personal computer today. One of those computers had fallen into the hands of some enterprising guys in El Segundo, and they were looking for things to work on, so I took it to them, and they said yes, they could analyze it. I designed, maybe not my first space frame, but close to it, and at the time it was the biggest in the United States.

RF: Was that a challenge, to design something so large and relatively new?

RB: The real challenge from the engineering point of view at the time was there were no fabrication outfits around that were making beautiful pieces to fit together—tubular structural members that fit into balls and clean joints, where today space frames are customized and quite beautiful. For the Pauley Pavilion, all I had to work with were regular structural members that were used for everything from bridges to buildings. Making wide flanges fit to make a connection that wasn't 8 or 10 feet long was difficult, and that's what I spent a lot of time doing, making it so the 8 members could terminate close together to the point where they could converge and not make a big, messy connection that would visually dominate everything.

RF: Is the strength of a space frame, then, that all of the forces of the members are resolved at those connections, so then it distributes those loads across all of the members?

RB: With an ordinary truss, it's a statically determinate object, meaning it has no redundant members. Every member is carrying the load, and that's all the members you have. With a space frame, you put in a whole bunch of members meeting at points in three dimensions instead of two, and the trick is to find how to make all of the members share in the load, so you get a very efficient joint. Until you had a computer to solve the simultaneous equations, of which you may get thousands, it was just impossible for humans to do it. It's a beautiful structural form, and you have a whole lot of extra members—or "redundant" is the engineering term for it—so I was able to take advantage of the times as they were to make it a space frame. Later on, the space frame guys went into business on their own doing nothing but space frames and developed their own structural shapes. I think now you get between 8 and 12 members meeting at a point.

RF: Was that the first project in which you used a computer?

RB: I think it was, yes. Of course, today, it's very clumsy compared to the refinements they have available now, but I loved it because I always wanted to use a space frame because they are so darned efficient. Whenever you do a new structural design or form, you're sure to run into some kind of problem you didn't anticipate. It comes with the territory. We had ours on the Pauley Pavilion. There were painters on the top level of seats that were painting the structure, and they had big pails of paint. Then they sent up welders, and, of course, the welders set the pails of paint on fire. The flames boiled up close to where the space frame came down toward the seats at the top edge, so they melted one of the members. And this presents an impossible predicament, because you can't just go in and take it out and put a new member in, because it won't be carrying any load.

RF: So you'd have to somehow "reset" the structure from no loads back to a fully loaded condition after you replace that member?

RB: But then you'd still not know what you had, because how do you shore the structure at each of the node points where the members intersected—there must have been 50 or 60—but how do you jack them all up so nothing is carrying any load? I thought, *What am I going to do with this thing?* I finally decided, to hell with it. It's a redundant member, they are all redundant members, so I'm never going to know what the new loads are, so we took the warped member out and replaced it with a new one, and at least it looks good. This is an important point in engineering: you don't really need to know the forces in something you're designing as long as you know they are less than some other design that would have higher loads that you know the answer for. I will never know what the forces are now, because when that one member is warped and changes its forces, every member in the structure changes its load. I know the structure is safe, but I don't know what the loads are.

RF: The space frame then sits on top of the concrete plinth and the shell of the seats, with all of the loads transferred into the concrete and foundation?

RB: Once you get down from the space frame reactions, there is plenty of concrete around, and there's no trick to get that to work.

RF: If you had a concrete base around the court, why not do a concrete shell for a roof?

RB: A concrete shell could have been done, but it would have been more expensive, materially, than this light steel framing. And I say it could have been done, with enough effort on the part of the structural designer—that's me—but you've got to be careful in using a shell in that you don't want to just say, "Oh I

have a structure here and I'm going to cover it and I want to use a shell."
Sometimes a shell is not appropriate. You cannot always get the right
combination of intersecting shapes to be efficient on a certain base.

RF: The underside of the stepped seating—the bottom of the slab—relies
on the quality of construction that you get in terms of the exposed finish of the
concrete. How did you and Becket manage to achieve something that could
be exposed? Was there a discussion about how it would be finished?

RB: I don't think either of us gave much thought to it. If Becket gave much
thought to it, I would have been brought in to weigh in on the formwork, but
I'm guessing they might have put a coat of plaster over it to make it smooth.
But I don't really know. That's the first time I've ever thought about it.

RF: Let me then ask you about the Tarzana Ice Rink, since the way it was
constructed is almost a perfect example of Brutalist architecture in the way
it was originally conceived.

RB: You used the right word: perfect. That was the most perfect building I
ever worked on because no one else had anything to do with it, including the
architect, which was Carl Maston. The job was for a daredevil ice skating jumper
who would jump over automobiles and people, and he wanted an ice rink so he
could start making some permanent money. He didn't have much money, so Carl
said it was going to be around a 100-foot span and around 200 feet long, and
he wanted something that was a feature, as opposed to a box, but the client had
no money.

RF: Can you describe the shape of the building—particularly the torus-shaped
shell roof panels?

RB: The shape is perfect for the building. As an ice rink you don't need a box
shape, you need an oval. You don't need a level roof in one direction, you can make
it slope down—in fact you want it to so the sun can't come in the ends. The torus,
which is defined as one circle being rotated like a tire of a car, a donut shape, is
actually modified. I knew I wanted to precast it to make it economical, so I knew
these precast pieces would have to stand there a while until they are joined
together. Once they are joined together, they are as strong as can be. I wanted to
corrugate it, to make it strong when each member was standing there by itself.

RF: Why not make the shell panels flat and smooth?

RB: As arches, the only way I could make them strong enough to support
themselves on their own was to corrugate them. If they had been flat, they would
have collapsed. There are two identical arches leaning together at the top that
will support each other as an arch as long as the arch has depth. If it was just a
flat shell, it would have been only 3 inches thick and spanning like 50 feet to the
center—it would just buckle somewhere. If it's corrugated, it can no longer be
a true torus because a torus consists of two circles surrounding each other,
where you get a smooth shape like a tire, not that this matters. I wanted to cast
them in the parking lot, so I had them dig to the corrugated shape; they poured
concrete over it for a base, and then poured the concrete panels inside. If you
want to cast a cylinder three-inches thick, the radius of the inner portion will be
whatever you decided, but then if you're going to cast another one on top of
that, it's going to be plus three inches, and then each successive one will creep
another three inches, and none of them will be the same shape.

RF: How did you solve that?

RB: If you were casting cylindrical shells, one over the other, say the radius is 60 inches, then your tendency would be to make the screed shape you pull along the top 60 inches also. But if you did that, you'd get this creep that I mentioned before. As long as the creep is of a tolerance you can live with, you don't care because you just have a shell with varying thickness. As you pile them up, each one is identical to the one below it, so when you pick them up and lean them against one another, each of the corrugations are exactly alike, but the variability is in the thickness. It may have varied as much as half an inch, which you'd never read architecturally. At the bottom, it fit into a serpentine groove in a continuous, conventional foundation. It was locked in, and then we could fill it in with concrete later on. I would have loved to put glass into it between the panels, but that would have been expensive. I think I was paid 4 percent of the contract, and I think I got $4,000 for it, but of course this was back in the 1960s.

RF: So the real efficiencies in the project are the concrete and the fact you were doing all fabrication on-site?

RB: And there was no formwork. But an interesting thing happened—there's always an interesting thing. The architect had called for some kind of paint on the concrete to reflect sunlight because it was in Tarzana, which is hot, and it has an ice floor. The paint didn't work right. The day I was out there after it opened, people were skating around and were wet because the ice kept melting on top. They had to get a new material to coat the structure—the sun going through three inches of concrete didn't really mean much. It was painted on the inside, so it looked uniform. Then I got sued on the job. It wasn't much, but the contractor took it to court, and I think it ended up costing me something, so I ended up doing the job for nothing. For every shell I did—I did about 100—every single one, I lost money on.

RF: Why is that? Contractors aren't well-versed enough in shell design to build them?

RB: Objectively, it's a moot question. Can you ask an engineer to determine all of those things when the contractor is going to shop the thing around to get the best price? Should you mandate things like erection and construction sequences, or should it be the contractor?

RF: In Los Angeles architecture, from the 1950s to the 1970s, it seems like there was a lot more opportunity for engineers like yourself to contribute to buildings where the structure expressed itself quite prominently. And then I think things shifted in the 1980s to an architecture of formal exuberance, but a much less pronounced role for structure. Why do you think the architects you worked with allowed structure to become so prominent?

RB: It certainly wasn't Carl Maston. When the Ice Rink was all done, when I talked to Carl about the torus, he just blanked out, he didn't give a shit. All of his stuff was all straight lines—he and I were the most incompatible architect and engineer that maybe ever existed—but then he won an AIA award for the project. A. Quincy Jones was the president of the AIA at the time, and I was doing A. Q.'s work, and most of the architects knew it wasn't Carl Maston's work, so the question came up that maybe they should make some recognition for Bradshaw for this, but they decided the award was only for architects, and so Carl got it.

Santa Anas

Anyway, this epoch, when we were doing space frames and shells, was the golden opportunity for engineers to step forward and have their design become the architecture of the building. Once shells went out, they just collapsed all of a sudden.

RF: So to speak. They didn't actually collapse, but fell out of favor.

RB: Yes, bad word. But when shells ended, in my opinion—and I'm the only guy who has ever given an opinion that has any value to it—it is because they were beaten to death. An architect would get a job and say, "I have to make a shell out of it." That's what happened to the airport [LAX]. Pereira was the architect, and it started out all shells. The only guy they could find in L.A. that was versatile in shells was me, but City Hall was so hostile to the schematics they saw that they decided not to go to shells. So the thing that finally lasted that had any sense of design was the Theme Building. Pereira just rolled over and played with them, so maybe he wasn't that committed to shells. Today, shells are still being done by Zaha Hadid—she does some pretty wild shells—and the Japanese and Chinese use them, but it's now just another form of structure. Once they went out, though, the tendency to make structure be the architecture declined a great deal. It has never really come back, although there are many opportunities for them. It wasn't so much that engineers were pushing it, but that the buildings demanded it.

RF: But even something like an office building, of which you did a considerable number, used to have a pronounced structure, whereas so many of them today conceal structure behind façade elements. The skyscrapers from the 1980s have completely hidden structures.

RB: I don't think it was an architecture of determination, I think it was just that shells were so dominant in determining the architecture of a building that we remember them. It wasn't that architects got tired of structure determining the architecture; it was that it wasn't that easy or economical to do anymore. Incidentally, the engineers really didn't have much to do with the dominance of shells. When I went into shells, I had very few engineers who paid any attention to what I was doing. Some of the more advanced ones, like professors in colleges, followed my work very closely, but mostly their attitude was, *Why are you trying to rock the boat with those crazy shapes, you're not going to make money on them*, which was certainly true. I just gave up on the engineers, ignored them, and went off on my own because I became fascinated with shells. So the engineers deserve very little credit for the proliferation of shells.

Mock Up:
The Persistence
of Beige

Tom Marble

After the city,
this (is how we live)
Pamphlet 4
2008

EXT. RSF HEADQUARTERS - DAY

The early morning light glints off the glass façade.

INT. WAR ROOM - DAY

The walls of the room are covered on three sides with aerial
photographs taken across much of Rancho San Felipe. The fourth
wall is a pin-up space filled with architectural renderings.

    NAT (V.O.)
This is the War Room. The heart and soul of the Architecture
& Planning division of the Rancho San Felipe Company. These
guys are presidents and vice presidents of everything related
to the physical planning of the Ranch: architecture, landscape
architecture, community design, planning, you name it. The
guy standing is Lloyd Butler, the President of Community
Design. He was part of the team that first produced the Rancho
San Felipe General Plan in the sixties.

Tall and lanky, LLOYD BUTLER, 64, presents the drawings.

    LLOYD
We've got the same Santa Barbara slash Palos Verdes theme
going on here, in the community elements.

Lloyd points to an entry gate with associated guardhouse.

    JACK
Remind me how a guardhouse is a community element.

    LLOYD
Fuck off, Jack.

The eight men around the room chuckle. Jack smiles.

> LLOYD
> You see it here in the entry to the neighborhood center. Here at the pool house. And, of course, the golf clubhouse itself. Any thoughts?

V.P. of Landscape Architecture, Hugh Macintyre, 41, round at the corners, speaks.

> HUGH
> How does the landscape figure in?

> LLOYD
> We're sticking with El Jefe's beach palette: Monterey Cypress, Italian Cypress, your occasional Phoenix canariensis; then Carissa, Myoporum, Ceanothus, etc. Anyone else?

Lloyd turns to Nat who, grinning, is lost in thought, sketching classical volutes on a legal pad.

> LLOYD (CONT'D)
> What about you?

All eyes turn to Nat. He looks up.

> NAT
> Me?

> JACK
> Gentlemen, meet the newest addition to A&P, Nat Fleming. V.P. of Architecture. He's not from Harvard like all you other fuckers, but he is Ivy League.

> LLOYD
> I hear you're the Mr. Fancy Pants L.A. architect. You must have an opinion.

Nat squints, reading the pinned-up drawings.

> NAT
> What style is the architecture?

> LLOYD
> Santa Barbara slash Palos Verdes. Like I said.

> NAT
> I don't really know what that means. Is it George Washington Smith meets, I don't know, Wallace Neff?

Lloyd looks at Jack.

> LLOYD
> Is he kidding?

> JACK
> (amused)
> It's, you know, Contemporary Traditional.

> HUGH
> Contempo-Trad: the local vernacular. Spanish Colonial, more or less

            NAT (V.O.)
I should have stopped talking, but these guys were patronizing
me.

            NAT
Spanish Colonial, really? Is it literally the Presidio complex
in Santa Barbara? Or is it a second-generation interpretation,
like what Neff and those guys were doing? I mean, it looks to
me like it could even be third or fourth generation.

            LLOYD
This is the shit El Jefe likes. If it offends your
architectural taste, I can live with that.

            NAT
But it might be interesting to go back to the original and…

            JACK
"Those who repeat the past are condemned to forget it."

All eyes turn to Jack.

            LLOYD
Who said that?

            JACK
I think it was Santana.

            NAT
I'm just saying, if we're at all interested in our place in
architectural history…

            LLOYD
                    (irritated, interrupting)
Look. I've been doing this shit for years. And in all humility
I can say I know more about architecture than most architects.
I know what its highest best function is. And at the end of
the day it's not about creating a (gesturing with his fingers)
"place in architectural history." It's about making a place
where people feel comfortable. It's not about challenging them
or making them feel stupid because they don't know the past.
Here, the past is history. Here, we live in the present.

Nat nods absently.

            NAT (V.O.)
Another mental note.

                    CUT TO:

INT. NAT'S OFFICE - DAY

Nat is at his computer, no longer grinning.

Jack pops his head through the open door. He hands Nat a sheet
of paper.

            JACK
This is a list of construction meetings I'd like you to
attend. To make sure shit gets built the way it's designed.

                NAT
          I'm still doing Design Review?

                JACK
          Of course. Design Guidelines, too. But this is where I really
          need help. On the front lines. So the Money Guys don't keep
          changing everything in the field. You up for it?

                NAT
          If you think I am.

Jack assesses Nat's mood.

                JACK
          Hey, you handled yourself great back there.

                NAT
          Really?

                JACK
          Don't worry about it. Those guys aren't used to people asking
          those kinds of questions. It was actually refreshing.

                NAT
          So you agree with me?

                JACK
          Let's not get carried away. You still have a lot to learn.

                NAT
          Like what?

Jack smiles.

                JACK
          When I was at Berkeley in the sixties, there was this guru
          character who said something I'll never forget.

                NAT
          What was that?

                JACK
          "Before you can change the world, you have to change your
          mind."

                NAT
          What is that supposed to mean?

                JACK
          Think about it.

And Jack is gone. Nat's face bends, attempting to make sense of his
comment.

CUT TO:

MONTAGE OVER MUSIC:

EXT. TWIN OAKS RETAIL - DAY

In the middle of nowhere, an L-shaped building is being framed around a parking lot at the intersection of two land highways. A construction trailer is nearby.

INT. TWIN OAKS CONSTRUCTION TRAILER - DAY

Mark Lambert and Nat are the only suits sitting at a table of contractors.

Mark gets up and goes to a model on a side table, and removes the top half of a clock tower. His gestures seem to say, "See, it's not so bad."

Nat stands, grabs the top of the tower, and puts it back on the model. He then sits as if to say, "The tower stays. End of discussion."

INT. NAT'S APARTMENT - NIGHT

Nat and Stephanie are in the kitchen. Nat is cooking up something in a large saucepan. He tastes it. Nods in approval. He dips the spoon again and feeds it to Stephanie. She spits it out in mock horror.

Nat isn't sure if she's kidding. Until she starts cracking up. She smiles. He kisses her, clears the dining table, and sets her on it, all without breaking their lip lock.

EXT. LOS ROBLES INDUSTRIAL PARK - DAY

Several tilt-up concrete slabs create a hollow, deck-of-cards complex of buildings in an isolated parcel. The façade of one of the buildings is divided into seven equal-sized bays, all painted different shades of beige.

Nat stands with Dave Bacci and the contractors looking at all the different colors. Nat points to one. The contractors nod. Bacci points to a different one.

Nat shakes his head. He points again to the one he likes. He makes eye contact with the head contractor who nods, writing in his notebook. Bacci fidgets.

INT. NAT'S APARTMENT - NIGHT

Nat and Stephanie are in the bath. It's a tight, formed plastic tub/ shower combo, but they don't seem to mind. Nat washes her back, scrubbing it with a sponge.

Then Nat reaches around with his sponge, washing her breasts. But it tickles her and she convulses. He takes the opportunity to tickle her more; she finally stops him by turning and kissing him.

The kissing escalates.

END MONTAGE.

EXT. EL ALISAL APARTMENT COMMUNITY - DAY

With just the belowground parking garage complete, the scope of
this massive complex is evident. On the edge of the parking structure
is a construction trailer.

INT. El ALISAL CONSTRUCTION TRAILER - DAY

Drawings of the apartment building are on the table.

Nat points to the roofs.

    NAT
All these pitches need to come down. Four in twelve maximum.
Personally, I'd prefer three in twelve.

Tim Gripp snickers.

    NAT
What?

    GRIPP
You know, of course, that the Chief likes six in twelve.

    NAT
Trust me. When he sees this, he'll love it.

    GRIPP
Just don't say I didn't warn you.

    NAT
Hey, just because he owns the company doesn't mean he's always
right.

    GRIPP
                    (glancing to the others)
Hey, good point.

Vic Henderson, 50, the fireplug of a head contractor, offers his
two cents.

    HENDERSON
Yeah. No, maybe you should tell him that.

    GRIPP
How do you define career suicide?

    NAT
No way. The Chief likes creative conflict. He thinks it makes
for a better product.

Gripp looks over to Henderson, drawing his index finger across
his throat.

CUT TO:

INT. NAT'S APARTMENT - NIGHT

Nat and Stephanie are on the couch spooning, watching TV. Nat flips channels.

He goes from Top Chef to Law & Order to a Lakers game.

Stephanie turns to Nat.

        STEPHANIE
You're not serious.

        NAT
You don't like basketball?

        STEPHANIE
Somehow I don't see you as the jock type.

        NAT
I was pretty good at sports. Back in eighth grade.

        STEPHANIE
Eighth grade?

        NAT
Sure. What I especially liked about it was being in the
moment, in three dimensions. You have to totally be aware of
where your body is in relation to all your teammates, the
opposing team, and the goal.

        STEPHANIE
I swear, you architects are borderline autistic.

        NAT
What do you mean?

        STEPHANIE
You may be brilliant with space but you have no idea what's
really going on. Especially with people.

        NAT
Gee. Thanks.

        STEPHANIE
No—I mean, not us. Even though there is no us.

        NAT
                          (smiling)
Of course not.

        STEPHANIE
But I'm betting it's true. If you looked back on your past
relationships…

Nat mutes the TV, thinking about it.

239

> NAT
>
> Well, let's see. My marriage? Spatially, it was fantastic; but as far as communication goes, you're right. It was a disaster.

> STEPHANIE
>
> There are ways to communicate other than words.

> NAT
>
> Do tell.

They share a smile, then a kiss.

                              CUT TO:

EXT. RSF HEADQUARTERS — DAY

A thick fog enshrouds the glass box of a building.

INT. NAT'S OFFICE — DAY

Nat is at his computer, checking his email. No new messages. He logs off, stands.

INT. A&P — DAY

Nat walks up to Jack's secretary, Kim.

> NAT
>
> Hey, Kim is Jack…

Nat glances over. Through the window he sees three men in dark coats sitting in Jack's office. Jack looks up, sees Nat, shrugs.

One of the men with his back turned glances back. It's Barrett Cash who, seeing Nat, smirks, then turns the blinds to close them.

> KIM
> (whispering)
> It's the police. They're talking to all the Direct Reports.

> NAT
>
> So, no Design Review today?

Kim shakes her head "no." Nat starts to leave.

> KIM
>
> Jack did want you to do something for him.

> NAT
>
> Name it.

Kim hands him a notebook. Nat regards it quizzically.

                              CUT TO:

EXT. ACQUARIA — DAY

Nat waits outside a restaurant under construction. He holds the notebook, which he reviews quickly.

ANGLE ON:

The notebook is full of paint chips. He looks at a page labeled "Acquaria." It is a grid of two dozen or so paint chips, all shades of beige.

Nat squints at the notebook.

Howard Kohl's black Mercedes pulls up to the curb. The Chief exits the car and crosses the parkway with the easy athleticism of a young Sean Connery.

He approaches Nat with his right hand extended. Nat shakes it.

          KOHL
     Mr. Fleming.

          NAT
     Mr. Kohl.

Kohl nods to the restaurant.

          KOHL
     What do you think?

          NAT
     Sir?

          KOHL
     Acquaria. What color should we paint it?

Nat looks at the Chief. Then down to the notebook. Then back to the Chief.

          NAT
     I'm thinking beige.

Kohl grimaces, clearly irritated with Nat's humor.

          KOHL
     I've been going over the palette and I can't figure it out.
     Polished Oak looks too pink and Tavern Taupe looks too green.
     Something in between would work, but what?

The two men peruse the notebook.

          NAT
     Hmmm. How about Antique Bisque?

          KOHL
     Isn't that pinker than Polished Oak?

          NAT
     I guess. What about Daplin?

          KOHL
     Too yellow.

          NAT
     Camel Tan?

                    KOHL
          Even yellower.

                    NAT
          It's hard to say, sir. What do you usually use around here?

Kohl, sneering with distaste, looks up at Nat.

                    KOHL
          Son, you do not inspire confidence.

                    NAT
          Sir?

                    KOHL
          You don't seem capable of making a decision.

                    NAT
          I'm just trying to understand what you want.

                    KOHL
          I want you to pick a color.

                    NAT
          Personally? I think you should go with something other than
          beige. Or tan. Whatever these all are.

                    KOHL
          What would you suggest?

                    NAT
          I don't know. Something more dynamic. To tell you the truth
          almost anything would make this building pop. Especially next
          to all the crap around it.

                    KOHL
                              (flustered)
          Just give me a paint name. That's all I'm asking.

                    NAT
          From these choices? I don't think I can. I mean, I could
          always go back and put together a new palette.

Kohl eyes Nat, grinding his teeth. He checks his watch.

                    KOHL
          Have Jack call me when you see him.

Kohl heads back to his car.

                    NAT (V.O.)
          This is when I was sure I'd blown it.

Nat panics. He glances quickly to the notebook.

                    NAT
          Boulevard might work…

                    KOHL
          Good day, Mr. Fleming.

Kohl enters his car and speeds off.

Nat deflates. He closes his notebook.

                NAT (V.O.)
      But then again, things happen for a reason.

                            CUT TO:

INT. OFFICE DIVISION - DAY

Nat and Jack emerge from the elevator. They walk with purpose down
the drab corporate hall lined with photos of drab corporate office
buildings.

                NAT
      What did they ask you?

                JACK
      I don't know. Some bullshit theory. They definitely have a
      hard-on for El Jefe.

                NAT
      Why?

                JACK
      Who the fuck knows? They find a dead body on the ranch and
      immediately they go after the Chief? Like that makes sense.

Nat opens the door for Jack. Jack starts in, then stops.

                JACK
      You met with him, right?

                NAT
      Yeah.

                JACK
      You picked a color?

                NAT
      Not quite.

                JACK
      Why not?

                NAT
      The colors were all bad. He definitely wanted you to call him,
      though.

Jack scowls at Nat before disappearing into the conference room.

INT. OFFICE CONFERENCE ROOM - DAY

The room is impeccably tasteful, clearly designed by a corporate
interiors firm. There is no pin-up space, just a stainless-steel rail
upon which sits two boards.

There are three other men. Dave Bacci is flanked by two of his
Minions, 30s, both wearing bespoke dark suits with expensive ties
and couture glasses.

Jack and Nat take seats opposite them.

>   JACK
> What are we looking at?

>   BACCI
> Gillette Technology. As you know, it's 16 buildings in
> clusters of four each surrounding parking groves.

>   JACK
> Where's the site plan?

>   BACCI
> We've already finalized that. Today we're looking at building
> articulation.

>   JACK
> But I need the site plan for reference.

>   BACCI
> If we could focus on the decision at hand.

>   JACK
> Why can't we see a site plan?

Jack looks to Nat for support. Nat shrugs blankly.

Bacci stands and goes to the board.

>   BACCI
> This is the product. Taste-Mod Flex-Tech, of course. With the
> colors Mr. Fleming approved.

Nat glances over to Jack who stares at the boards, squinting.

>   JACK
> Why are the windows so small?

>   BACCI
> The windows aren't the issue, Jack.

>   JACK
> I don't care. How did we get to the decision on the windows?

Bacci nods to one of the Minions who slides over a sheet of paper
with tables.

>   MINION 1
> Here is a record of each decision made, why, and when.

>   MINION 2
> If you recall, the size of the windows was determined by a
> complex algorithm taking into account structural requirements,
> the cost of reinforcing the openings, and the need to
> implement standard window sizes.

                    JACK
          I thought we agreed on 50 percent; this looks more like 35.

                    MINION 2
          Thirty-four, actually.

                    JACK
          That's totally unacceptable.

                    BACCI
          It is what it is.

                    JACK
          No. It's not what it's not. And it's definitely not 34 percent.

                    BACCI
          Jack, that ship has sailed. I've already run this by the Chief.

Jack just stares at him.

                    JACK
          What, do you actually think you can make design decisions
          without me?

                    BACCI
          It's not what I think that matters, is it, Jack?

                    JACK
          You got that right.

Jack and Bacci lock eyes. Nat diffuses the tension.

                    NAT
          What are we looking at today?

Minion 1 slides over two 11×17 booklets with pages of facade
renderings, which Jack and Nat flip through.

                    MINION 1
          Last time you said you wanted to see more articulation in the
          building panels.

                    BACCI
          Each tilt-up panel is 20 feet wide. We asked the architects
          to come up with a few ideas of how we might give it the base-
          middle-top differentiation you felt was necessary.

                    JACK
          What are these lines?

                    BACCI
          That's the articulation.

                    JACK
          I can barely see it.

                    MINION 1
          After several cost-benefit analyses, we determined that we have
          three-quarters of an inch of concrete to play with. These
          schemes take advantage of that.

                    JACK
          Wow. A full three-quarters?

                    BACCI
          I know it doesn't sound like much, but you can score the
          panels to cast shadows like this.
                              (flipping the page)
          Which makes the bottom feel—what was it you said? Rusticated?

                    JACK
          No. This isn't enough.

                    BACCI
          Which isn't enough?

                    JACK
          None of them. I'm sorry, but I want more. More windows, more
          articulation, more, more.

                    BACCI
          No, I'm the one who's sorry, Jack. The construction schedule
          is already set. If you don't—today, right now—pick one of
          these options, I'll be forced to do it myself.

Jack stares down Bacci who does not flinch.

                    NAT (V.O.)
          Something was wrong. These guys usually buckled under when
          Jack confronted them. But that day they were solid, totally
          in control.

Jack stands, grabbing a handout.

                    JACK
          We'll see about that.

INT. SEVENTH FLOOR LOBBY — DAY

Jack vaults out of the elevator. Nat follows.

Jack walks right up to Kohl classically beautiful Girl Friday,
GLADYS, 40.

                    JACK
          Gladys, hi. I need to see the Chief.

                    GLADYS
          He's in a meeting, Mr. Weber. Would you like to wait?

Jack, frustrated, sighs loudly. He sits in one of the Barcelona
chairs by the window. Nat sits by him.

Suddenly the door to Howard Kohl's suite opens. Out strides Stephanie
Talbott-Kohl who almost collides with Jack as he erupts from his
seat.

                    STEPHANIE
          Excuse me!

Jack bolts into the office without acknowledging Stephanie.

                    GLADYS
          Mr. Weber!

Stephanie, amused by Jack's abruptness, glances to Gladys who shakes
her head.

                    STEPHANIE
          That man needs a leash.

Gladys smiles, nodding.

As Stephanie walks toward the elevator Nat smiles, starts to get up.
Stephanie subtly but firmly shakes her head "no." Nat obeys, settling
back in his seat.
Stephanie, in the elevator, waves to Gladys.

                    STEPHANIE
          Good night, Gladys.

                    GLADYS
          Good night, Mrs. Kohl.

As the elevator doors close, Gladys glances at Nat before returning
to her work.

Nat's face crumples, trying to make sense of what just happened.

Jack's voice BOOMS from within Howard Kohl's office.

                    JACK (O.S.)
          I just want to know what the hell is going on.

Nat stands. He pretends to look at the art, all contemporary: a
Damien Hirst dot painting, an Ed Ruscha photo series, a Jorge Pardo
ladder.

Nat makes his way closer to the office. He manages to get a glimpse
inside.

The two men talk quietly.

Nat approaches the door to hear them.

                    KOHL
          Sure, part of it's the economy. But part of it's you.

                    JACK
          Me?

                    KOHL
          You crossed the line, Jack

                    JACK
          How?

                    KOHL
          I don't think I can trust you anymore.

                    JACK
I'm the guy you should trust the most. I'm the only guy
protecting your vision. I'm the only guy who would break you
out of a third-world prison. All these other knuckleheads care
about is getting the hugest bonus possible.

                    KOHL
Motivation that I completely understand. But you. What are you
in this for?

                    JACK
What?

                    KOHL
Why are you here?

Gladys suddenly appears at Nat's side.

                    GLADYS
Excuse me.

                    NAT
Sorry.

Nat steps back. Kohl and Jack see Nat lurking outside. Jack scowls
at him.

                    GLADYS
Sir, I have the document you requested.

                    KOHL
Thanks. And Gladys?

                    GLADYS
Yes?

                    KOHL
Close the door behind you.

Gladys nods, handing the document to Kohl. She exits, pulling the
door behind her.

Gladys shoots Nat a hard look. He smiles insecurely.

                         CUT TO:

INT. A&P - NIGHT

Nat exits the elevator. The place is quiet. All of the secretaries
have gone home.

INT. NAT'S OFFICE - NIGHT

Nat takes off his coat, then plops down in his seat.

ANGLE ON:

Computer Screen.

Nat wakes his computer from sleep. His eyes light up.

                    NAT
          No way.

                    NAT (V.O.)
          Alison finally responded to my email.

ANGLE ON:

Email Message Box.

"Is this THE Nathanael Fleming? From high school?"

Nat hits REPLY. Types.

"It is indeed. So, how are you? Where are you?"

Nat hits SEND.

                         CUT TO:

INT. NAT'S APARTMENT - NIGHT

Nat, in his T-shirt and underwear, is on the computer.

ANGLE ON:

Email Message Box.

"I think I remember you. We dated a few times, right?"

                    NAT (V.O.)
          Maybe I had a different take on our quote unquote
          relationship...

Nat hits REPLY. Types.

"More than a few times. Remember the prom?"

Nat hits SEND.

INT. NAT'S OFFICE - DAY

Nat, in a suit and tie, is on the computer, annoyed.

ANGLE ON:

Email Message Box.

"The prom, really? I went with Turner Newton to my prom. Wait.
Did I go with you to yours?"

Nat hits reply. Types.

"Yes. I guess it meant more to me than you."

DELETE.

He shakes his head, fuming. He types again.

"That's total bullshit. As if you can't remember."

DELETE

Nat sighs. He pauses, thinking. He types again.

"I'm pretty sure it was you."

Nat grins. Hits SEND.

INT. NAT'S APARTMENT - MORNING

Nat, freshly showered, is on the computer again.

ANGLE ON:

Email Message Box.

"I was kidding. Of course I remember you. I remember everything."

Nat smiles.

   NAT (V.O.)
  ...then again, maybe not.

Biographies

Robert Adams is the Director of the Master of Science in Design and Health, and Associate Professor of Architecture at the University of Michigan, Taubman College of Architecture and Urban Planning, and the Stamps School of Art and Design. He is Chair of the University of Michigan Initiative on Disability Studies.

Rachel Allen is principal of Rachel Allen Architecture in Los Angeles. She was the 2002–2003 recipient of the Mercedes T. Bass Rome Prize in Architecture from the American Academy in Rome. She is currently the Mayor's Appointee to the Board of the Lincoln Heights Historic Preservation Overlay Zone.

Rob Berry is principal of Berry and Linné and Lecturer at the University of Southern California School of Architecture.

Aaron Betsky is a critic and curator of art, architecture, and design. He is currently Dean of the Frank Lloyd Wright School of Architecture. Previously he was Director of the Cincinnati Art Museum and the Netherlands Architecture Institute and Curator of Architecture and Design at the San Francisco Museum of Modern Art. Betsky directed the 11th Venice International Biennale of Architecture in 2008.

Richard Bradshaw is a retired structural engineer whose eponymous firm designed such landmarks as the Theme Building at LAX and the Terminal 1 rotunda of the McCarran International Airport in Las Vegas.

Central Office of Architecture was an architecture practice in Los Angeles led by architects Ron Golan, Eric A. Kahn, and Russell N. Thomsen.

Marco Cenzatti is Lecturer in Architecture and City and Regional Planning at the University of California, Berkeley, College of Environmental Design. His research and writings gravitate around the reciprocal influence of social relations producing space and space-shaping social relations.

John Chase was a writer, architect, and urban designer for the City of West Hollywood, California. Chase was editor, with Margaret Crawford and John Kaliski, of *Everyday Urbanism* (Monacelli, 1999). A selection of his essays on architecture, urbanism, and Los Angeles, among other things, are collected in the book *Glitter Stucco and Dumpster Diving* (Verso, 2000).

Margaret Crawford is Professor of Architecture at the University of California, Berkeley, College of Environmental Design. She teaches courses in the history and theory of architecture, urbanism, and urban history as well as urban design and planning studios focusing on small-scale urbanity and postmodern urbanism. Her research focuses on the evolution, uses, and meanings of urban space.

Chava Danielson is a principal of DSH // architecture in Los Angeles and Adjunct Professor in the Architecture/Landscape/Interiors Department at Otis College of Art and Design, where she teaches design studio and courses in urban history and theory.

Mike Davis is Professor Emeritus in the Department of Creative Writing at the University of California, Riverside. He is the author of *City of Quartz* (Verso, 1990) and *Ecology of Fear* (Metropolitan Books, 1998), among many other works. He was named a MacArthur Fellow in 1998.

Joe Day designs and writes in L.A., where he leads deegan-day design and teaches at SCI-Arc. He is the author of *Corrections & Collections: Architectures for Art and Crime* (Routledge, 2013). Day contributed a foreword to the new edition of Reyner Banham's *Los Angeles: Architecture of the Four Ecologies* (University of California, 2009).

Jessica Fleischmann is Founder and Creative Director of the graphic design studio Still Room. She is also a co-founder of X Artists' Books, a small art book press based in Los Angeles.

Steven Flusty is faculty at the Evergreen State College; adjunct professor, Department of Geography, faculty of Liberal Arts and Professional Studies, York University; and faculty of Graduate Studies, York University. His expertise include quotidian imperialisms, intermetropolitan geography, and *détournement*.

Russell Fortmeyer teaches at SCI-Arc and leads sustainable design for the L.A. office of the global engineering firm Arup.

Todd Gannon is an architect and writer. He is Professor and Section Head of Architecture at the Austin E. Knowlton School of Architecture at The Ohio State University. Gannon is the author of *Reyner Banham and the Paradoxes of High Tech* (Getty Research Institute, 2017).

Frank Gehry is an architect and a partner at Gehry Partners, LLP, in Los Angeles.

Thurman Grant is an architect and educator. He is an adjunct faculty member of the Interior Architecture Department at the Woodbury University School of Architecture. He is an editor of *Dingbat 2.0: The Iconic Los Angeles Apartment as Projection of a Metropolis* (DoppelHouse Press, 2016).

Alan Hess is the author of *Palm Springs Weekend* (Chronicle, 2001) and the architecture critic for the *San Jose Mercury News*. His landmark books include *Googie* (Chronicle, 1985) and *Viva Las Vegas* (Chronicle, 1993).

Craig Hodgetts is founding principal and creative director of Hodgetts + Fung. He is presently a professor at the UCLA Graduate School of Architecture and Urban Planning, and previously was a founding dean of the School of Design at the California Institute of the Arts.

Victor Jones is principal of Los Angeles–based design firm Fièvre + Jones, and a writer. The relationships between architecture, infrastructure, and the urban experience play a crucial role in both his creative and intellectual pursuits. Jones is the author of *Un pont apart / A Distant Bridge* (Métispresses, 2016).

Ted Kane is principal and design director of Kane Architecture and Urban Design. He is editor of the journal *Polar Inertia*, which focuses on contemporary urbanism and nomadic culture.

Sylvia Lavin is a critic, curator, and historian. She is the Director of the Critical Studies and MA/PhD programs in the Department of Architecture and Urban Design at UCLA. Lavin is the author of *Kissing Architecture* (Princeton University Press, 2011) and curator of the exhibition *Everything Loose Will Land* (MAK Center for Art and Architecture, 2013).

Douglas MacLeod is Chair of the RAIC Centre for Architecture at Athabasca University. He is a contributing editor to *Canadian Architect* magazine and the former Executive Director of the Canadian Design Research Network.

Tom Marble is principal of Tom Marble Architecture. He is currently working on *The Expediter*, an architectural film noir exploring the role of real estate development in the formation of contemporary Los Angeles.

Duane McLemore is a designer and educator based in Los Angeles. He is a founder of the design studio X Over Zero and teaches in the architecture program at Woodbury University.

Catherine Opie is a photographer and Professor of Photography in the Department of Art at UCLA. Her work is included in the collections of the Museum of Modern Art, the Whitney Museum of American Art, the Los Angeles County Museum of Art, and the Museum of Contemporary Art (Los Angeles), among many others. She lives and works in Los Angeles.

Michael Sweeney is a practicing architect in Los Angeles with Assembledge+.

Christopher Tandon is an art director and production designer. He is known for his work on *Kill Bill: Vol. 1* (2003), *Kill Bill: Vol. 2* (2004), and *Drive* (2011).

Kazys Varnelis, Ph.D. is the Director of the Network Architecture Lab. He is a historian, artist, and maker of architecture. With Robert Sumrell, he runs AUDC.

Mimi Zeiger is a Los Angeles–based critic, editor, and curator. She has covered art, architecture, urbanism, and design for a number of publications including *The New York Times*, *Domus*, and *Architectural Review*. She is a contributing editor of *Architect* and a regular opinion columnist for *Dezeen*. Zeiger teaches in the Media Design Practices MFA program at Art Center College of Design.

Peter Zellner is principal of ZELLNERandCompany in Los Angeles. He is a faculty member at the University of Southern California School of Architecture and an executive board member of From Lot to Spot, a green space equity organization. In 2016, he founded the Free School of Architecture.

Publication History

Newsletters

Early newsletters were numbered beginning with #3 and continuing intermittently through #16.

Newsletter (unnumbered/3) "Summer/Fall;" Natalie Shivers, editor. Undated (ca. 1988).

Newsletter (unnumbered/4); Natalie Shivers, editor. Fall 1988.

Newsletter #5; Natalie Shivers and Aaron Betsky, editors. November 1988.

Newsletter #6 "Winter;" Natalie Shivers and Aaron Betsky, editors. Undated (ca. 1989).

Newsletter #7 "Spring;" Natalie Shivers, editor. Undated (ca. 1989).

Newsletter #8; Aaron Betsky, Ben Caffey, Randall Cloud, Christian Hubert, and Kris Muller, contributing editors. 1989.

Newsletter #9; Natalie Shivers, editor. December 1989.

Newsletter #10; publication lost.

Newsletter #11; publication lost.

Newsletter #12; publication lost.

Newsletter #13; Aaron Betsky, Ben Caffey, John Chase, Randall Cloud, Douglas MacLeod, and Kris Miller, contributing editors. October/November 1990.

Newsletter (unnumbered/14) "Spring;" Aaron Betsky, Ben Caffey, John Chase, Randall Cloud, Douglas MacLeod, and Kris Miller, contributing editors. Undated (ca. 1991).

Newsletter #15; Aaron Betsky, Ben Caffey, John Chase, Randall Cloud, Douglas MacLeod, and Kris Miller, contributing editors. June/July 1991.

Newsletter (unnumbered/ 16) "Fall/I Like X"; Aaron Betsky, Ben Caffey, John Chase, Randall Cloud, Douglas MacLeod, and Kris Miller, contributing editors. Undated (ca. 1991).

Newsletter "Spring Collection"; Natalie Shivers, editor, Sylvia Lavin, guest editor, Spring 1992.

Newsletter; Sylvia Lavin, editor. September 1992.

Newsletter; Sylvia Lavin, editor. February 1993.

Newsletter; Sylvia Lavin, editor. August 1993.

Newsletter; Chava Danielson, editor. February 1994.

Newsletter; Chava Danielson, editor. May 1994.

Newsletter; Chava Danielson, editor. October 1994.

Newsletter; Chava Danielson, editor. May 1995.

Newsletter; Chava Danielson, editor. December 1995.

Newsletter; Chava Danielson, editor. Summer 1996.

Newsletter; Chava Danielson and Joe Day, editors. Summer 1997.

Newsletter; Chava Danielson, editor. Late Fall 1997.

Newsletter; Barbara Bestor, editor. Late Spring 1998.

Catalog: "Unfinished Business: 25 Years of Discourse in Los Angeles," John Southern and Mimi Zeiger, editors. Summer 2012.

Newsletter: "L.A. Confidential;" James Black, Thurman Grant, Duane McLemore, Michael Sweeney, and Mimi Zeiger, editors. Spring 2013.

Newsletter: "Public. Civic. Urban. Community;" Orhan Ayyüce, Nathan Bishop, Rob Berry, James Black, Matthew Gillis, Thurman Grant, Duane McLemore, Michael Sweeney, and Mimi Zeiger, editors. Fall 2013.

Newsletter: "And Also Here;" Rob Berry, James Black, Martina Dolejsova, Matthew Gillis, Duane McLemore, Michael Sweeney, Mimi Zeiger, editors. Summer 2014.

Newsletter: "Concrete Architectural Monuments of Los Angeles;" Orhan Ayyüce, Rob Berry, James Black, Russell Fortmeyer, Matthew Gillis, Duane McLemore, Michael Sweeney, and Mimi Zeiger, editors. Summer 2015.

Newsletter: "Interior Urbanism;" Jonathan Crisman and Mathew Gillis, editors. Fall 2016.

Newsletter: "In Defense / Indefensible;" Wendy Gilmartin and Mimi Zeiger, editors. Winter 2016.

Newsletter: "The Essence of the City;" Orhan Ayyüce, editor. Summer 2016.

Newsletter: "Space made Public;" Astrid Sykes and Christopher Torres, editors. Summer 2017

Books

Hodgetts, Craig. *Swimming to Suburbia: Some Thoughts on the New City and How It Came to Be That Way*, Forum Publication #1, 1987.

Mumford, Grant with Paige,Gary ed.. *35mm Works*, Forum Publication #2, 1988.

Crawford, Margaret. *The Ecology of Fantasy*, Forum Publication #3, undated ca. 1988 or 1989.

Central Office of Architecture. *Recombinant Images in Los Angeles*, Forum Publication #4, undated ca. 1988 or 1989.

Suisman, Douglas R. *Los Angeles Boulevard: Eight X-Rays of the Body Public*, Forum Publication #5, 1989. revised and expanded ORO Editions, 2014.

Betsky, Aaron. *33-D6-E6*, Forum Publication #6, 1990. distributed by Princeton Architectural Press.

MacLeod, Douglas & Betsky, Aaron. *ARCHINFO: Architecture and Information*, Forum Publication #7, undated ca. 1990 or 1991. Diskette and collection of postcards.

Betsky, Aaron, Whiteson, Lean & John Chase, John eds. *Experimental Architecture in Los Angeles*, Forum Publication #8, 1992. published by Rizzoli International.

[Publication #9?] Paralogical Prototypes, by Neil Denari. Book, 1993.

Cenzatti, Marco. *Los Angeles and the L.A. School: Postmodernism and Urban Studies*, Forum Publication #10, 1993.

Flusty, Steven. *Building Paranoia: The Proliferation of Interdictory Space and the Erosion of Spatial Justice*, Forum Publication #11, 1994.

Chase, John, Crawford, Margaret & Kaliski, John eds. *Everyday Urbanism*, Forum Publication #12, Published by Monacelli, 1999; revised 2nd ed., 2008.

Mangurian, Robert & Ray, Mary-Ann WRAPPER: 40 possible city surfaces for the Museum of Jurassic Technology, Forum Publication #13, William Stout Publishers (San Francisco) and Rice School of Architecture (Houston), 1999.

Portfolio / Forum Memo 2002-2003. Folio of eight 15 × 22" prints, 2003.

Varnelis, Kazys ed. *Forum ANNUAL 2004*. Anthology of articles from online Forum Issues, self-published pamphlet, 2004

Martin, Elizabeth ed. *cityworksLosAngeles: HANDBOOK*, Forum Press, 2005.

Techentin, Warren, curator. *Portfolio 2006*. Jessica Bronson, Catherine Opie, Alex Slade, and James Welling, artists. Folio of 4 15x22 inch prints, 2006.

Varnelis, Kazys, ed. The *Infrastructural City: Networked Ecologies in Los Angeles*, Actar, 2008.

Grant, Thurman & Stein, Joshua G. eds. *Dingbat 2.0: The Iconic Los Angeles Apartment as Projection of a Metropolis*. DoppelHouse Press, 2016.

Pamphlets

Techentin, Warren ed. *Dead Malls*, Forum Pamphlet 1, 2004.

Crosher, Zoe. *Out the Window (LAX)*, Forum Pamphlet 2, 2006.

Kane, Ted & Goldin, Greg eds. *Polar Inertia: Migrating Urban Systems*, Forum Pamphlet 3, 2007.

Marble, Tom, *After The City, This (Is How We Live)*, Forum Pamphlet 4, 2007.

Gannon, Todd ed. *Pendulum Plane: Oyler Wu Collaborative*, Forum Pamphlet 5, 2009.

Jones, Wes & Gannon, Todd ed. *Meet the Nelsons! The Any Years: Issues 10-27 (1994-2001)*, Forum Pamphlet 6, 2010.

Online Publications:
Forum Issues [1999-2004]

Bestor, Barbara ed. *Forum Issue 0*. 10 December 1999, https://web.archive.org/web/20040311024554/
http://www.laforum.org:80/issues/issue0.php
Accessed 20 June 2017

Allen, Rachel & Burnett-Stuart, Jack eds. *Forum Issue 1*. 10 October 2000, https://web.archive.org/web/2
0040405201556/http://www.laforum.org:80/issues/
issue1/new.html Accessed 20 June 2017

Durfee, Tim & Burnett-Stuart, Jack eds. *Forum Issue 2: Gehry and Moneo Under Construction* 30 September 2001, http://laforum.org/publication/forum-issue-2-gehry-and-moneo-under-construction/ Accessed 20 June 2017

Lamprecht, Barbara ed, *Forum Issue 3: Rethinking Housing, Prototypes and Proposals* 20 March 2002, https://web.archive.org/web/20040302064254/http://
www.laforum.org:80/issues/issue3.php Accessed 20 June 2017

Loomis, Alan ed. *Forum Issue 4: Consuming the City* 22 February 2003, https://web.archive.org/
web/20040224082456/http://www.laforum.org:80/
issues/issue4.php Accessed 20 June 2017

Loomis, Alan & Mogul, Lize eds. *Forum Issue 5: Parks* 5 June 2003 http://laforum.org/publication/forum-issue-5-parks/ Accessed 20 June 2017

Loomis, Alan & Bharne, Vinayak eds. *Forum Issue 6: A Note on Downtown* 1 February 2004 http://laforum
.org/publication/forum-issue-6-a-note-on-downtown/
Accessed 20 June 2017

Marble, Tom ed. *Forum Issue 7: Late Moderns* 11 Septtember 2004 http://laforum.org/publication/
forum-issue-7-late-moderns/ Accessed 20 June 2017

Image Credits

Forum Memos [2002-2003]

Marble, Tom ed. *Forum Memos: 00-07* https://web
.archive.org/web/20040612050755/http://laforum
.org:80/forumemo.php Accessed 20 June 2017

Online Features [2001-2002]

Leclerc, David & Lamprecht, Barbara. "Goodbye,
Modern" 10 September 2002 https://web.archive.org/
web/20060113202654/http://www.laforum.org:80/
features/goodbyemodern.php Accessed 20 June 2017

Singley, Paulette and Varnelis, Kazys. "LACMA on Fire"
6 August 2002 https://web.archive.org/
web/20060113202654/http://www.laforum.org:80/
features/lacma.php Accessed 20 June 2017

Day, Joe. "Meiered: MOCA's 'What's Shakin': New
Architecture in LA" 12 February 2002 https://web.
archive.org/web/20060113202654/http://www.laforum.
org/more.php?id=42_0_1_0_M7 Accessed 20 June 2017

Bailey, Dave Hullfish. "Schindler Shelter" 7 November
2001 https://web.archive.org/web/20060113202654/
http://www.laforum.org:80/features/bailey/index.html
Accessed 20 June 2017

Leclerc, David. "Sorry Rudy!: A visit to MOCA's 'The
Architecture of R.M. Schindler" 4 May 2001 https://web.
archive.org/web/20060113202654/http://www.laforum.
org/more.php?id=44_0_1_0_M7 Accessed 20 June 2017

Allen, Rachel. "A Model Staging Area Or, Why Ann
Bergren's Thesis Is So Beautiful" *Forum Special Feature*
19 February 2001 https://web.archive.org/
web/20060113202654/http://www.laforum.org:80/
features.php# Accessed 20 June 2017 `

p. 112-3: Newsletter #5; Natalie Shivers and
Aaron Betsky, editors. November 1988.

p. 114-115: Newsletter; Chava Danielson, editor.
May 1995.

p. 116-117: Newsletter #7 "Spring;" Natalie Shivers,
editor. Undated (ca. 1989).

p. 118-119: Newsletter #9; Natalie Shivers, editor.
December 1989.

p. 120-121: Newsletter "Spring Collection"; Natalie
Shivers, editor, Sylvia Lavin, guest editor, Spring 1992.

p. 122-23: Newsletter; Sylvia Lavin, editor.
February 1993.

p. 124: Newsletter; Chava Danielson, editor.
February 1994.

p. 125: Newsletter: "Public. Civic. Urban. Community;"
Orhan Ayyüce, Nathan Bishop, Rob Berry, James Black,
Matthew Gillis, Thurman Grant, Duane McLemore,
Michael Sweeney, and Mimi Zeiger, editors. Fall 2013.

p. 126-27: Newsletter; Chava Danielson and Joe Day,
editors. Summer 1997.

p. 128-29: Newsletter; Chava Danielson, editor.
Late Fall 1997.

p. 130-31: Newsletter: "L.A. Confidential;" James Black,
Thurman Grant, Duane McLemore, Michael Sweeney,
and Mimi Zeiger, editors. Spring 2013.